HOW TO
LOSE
FRIENDS &
ALIENATE
PEOPLE

Author's Note

This book was written before the terrorist attack on the World Trade Center and, given how New Yorkers responded to that tragedy, my attitude towards them may strike some readers as a bit uncharitable. Clearly, not all the residents of Manhattan are the shallow, narcissistic creatures I encountered. Many of them have shown themselves to be quite the opposite. All I can say is that, in the years I lived there (1995–2000), New Yorkers gave little indication that they were capable of behaving so compassionately. I left with the impression that they were primarily interested in advertising their own importance, whether by snagging a good table at Balthazar, spending the weekend on St Bart's or getting hold of the latest pair of designer sunglasses. It was the Age of Conspicuous Consumption.

It's too early to say whether this era has now been consigned to the dustbin of history. There were indications that it was drawing to a close even before the World Trade Center disaster. The gaudy, bacchanalian atmosphere of the late nineties coincided with the biggest boom in Wall Street's history and, after the collapse of various high-profile stocks, people seemed to sober up a bit. As I discovered, it's only when your fortunes take a turn for the worse that you realise what's really important in life – and it doesn't include hanging out with Puff Daddy. With a bit of luck, this book will begin to read like an historical document rather than an account of what it's like to live in contemporary Manhattan. But I wouldn't bet on it.

Toby Young
September 2001

HOW TO
LOSE
FRIENDS &
ALIENATE
PEOPLE

TOBY YOUNG

LITTLE, BROWN AND COMPANY

To Caroline

A *Little, Brown* Book

First published in Great Britain in 2001
By Little, Brown and Company
Reprinted 2001 (twice)

A CIP catalogue record for this book
is available from the British Library.

ISBN 0 316 85791 2

Extract from 'Letter to Lord Byron' by W.H. Auden (*Collected Poems*)
reproduced by kind permission of Faber & Faber Ltd.

Typeset in Sabon by Palimpsest Book Production Ltd,
Polmont, Stirlingshire

Printed and bound in Great Britain by
Clays Ltd, St Ives plc

Little, Brown and Company (UK)
Brettenham House
Lancaster Place
London WC2E 7EN

CONTENTS

PROLOGUE

To anyone within a ten-block radius of Mortons, the West Hollywood power restaurant, it was obvious something was going on that night. Monday evenings at Mortons usually attract some big industry players, but on this particular Monday – 28 March, 1994 – it was as if the entire Hollywood A-list had decided to assemble on the corner of Melrose and Robertson. Lines of police officers struggled to hold back the crowds as wave upon wave of movie stars converged on the restaurant's entrance, some of them clutching gold statuettes. It was the night of the 66th Annual Academy Awards and *Vanity Fair* was throwing its first ever Oscar party.

I checked my watch: 11.25 p.m. In five minutes' time I'd have to approach the clipboard Nazi guarding the entrance and convince her to let me in. I busied myself with picking specks of dirt off my dinner jacket in an attempt to calm my nerves. Of all the Oscar parties taking place that night, this was undoubtedly the one to be at. That distinction used to belong to the party hosted by Irving 'Swifty' Lazar at Spago, but the legendary superagent had died the previous December. One of the reasons Swifty's party had been so hot was because the guest list was restricted to a limited number of VIPs. Those deemed insufficiently important were fobbed off with the excuse that the Los Angeles fire marshals had decreed that no more than 300 people were allowed to attend, a ruse dreamt up by the

1

wily agent to keep the numbers down. As a result, the atmosphere at the party had been surprisingly intimate. My friend Alex de Silva had gatecrashed the soirée in 1992 and, in the space of ten minutes, had met Sharon Stone, Michael Douglas and Tom Cruise. Indeed, Cruise had actually marched up and introduced himself, assuming that if Alex was at the party he must be someone important. In fact, he was a freelance British hack who'd flown in to town for the sole purpose of attending the Oscar parties.

The reason the *Vanity Fair* party had emerged as 1994's hot ticket was a combination of happenstance and extremely hard work on the part of the magazine's party planners. Swifty's death from liver failure at the age of eighty-six had set off a mad scramble to fill his shoes. According to Wolfgang Puck, the owner of Spago, people had started calling up and attempting to book the restaurant while the agent's body was still warm. In the end Puck had decided to close Spago on Oscar night as a mark of respect for Swifty, leaving the field wide open to his rival Peter Morton. Once Graydon Carter, the editor of *Vanity Fair*, had secured Mortons, his crack team of party planners had set to work. Jane Sarkin, the magazine's chief 'celebrity wrangler', had spent the best part of three months in tense negotiations with agents, managers and publicists, making sure their A-list clients agreed to show up. Once a sufficient number of show ponies have been rounded up and placed in the paddock it's only a matter of time before the rest are scrabbling to join them. A good celebrity wrangler concentrates her efforts on a few prize animals and the Hollywood herd instinct takes care of the rest.

When I had called Beth Kseniak the previous week, I'd thought the fact that I'd written a short piece for *Vanity Fair* a year before would give me some leverage, but I was wrong. 'What kind of coverage are you planning to give the party?' she asked. I hadn't been planning on giving it any – I was in LA accompanying Alex de Silva on his annual party pilgrimage – but after my conversation with Kseniak I called up a friend on the *Daily Telegraph* and persuaded him to commission a piece. Even that failed to impress the hard-nosed publicist. 'I'll have a word with Graydon,' she sighed, 'but I'm not making any promises.'

She'd gotten back to me on Friday, tentatively agreeing to let me come provided I arrived no earlier than 11.30 p.m. She explained that in order to accommodate all the guests, invitations had to be staggered over the course of the evening. The first lot of people – the *crème de la crème* – had been invited at 5.30 p.m. so they could watch the Oscars on little television sets at their tables while enjoying a four-course meal. From 9.30 p.m. onwards, different categories of guests were invited at half-hourly intervals in descending order of importance. 11.30 p.m. was the final timeslot of the evening, half an hour before the party ended. As a member of the 'foreign press' I was at the bottom of the Hollywood food chain, but that didn't bother me. I was on the list.

My sense of triumph was compounded by the fact that Alex hadn't been able to get on it in spite of offering to write a piece for the *Daily Mail* which, as he pointed out to Kseniak, had a higher circulation than the *Telegraph*. Frustratingly for him, she didn't rule out the possibility that circumstances might change at the last minute – it was just 'very, very unlikely'. Needless to say, I'd teased him about this the entire weekend. Every time a phone rang I said, 'You'd better get that. It could be Kseniak.' By the time Monday rolled around and he still hadn't heard from her, he was climbing the walls.

Then disaster struck. I returned to my hotel at 4 p.m. on Monday after a long, boozy lunch with Alex to find the message light blinking in my room. Kseniak had called while I was out. 'I'm sorry to have to tell you this,' she began, 'but it's not going to be possible to accommodate you tonight. There just isn't enough room. The Los Angeles fire marshals have said that no more than 300 people are allowed to come. I'm terribly sorry.'

I rushed over to Alex's room in a state of high dudgeon, only to be greeted by a grinning, dancing fool. He, too, had been

3

called by Kseniak while we were out, only his message had informed him that, provided he arrived no earlier than 11.30 p.m., he could come. The little bastard had been given my place on the guest list!

I was devastated. Up until this point, I'd been exaggerating how much I cared as a way of needling Alex. In common with most intelligent, educated people, he considered it incredibly uncool to get excited about the prospect of hanging out with celebrities. 'Who wants to jump through a series of hoops just to rub shoulders with Michael Caine?' he drawled when it looked as though he wasn't going to make it on to the list. Among my peer group, admitting that you were dazzled by movie stars was on a par with confessing to having a soft spot for the Royal Family – it simply wasn't done. Celebrities were just the trained monkeys of the entertainment moguls who ran the media-industrial complex and sophisticated people like us weren't supposed to be impressed by them.

In reality, of course, Alex was no more capable of resisting the allure of movie stars than a fourteen-year-old schoolgirl. The attitude of all my friends towards celebrities was completely phoney. They might claim to be indifferent, but they became forelock-tugging serfs the moment a famous person entered the room. They worshipped at the altar of celebrity just like everyone else; they were just too embarrassed to admit it. Consequently, I made a point of erring in the opposite direction. I hammed up my obsession with A-list stars as a way of letting my friends know I found their pretence at insouciance totally unconvincing. If Sylvester Stallone graced me with his presence, I liked to say, I'd drop to my knees and unzip his flies. But this was just a way of shocking people. At least, I hope it was. I don't think I would have been *that* bowled over by the *Rambo* star.

However, now that I'd been categorically excluded from the party, I began to get a little frantic. This was partly just a natural human reaction: I wanted what I couldn't have, particularly now that it had been snatched away from me and given to Alex.

But I was also starting to buy into the general mystique that had grown up around the party. *Vanity Fair*'s party planners had done their job well: this was the only game in town. If everyone else was clamouring to get on the list, who was I to say it wasn't a privilege worth fighting for? Now that I'd been made to jump through a series of hoops, the prospect of rubbing shoulders with Michael Caine seemed very appealing. There was no way I was going to come this close, only to be excluded at the last minute.

One way or another, I would go to the ball.

At 11.30 p.m. on the dot, I straightened my bow tie one last time, summoned up as much self-confidence as I could muster and pushed my way past the police barrier until I was face to face with the clipboard Nazi. Two enormous bouncers loomed on either side of her.

'Can I help you?' she asked, looking me up and down as if I was a homeless man who'd just emerged from a crack in the pavement.

'Alex de Silva, *Daily Mail*,' I replied, thrusting out my hand. 'I'm on the list.'

She ignored my outstretched paw and went through the motions of checking the guest list. She was clearly unconvinced that a balding, British hack in a rented dinner jacket had any place on Mount Olympus.

'Your name's not on *my* list,' she said. 'I'm going to have to ask you to move on. We need to keep this area clear.'

I could hear a few titters from the crowd behind me. Watching pushy young men like me getting their comeuppance was all part of the evening's entertainment for them.

'There must be a mistake,' I spluttered. 'Beth Kseniak called me only this afternoon to tell me I could come.'

'Look, if Beth told you you could come your name would be on my list and it's not here. You're going to have to move along.'

By now, the titters had turned into jeers and catcalls. The

crowds outside these events are referred to by people on the inside as 'looky-loos' and their devotion to celebrities is matched by their hostility towards those they consider interlopers. I was just a civilian. I didn't belong on the other side of the velvet rope. I belonged behind the police barrier with them.

The bouncers began to eyeball me suspiciously.

'Could you please check one more time?' I pleaded. 'I'm sure my name's on there somewhere.'

The clipboard Nazi ran her eye over the list again, this time even faster.

'Not here,' she concluded. 'Bye, bye.'

What was going on? Had Kseniak forgotten to take my name off and replace it with Alex's? I couldn't very well tell her to check under the name 'Toby Young' now that I'd identified myself as Alex de Silva. I was fucked.

At that moment I sensed a commotion behind me and turned to witness the arrival of Anna Nicole Smith accompanied by a retinue of half-a-dozen hangers-on. This was her 'conga line', an essential accessory of any celebrity, however minor.[1] The crowd erupted, while the clipboard Nazi shoved me to one side and lifted the velvet rope. Suddenly, from being a ferocious gate-keeper, she morphed into an obsequious maitre d'.

'Miss Smith! How good of you to come!'

'I'm with a few friends,' said the *Playboy* centrefold, motioning to her entourage. 'Is that a problem?'

'Don't be absurd,' laughed the clipboard Nazi, as if stopping anyone from entering the party was the furthest thing from her mind. 'Go right in.'

After Anna Nicole Smith and her six friends had filed past, the clipboard Nazi replaced the velvet rope and turned her attention back to me. She gave me a look as if to say 'you still here?' I decided to give it one last try.

---

[1] As a general rule, the more insecure the celebrity, the larger their 'conga line'. When Jennifer Lopez appeared on BBC1's *The National Lottery Stars* on 16 December, 2000 she was accompanied by an entourage of 72 people.

'Would it be possible to check with Beth? Alex de Silva from the *Daily Mail*.'

'Okay,' she sighed, 'but it won't make any difference.'

She unclipped a walkie-talkie from her belt and asked to speak to her boss. There was no reply. I checked my watch: 11.35 p.m.

Suddenly, I heard a familiar voice: 'Toby? Is that you?'

It was Alex.

From what I could tell he was standing behind the police barrier, but I didn't dare turn round. I looked imploringly at the clipboard Nazi, but her attention was focused on Alex. He piped up again.

'Toby, if that's you, will you tell that nice lady to tell this nice policeman that I'm on the guest list? He's refusing to let anyone through without an invitation.'

'D'you know that guy?' asked the clipboard Nazi.

I pretended to be miles away.

'I'm sorry, what?'

'That guy over there. D'you know him?'

I shot a glance in Alex's direction.

'Oh, *that* guy. Yeah, he's a notorious gatecrasher. Tries to get into everything. I wouldn't let him anywhere near the place if I were you.'

By now Alex knew for certain it was me.

'Toby, why won't you acknowledge me, you prat?'

The clipboard Nazi continued to stare in Alex's direction.

'Look, could you try Beth again?' I pleaded. 'I'm not making it up. She phoned me this afternoon to tell me I could come.'

Without taking her eyes off Alex, she summoned her boss once again on her walkie-talkie. This time she got a response.

'This is Beth. Go ahead.'

'I've got a young man here called Jack Silver from the *Dayton Mail*.'

'ALEX DE SILVA,' I shouted, leaning into the walkie-talkie so Kseniak could hear me. 'From the *Daily Mail*. You left a message on my hotel voicemail this afternoon.'

Before she could reply, Alex started screaming.

'HE'S PRETENDING TO BE ME. I'M ALEX, NOT HIM. HIS NAME'S TOBY YOUNG. DON'T LET HIM IN.'

Did the clipboard Nazi hear him? I couldn't tell.

The walkie-talkie crackled back into life.

'Yeah, I remember. Okay, he can come in.'

Still staring at Alex, she absent-mindedly lifted the velvet rope. Against all the odds, I'd made it.

'A word of warning,' I said, just before heading into the party. 'One of that gatecrasher's favourite tricks is to pretend to be someone else. Don't believe a word he says.'

It wasn't long before I got an inkling of what the remainder of the evening held in store. In order to actually enter the party you had to walk along a red carpet with velvet ropes on either side while television crews, journalists and dozens of paparazzi all craned their necks, squinting to see if you were anyone important. Even Barry Norman was there, clutching a microphone. When Anna Nicole Smith had set foot on the carpet, pandemonium had broken out. People in the crowd started screaming out her name, the cameramen switched on their powerful spotlights and she responded by thrusting out her breasts and batting her eyelids into the glare. My turn to run this gauntlet coincided with the last member of Smith's entourage slipping into the party and, as a result, I had everybody's full attention. That was unfortunate. Still, it couldn't be helped. I stuck my chin out, threw back my shoulders and took the plunge.

It was at this point that one of the looky-loos behind me decided to get his revenge.

'Who is it?' he cried.

I felt several thousand pairs of eyes scrutinising me at once.

'Ah, it's *nobody*,' he concluded. 'Just some bald guy.'

A moment later the area was plunged into darkness and I was almost swept off my feet by a powerful blast of air. For a second I thought a small tornado had caused a power cut. Then I realised what had happened. On discovering that I was

8

a nobody, not only had all the cameramen switched off their spotlights, but all the paparazzi had lowered their telephoto lenses simultaneously, thereby creating a gale-force gust of wind. I ended up stumbling into the party like a drunk on the deck of a North Sea trawler.

The first thing that struck me after my eyes had adjusted to the light was the sheer number of movie stars. Everywhere I looked, there were rows of white teeth, wheat fields of expensively coifed hair and acres of glowing, sun-kissed flesh. It was like walking into the pages of *Hello!* Within seconds of arriving I spotted Tom Cruise, Nicole Kidman, Leonardo DiCaprio, Sharon Stone, Ralph Fiennes, Alex Kingston, Liam Neeson and Natasha Richardson – and that was just in the bar area. Elsewhere, I later discovered, the guests included David Copperfield, Claudia Schiffer, Kurt Russell, Goldie Hawn, Prince, Anjelica Huston, Gabriel Byrne, Shirley MacLaine, Kirk Douglas, Rosie O'Donnell, Gore Vidal and Nancy Reagan. It's not an exaggeration to say that in the party as a whole celebrities outnumbered civilians by a ratio of 2:1. No wonder I had difficulty getting in. It was nothing short of miraculous that so many huge egos had managed to squeeze into such a small space.

It was disconcerting being at an event at which I knew everyone and no one knew me. Who was I supposed to talk to? I decided my first priority was to get a drink. I edged my way towards the bar, receiving a sharp jab in the ribs from the Oscar Holly Hunter had just won for her role in *The Piano*, and asked the barman for a Black Label on the rocks. As he was getting it, I noticed an extremely attractive woman in her early twenties standing on my right, apparently on her own. It was Amanda de Cadanet, the ex-*Word* presenter, wearing a ridiculously low-cut dress. Her tits were popping out like two scoops of ice cream.

'What were you nominated for?' I asked, struggling to make myself heard above the din. 'Best Supporting Dress?'

She gave me a blank look.

'I wasn't nominated for anything.'

'I know. That was just my way of saying you look great.'

'I'm sorry, what?'

She turned her head so her left ear was next to my mouth.

'YOU LOOK GREAT IN THAT DRESS.'

'Thanks,' she said, recoiling. 'Will you excuse me? I've just seen someone I know.'

Before I could respond, she bolted to the other side of the restaurant. That hadn't gone very well. Still, perhaps that was because she was such a D-list celebrity. The smaller the star, the more standoffish they are, I told myself.

I picked up my drink and surveyed the crowd, searching for a bigger target. My eyes immediately lighted on Kenneth Branagh. His wife, Emma Thompson, had been nominated in two categories that year – Best Actress and Best Supporting Actress – but she was nowhere to be seen. Indeed, as far as I could tell he wasn't talking to anyone. I gulped down some Scotch and made my way across the room.

'Toby Young, the *Daily Telegraph*,' I said, planting myself squarely in front of him.

He nodded and looked at me expectantly. What was it I wanted? Clearly, he was in no mood to make polite conversation with a member of the British press. I desperately tried to think of something funny to break the ice.

'So, how many unlettered Hollywood executives have come up to you this evening and said' – I put on my thickest American accent – 'I jes lurved you in that Shakespeare thang?'

He tilted his head quizzically.

'Which Shakespeare thing?'

Evidently, he hadn't heard me properly. I could feel a wave of panic rising up from my abdomen. I couldn't remember a single one of the half dozen or so adaptations he'd starred in. I slipped back into my normal voice.

'Er, *Hamlet*?'

'That wasn't me. That was Mel Gibson.'

'God, what am I on about?' – I slapped my forehead – 'I mean *Prospero's Books*.'

'That was John Gielgud.'

10

I took a slug of Scotch.

'This isn't going very well is it?'

'No, it's not.'

'Can we start again?'

'Only if you can tell me the name of my most recent Shakespeare *thang*.'

He spat out the last word as if it was a cyanide pill. I racked my brains. It was no good. The only film of his I'd ever seen was *Dead Again*. When it became obvious that I wasn't going to come up with anything he dismissed me with a little shrug. Reluctantly, I turned round, tucked my tail between my legs and crawled back to the bar.

I ordered another Black Label on the rocks. This wasn't nearly as much fun as I'd anticipated. I'd imagined that the usual chasm that separates celebrities from ordinary mortals would disappear in an atmosphere of alcohol-fuelled informality. Hadn't Tom Cruise actually introduced himself to Alex at Swifty's party? Looking at Tom Cruise now, receiving courtiers like some all-conquering Renaissance prince, it struck me that Alex was almost certainly lying about this. If anything, the rigid Hollywood pecking order was even more pronounced than usual. I may have been standing only a few feet away from some of the biggest names in show business, but the distance between us had never been greater.

Then, out of the corner of my eye, I saw someone who looked almost as out of place as me: the figure skater Nancy Kerrigan. This beautiful, 24-year-old girl had shot to fame the previous January when she'd been clubbed on the knee with a 'retractable baton' – that's what the press called it – by an unknown assailant while practising for the 1994 Winter Olympics. When it emerged that the man was associated with Tonya Harding, a rival figure skater, the whole saga became a huge tabloid news story.

'Pretty impressive crowd, eh?' I said, flashing her my most winning smile.

'Absolutely,' she replied, smiling back. 'I feel like I'm watching a movie or something.'

11

'Me too. I just asked the barman for some popcorn and a large Coke.'

To my astonishment, she burst out laughing. At last, I'd found a receptive audience!

'Toby Young,' I said, sticking out my hand. 'I'm covering this event for a British newspaper.'

'Nancy Kerrigan,' she replied, clasping it in both of hers. 'Great to meet you.'

My self-confidence came flooding back. I began fantasising about taking this mouth-watering slice of American cheesecake back to my hotel room. I'd knock on Alex's door on the way to my room with this goddess on my arm and bid him good-night. *Talk about a Kodak moment!*

Then, out of nowhere, I felt a sharp tap on my shoulder.

'Excuse me, sir, but can I have your name?'

It was a bouncer.

'Not again,' I protested. 'I've just been through all this with the woman at the door.'

He laid one of his enormous mitts on my shoulder.

'If you follow me, sir, I'm sure we can resolve this matter to everyone's satisfaction.'

I looked back at Nancy. Her eyes were wide with alarm as if I might at any moment whip out a 'retractable baton' and start pounding away at her knee.

'Let's go,' said the bouncer, tightening his grip. 'RIGHT NOW.'

How had I been rumbled? I looked over his shoulder and, sure enough, there was Alex with a huge grin on his face. Somehow, he'd managed to persuade the clipboard Nazi not only to let him in, but to empower him to have me thrown out as well. He always had been a smooth-talking bastard.

'Okay, okay,' I said. 'I'll go quietly.'

Thirty seconds later I was back on the other side of the police barrier, indistinguishable from any of the other looky-loos. Luckily, none of them recognised me.

*

Reflecting on the evening back in my hotel room, I'd like to say I came to the conclusion that this brave new world wasn't worth conquering. I would have saved myself a great deal of trouble. But the truth is my bitterness about being thrown out of the party didn't last long. I was overawed by the sheer spectacle of it. The sight of all those celebrities under one roof, besieged by journalists and photographers, had been overpoweringly seductive. Even the looky-loos had their role to play. It was like a scene out of *La Dolce Vita*. This was the life I'd fantasised about as I sat in my bedsit in Shepherd's Bush.

Why did I find this world so appealing? In part, it was because I knew I wasn't supposed to. People from my background – I come from the class that Keynes called 'the educated bourgeoisie' – are expected to see through this tawdry, showbiz glamour. My father's a member of 'the Great and the Good' who was made a life peer in 1977 for his services to successive Labour governments, including setting up the Open University. My mother had written a prize-winning literary novel and edited an educational magazine. Attending the *Vanity Fair* Oscar party would have been their idea of hell.

At Oxford, even people my own age thought this kind of 'Hollywood bullshit' was beyond the pale. Popular culture was strictly divided between the stuff it was okay to like – independent films, alternative rock, any form of cultural expression associated with minorities – and the mindless pap produced by the American entertainment industry. In order to pass muster, something had to be 'real'; it had to have 'an edge'. Mainstream popular culture was 'plastic' and 'safe'. If it was enjoyed at all it was strictly in a spirit of camp condescension. *Baywatch*, for instance, was regarded as 'hilarious' because it fell into the 'so-bad-it's-good' category.

I balked at this. I turned this hierarchy on its head, rejecting anything that was considered remotely authentic in favour of pure, escapist entertainment. I liked popcorn movies; my favourite actors were Charlton Heston, Clint Eastwood and Arnold Schwarzenegger. When it came to music, I was more

13

interested in disco than reggae. Commercial pop music, the kind that was played on FM radio stations all across America, that was the stuff I liked. Unlike most of my contemporaries, I didn't read *The New Musical Express* or *Sight & Sound*; I read *Smash Hits* and *Playboy*. Mainstream popular culture was my religion and Hollywood was my Mecca.

In this light, being at the *Vanity Fair* Oscar party was like attending a rally of fellow believers. For the first time in my life, I was surrounded by people who thought as highly of Hollywood blockbusters as I did. (The winners that year included *Jurassic Park*, *The Fugitive* and *Mrs Doubtfire*.) Of course, I was dimly aware that, for these people, claiming to like big-budget, commercial movies wasn't a way of advertising their hostility to the liberal intelligentsia; no, these people actually *liked* them. But somehow that didn't seem to matter.

Still, that was only part of the reason I'd been blown away. In addition, being in such close proximity to all those movie stars had left me feeling strangely elated. Seeing Tom Cruise in the flesh, no more than ten feet away, had had an almost narcotic effect. I felt like Alan Clark did when he came face to face with Margaret Thatcher in 1986: 'At the end, when she spoke of her determination to go on, and her blue eyes flashed, I got a full dose of personality compulsion, something of the *Führer Kontakt*.'

In the past, I'd rationalised my enthusiasm for various Hollywood celebs by telling myself it was just a way of letting my snobbish friends know what I thought of their aloofness. *Unlike you, I'm not ashamed to admit that I'm just an ordinary, common-or-garden fan*. But deep down I really didn't think I'd be *that* impressed if I happened to be in the same room as them. Well, being at the *Vanity Fair* party had put paid to that. My first impulse on spotting Tom Cruise had been to genuflect. When it came down to it, I was just another salivating starfucker, a looky-loo who'd managed to get past the police barrier.

It was a world away from my bedsit in Shepherd's Bush. Even

by West London standards, W12 is a fairly sleazy neighbourhood; compared to West Hollywood, it's a Third World ghetto.
Indeed, Britain as a whole seemed a bit shabby and second-
rate after that night. What celebrities do we have to compete
with the likes of Tom Cruise and Sharon Stone? Next to them,
the cast of *Coronation Street* look like a bunch of contestants
on *Stars in Their Eyes*. We're no more of a global superpower
in popular culture than we are in international politics. The
Brits have lost an Empire and failed to find a role – unless you
count being cast as villains in Hollywood movies. Contrary to
Harold Macmillan's hope, Britain has never succeeded in
playing Greece to America's Rome; Ancient Britain to their
Rome is more like it.

Sitting in my hotel room that night, I made up my mind up
to try and seek my fortune in the New World. Many Brits
who've elected to ditch the old country have described how
constrained they felt by their humble class origins. In my case,
it was almost the other way round. Back in London, in spite
of my immersion in mainstream popular culture, I'd never been
able to entirely escape my parents' clutches. I'd always had a
sense of them looking over my shoulder, shaking their heads in
disapproval. Perhaps in America, 3,000 miles away, I'd finally
be able to expunge the guilt I felt about not doing something
more worthwhile with my life, like working for Oxfam or setting
up a shelter for the homeless. My idea of heaven was being
able to roll around naked in a huge pile of money with Anna
Nicole Smith *without feeling the slightest pang of conscience.*

Of course, I didn't admit that the reason I wanted to come
to America was because I wanted to plunge headfirst into the
cesspool of celebrity culture. I told myself that the world I'd
just glimpsed would make a great subject for a comic novel or
a satirical play; that as a writer I had a duty to capture it in
all its tacky splendour. That's why I wanted to live in the States:
for the *material*.

In reality, though, being at the party had had a strange effect
on me. Some form of transference had taken place and I'd ended

up fully embracing the belief-system I'd only flirted with before. In some weird sense, I became an American. I didn't want to move amongst these potentates, notebook in hand, recording their excesses for posterity; I wanted to be one of them. I had no burning desire to write a book that would offer the looky-loos a glimpse behind the velvet rope; I wanted them to prostrate themselves before me. I couldn't wait to strut about in my Armani dinner jacket, waving around the gaudy symbols of my success for all the world to see. *Check out my Rolex! Get a load of the tits on my girlfriend! Am I cool, or what?*

My time had come. I wanted to be a SOMEBODY.

1

'MILLIONS ARE TO BE GRABBED OUT HERE AND YOUR ONLY COMPETITION IS IDIOTS.'

It was the afternoon of 8 June, 1995 when I finally got the call.

'This is Dana Brown from Graydon Carter's office. Is this Toby Young?'

'Er, yes.'

'One moment please.'

Pause.

'Toby? It's Graydon. How'd you like to come hang out for a month?'

This was it, the one I'd been waiting for. Ever since the night of the *Vanity Fair* party fifteen months earlier, I'd been assiduously cultivating the magazine's editor. I'd written three pieces for him at this stage and whenever I bumped into him on one of his regular jaunts to London I'd done my best to charm him. The fact that he was offering me no more than a month's work was largely academic. It was a one-month trial and, provided I didn't screw up, it would lead to a full-time job. I felt like Boot being summoned by *The Daily Beast*.

To me, *Vanity Fair* wasn't just another glossy New York magazine. It was a link to Manhattan during its golden age, the era of the Algonquin Round Table. During *Vanity Fair*'s

17

first incarnation, from 1914–36, its contributors had included Dorothy Parker, Edmund Wilson, Robert Benchley, D.H. Lawrence, T.S. Eliot, Colette, Cocteau, Herman J. Mankiewicz . . . the list is endless. Even Houdini had written for *Vanity Fair*. It had been resurrected in 1983 by S.I. Newhouse Jr, the billionaire owner of Condé Nast, and from 1984–92 it had been edited by Tina Brown, formerly at the helm of *Tatler*. Tina was thirty when she received the call from Si, as he's known, and she went on to edit *The New Yorker*, the most prestigious job in American journalism. Under Tina, *Vanity Fair* had become the monthly bible of the Jet Set, an eclectic combination of Hollywood glamour, high society and true crime that Tina referred to as 'the mix'. It wasn't exactly the highbrow, literary magazine it had been, but it was still a damn sight more sexy than any of its British rivals.

I first met Graydon in 1993 at a *Sunday Times* lunch about a year after he'd succeeded Tina. I was twenty-nine at the time and had already worked for a wide cross-section of British publications, from the *Literary Review* to *Hello!*, but I'd never encountered a magazine editor quite like him. With his threadbare, Savile Row suit and slightly dog-eared Jermyn Street shirt, not to mention his eccentric hairstyle, he had a slightly raffish air, more reminiscent of the *Spectator* than one of the glossies. When he spoke, though, he sounded like a Chicago newspaperman of the old school, spitting out one-liners like a character in *The Front Page*.

For instance, after a few glasses of wine I suggested that *Vanity Fair* should run a photographic feature on 'literary London' featuring headshots of Britain's most distinguished authors in their favourite pubs. The idea was to illustrate the connection between alcohol and London literary life.

'What, are you kidding?' he responded. 'It'd look like a fucking dental textbook.'

The impression he gave was of a man who'd gone to a great deal of trouble to cultivate a particular image – a faintly bohemian Wasp with literary aspirations – but was only too happy to contradict it the moment he opened his mouth. As far as I could tell, his stream of seditious wisecracks, punctuated by expletives, was a way of letting you know that he was on your side even if he appeared to be a member of the Establishment.

I hoped it was true.

Every Fleet Street hack I know has, at one time or another, fantasised about working for a New York magazine. Getting that call from Tina Brown or Graydon Carter is the equivalent of the telegram Herman J. Mankiewicz sent Ben Hecht from Hollywood in 1925:

WILL YOU ACCEPT THREE HUNDRED PER WEEK TO WORK FOR PARAMOUNT PICTURES? ALL EXPENSES PAID. THE THREE HUNDRED IS PEANUTS. MILLIONS ARE TO BE GRABBED OUT HERE AND YOUR ONLY COMPETITION IS IDIOTS. DON'T LET THIS GET AROUND.

In my case, the call came at just the right time. Exactly two weeks earlier I'd taken the decision to close *The Modern Review*, the magazine I'd been editing for the last four years, without telling my co-proprietor Julie Burchill. 'Toby has no future here,' she thundered in *The Times* when she found out. 'He'll have to leave the country, like everyone else who falls out with me.' Julie and I had quarrelled after she'd left her husband, Cosmo Landesman, for Charlotte Raven, a 25-year-old contributor to the magazine. Charlotte, a bisexual feminist, had re-awakened Julie's radical conscience and Julie wanted to make her the editor. Together they were going to turn it into a cross between the *New Statesman* and *Spare Rib*. I felt like an old-fashioned Labour MP facing a takeover of his local constituency party by the Militant Tendency. I'd decided to close the magazine rather than let it fall into enemy hands and the upshot was that I was now unemployed.

By rights I should have been depressed: *The Modern Review* was my life. Julie, Cosmo and I had founded it in 1991 and in the intervening years we'd produced twenty issues. The original idea was to provide a forum for journalists and academics to write long, scholarly articles about the likes of Bruce Willis and Stephen King – the magazine's motto was 'Low Culture for Highbrows'. The point, of course, was to champion the kind of mainstream schlock that the chattering classes regarded as beneath contempt. Today, there is less of a division between respectable and unrespectable popular culture, but in 1991 writers in the broadsheet press still treated Hollywood blockbusters and bestselling novels as the equivalent of junk food. *The Modern Review* set out to *épater* the educated bourgeoisie.

In the first issue we published authors like Nick Hornby, Pauline Kael, Mark Steyn and James Wood on such important icons of our time as Adrian Mole, Kevin Costner, Michael Caine and Hannibal Lecter. Typical articles included a bibliography of Arnold Schwarzenegger by the magazine's literary editor and a piece by a young Cambridge don wondering if Paul Gascoigne was suffering from Tourette's Syndrome: 'Wazza mazza wiz Gazza?'[1] It even contained a book review by an unknown Cambridge graduate called Chris Weitz who, along with his brother Paul, went on to make *American Pie* nine years later. After flicking through it for the first time, Julie described it as being like an issue of *Smash Hits* edited by F.R. Leavis.

The magazine got off to a flying start when Robert Maxwell applied for an injunction against it. It was the autumn of 1991 and in the course of putting together the first issue I smuggled my staff into the offices of the *European*, a newspaper that was then owned by the socialist millionaire. We needed to use its

---

[1] 'One can see why wealth and fame might induce anyone to drink and screw around a bit, but Gazza's indiscretions – swearing, gesticulating, pulling faces, lunging – are so trivial and so sort of pleasureless that it is easy to wonder why anyone would persist in them unless he had to.' David Runciman, 'Wazza mazza wiz Gazza?', *The Modern Review*, Autumn, 1991.

high-tech production facilities to prepare a camera-ready copy of the magazine for our printers. No one was around – it was the weekend – and we would have got away with it if we hadn't left some page proofs lying about to be discovered by the paper's staff. Even then Maxwell might not have minded, but I had insisted on including his name in the list of people we thanked on the contents page, an act of mischief that would cost me dear. According to the managing editor of the *European*, Maxwell 'completely lost it' when he saw this, claiming it was 'like burglars leaving a calling card'.

It wasn't long before a letter from his solicitors was winging its way to my bedsit in Shepherd's Bush. It accused me and my staff of breaking the law and said that unless I gave a 'written undertaking' that the first issue would be shelved they would 'apply to the High Court tomorrow for an injunction to restrain publication of *The Modern Review*' and 'report the matter to the police'.

After several glasses of whisky, I got up the courage to tell Maxwell to piss off. He was a James Bond villain and I wasn't about to pulp the first issue just because we'd injured his vanity. Still, it was a high-risk strategy, not least because the magazine could ill afford an expensive legal battle. In its first year, *The Modern Review* had to limp along on an initial investment of just £16,666.50. Over the course of its four-year life, the total investment in the magazine was £42,683 – roughly half of what Graydon Carter spends on limousines in a single year. It only managed to survive by having very low overheads. It wasn't so much a cottage industry as a bedsit industry, being produced out of my flat in Shepherd's Bush. The 'office' consisted of two Apple Macs and an Amstrad telephone/fax. When people called up and asked for the 'subscription department' I simply handed the phone to Ed Porter, the deputy editor. He and I were the only full-time employees and we paid ourselves a grand total of £3,000 a year. No one could accuse us of being in it for the money.

Luckily, I was used to putting out magazines on miniscule

21

budgets. I'd produced my first magazine in primary school – the *Outlaw* – and went on to launch another at William Ellis, the grammar school I'd been to in North London, and then another at Oxford. Since all undergraduate magazines were named after rivers – *Isis, Cherwell, Tributary* – I had called mine the *Danube*. My thinking went like this: the bigger the river, the bigger the magazine.

It folded after two issues.

I was twenty-seven when *The Modern Review* launched, but all this experience enabled me to joke that I'd been in the magazine publishing business for seventeen years. In fact, beyond the nuts and bolts of laying out pages, I knew almost nothing about running a magazine.

Towards the end of 1991 things were looking bleak. Maxwell's application for an injunction against *The Modern Review* had been rejected, but he'd brought a civil case against me personally and that was looming. In the meantime, the lawyers I'd hired to fight the case had presented me with a bill for £17,132.53 and were threatening me with a lawsuit of their own if I didn't settle it immediately. I'd never seen *that* on *LA Law*. Then, just when it looked as though I was going to have to take out a second mortgage on my flat, something happened on the other side of the world that completely changed my fortunes. I first heard about it from my friend Aidan Hartley, a journalist based in Nairobi, who called me at 4 a.m. on 5 November. He'd just seen something on the wire he thought might interest me.

'This better be good,' I said.

'It is. Robert Maxwell's missing at sea.'

Maxwell's death put an end to his lawsuit. As for *The Modern Review*'s solicitors, they reduced their bill to £14,100 and agreed to let the magazine pay in instalments. We never heard anything from the police.

Having got over that hump, *The Modern Review* survived for another four years. Nothing ever happened to match the excitement of those first few weeks, but there were some highs. In the summer of 1992 I dispatched an undercover female reporter to Cornwall to receive some personal instruction from D.M. Thomas on the art of erotic writing. As expected, he misbehaved himself. In 1993 the magazine published the unexpurgated transcript of an increasingly acrimonious fax correspondence between Julie Burchill and Camille Paglia that ended with Julie calling the Humanities Professor a 'crazy old dyke'. You can still find the whole exchange on the Internet. My proudest achievement was persuading Rob Long, an executive producer of *Cheers,* to write a regular column in which he documented his strange relationship with his agent. The columns formed the basis of an hilarious book – *Conversations With My Agent* – which made it on to the *Los Angeles Times* bestseller list.

There were also some lows. I was threatened with another lawsuit in 1994, this time by Elizabeth Hurley. She'd got wind of the fact that I intended to print some semi-nude photographs of her and hired the firm of Schilling & Lom to put the frighteners on me. I thought that was a bit rich considering she'd posed for similar photographs in *GQ*, *Esquire* and *Loaded*, but then that was before she'd become famous for wearing *that* dress to the premier of *Four Weddings and a Funeral*. Elizabeth Hurley is the first actress in history who didn't get noticed until she put her clothes on.

The biggest low by far was my quarrel with Julie Burchill. I first met Julie in 1984 when she left Tony Parsons and moved in with Cosmo Landesman, a 29-year-old American journalist who happened to be my next-door neighbour. Julie became – quite literally – the girl next door and we instantly turned into New Best Friends. I think she liked the fact that I was so obnoxious. I was a 20-year-old Oxford undergraduate at the time suffering from what I diagnosed as 'negative charisma' – I only had to walk across a crowded room in which I knew nobody and nobody knew me and already I had made enemies. Julie probably took to me because detesting me would have been far too obvious. She always liked doing the opposite of what was expected of her. Whatever the reason, I was grateful for her friendship. I was desperate to break into journalism and in spite of being only twenty-five Julie was one of the most famous journalists in the country with columns in *The Face, Time Out* and *The Sunday Times*. I remember one occasion, a few months after meeting her, when I stood on the window ledge of Cosmo's fourth-floor flat and said she only had to give the word and I'd jump: her friendship meant that much to me.

'Go on then, jump,' she giggled.

Rather sheepishly, I climbed back into the room.

Nevertheless, she was supportive in her own way. When she got bored of doing her *Time Out* column she suggested that I ghost it and we'd split the money. This arrangement only produced one piece but she was so pleased with the result she included it in *Love It or Shove It*, a 'Greatest Hits' collection of her journalism.[1] She also kept up a stream of sisterly advice in letters to me while I was still at Brasenose, my Oxford college. 'How do you convince women you are not merely a cuddly teddy-bear surrogate, with that 12-year-old's nose of yours?' she wrote in 1986. 'Cosmo says the answer is sodomy – no woman can fail to take a man seriously after being sodomized. For a liberal democrat he can be very BASIC at times.'

Julie could be very funny. She was once at a dinner party with Katherine Hamnett when the designer announced – with the air of someone making a profound observation – that the young poor were better dressed than the young rich. 'Only because they can't afford your clothes,' quipped Julie. Cosmo called her 'my Queen' and there was undoubtedly something regal about her. She had a natural authority, which was rather surprising given her cartoonish appearance and squeaky, high-pitched voice, but few dared to contradict her. Like Evelyn Waugh, she had the effect of making people want to please her. It had something to do with her journalistic reputation as a ferocious attack dog – no one wanted to get on her bad side.

---

[1] 'Waiting for the revolution', *Love It or Shove It* (London: Century, 1985).

She only had to refrain from attacking someone in order for them to feel immensely flattered. Seeing her at a party, usually seated with a glass of champagne while the great and the good lined up to kiss her ring, you had the impression she was one of the great personalities of the age. At the time I thought of her as having 'movie-star charisma' but I've met dozens of movie stars since and none of them have had her force of personality.

The reason this is all in the past tense is because I haven't seen or spoken to Julie since 1995. Our quarrel began when the *Guardian* expressed an interest in buying *The Modern Review* in March of that year. Several newspapers had incorporated elements of the magazine into their make-up – *The Sunday Times* based its 'Culture' section on *The Modern Review* – but none had offered to buy it before. However, the *Guardian* made it clear that the magazine's original formula – smart writers on dumb things – would have to be updated if they were to remain interested. Too many broadsheet journalists were now pulling the same stunt. It no longer gave us a distinctive editorial identity.

I convened a series of meetings with the magazine's staff to discuss what direction we might take it in. I thought they'd all be delighted that I'd managed to find a newspaper interested in buying it. Proper wages at last! What I hadn't anticipated was that the possibility that *The Modern Review* might be moved out of my flat meant that someone else might edit it. A focus of opposition soon emerged and, to my astonishment, that person was Charlotte Raven. Charlotte was only twenty-five. She was a lively, intelligent writer, but she'd never edited anything before in her life. Her main task in the office was typing! However, she had an advantage that the other potential candidates lacked: she was sleeping with Julie Burchill.

Then several things happened at once. As quickly as it had arisen, the *Guardian*'s interest in *The Modern Review* fizzled out and Wallace Kingston, the magazine's ad salesman, was struck down by a mysterious illness. (Diabetes, it turned out.) He confessed that he'd only managed to sell £1,147.50 of space in the next issue, a figure somewhat short of his usual average of £10,000. Suddenly, the magazine was in the throes of a financial crisis. Faced with the prospect of my kingdom falling into enemy hands, and with nothing left in my treasury, I was sorely tempted just to torch the place. The more I thought about it, the more the idea appealed to me. *The Modern Review* had entered the world in a blaze of publicity – why not leave it that way too? I decided to consult a lawyer friend of mine. Was I legally entitled to close it down, given that Julie owned half the voting shares?

'Strictly speaking, no,' he said. 'But you'd probably get away with it.'

What lingering doubts I had were swept away when Julie threatened to break a commitment she'd made to put in an appearance at a *Modern Review* seminar at the Design Museum. Several thousand pounds of sponsorship money were riding on her attendance: if she didn't turn up, the magazine wouldn't get the cash. Why wouldn't she come?

'Because I never want to see your ugly little face again,' she explained, matter-of-factly. 'You've been an embarrassment to me for years.'[1]

Click. Dial-tone.

Okay, I thought, you've asked for it. I held an emergency meeting of those members of staff who were still loyal to me – all three of them – and told them what I wanted to do: close the magazine down in secret without telling Julie or Charlotte. Miraculously, they agreed to help. Over the next two weeks we secretly put together a 'Greatest Hits' issue and smuggled it down to our printers. I wrote a 2,000-word editorial announcing that this would be the last ever issue of *The Modern Review*

---

[1] This comment seemed to come out of nowhere. Relations between us weren't particularly good at this point, but I was totally unprepared for such a cold-hearted dismissal. It was as if my mother suddenly decided to headbutt me. Until this point, it never would have occurred to me that our friendship could be dissolved by a single, cruel remark – but it could and it was.

and described the dramatic circumstances that had led to its demise: Julie was having a lesbian affair with one of the contributors. On the cover were the words: 'That's all Folks!'

As soon as the issue hit the newsstands, the press went nuts. According to one media critic, my dispute with Julie received forty-eight yards of column inches, making it the second biggest story of the week after Bosnia.[1] The press first reported it as a news story then followed up by asking whether a spat between two journalists should have received so much coverage. In some ways, I wished it hadn't. The publicity was far from favourable. I joked at the time that there was only one thing worse than being talked about and that was being Toby Young. Among other indignities, I was compared to Hitler in the *Independent on Sunday*.[2] During the week the scandal raged I lost half a stone – the public humiliation diet!

Julie's line, repeated in endless interviews, was that I had thrown some sort of tantrum and destroyed the magazine in a jealous rage. 'He has acted like a spoilt child whose favourite toy is in danger of being taken away,' she told the *Evening Standard*.

She had a point. I'd sweated blood to produce *The Modern Review* and this was the thanks I got? How dare members of the magazine's staff, people I'd personally plucked out of obscurity, turn on me? Did they really think that Charlotte had the energy, the patience and the talent to put out a new

---

[1] 'One of our researchers has been up all night measuring the Burchill/Young coverage and has come up with a figure of 1,705 inches, or 48 yards, second only to Bosnia.' Stephen Glover, 'Such a small earthquake', *Evening Standard*, 7 June, 1995.

[2] It was Charlotte Raven who made the comparison. 'I have been cast as the bimbo from hell, the typist with misplaced ambitions who would stop at nothing, least of all the ensnaring of the affections of the proprietress, in order to build up my empire,' she was quoted as saying. 'What can I say? It is a case of Toby's paranoia and obsession with us. It is Hitler in his bunker, flailing about.' Quoted by Decca Aitkenhead, 'Two's company, but three's an interview', *Independent on Sunday*, 4 June, 1995.

issue of the magazine every other month? What ingratitude!
Harrumph!

But it was Julie I felt most betrayed by. How could she reject
me for Charlotte? I believed in the oath we'd sworn again and
again, whenever we got drunk, in which we'd promised undying
loyalty to each other. There was something absurdly sophomoric about it – I'd lost count of the times we'd sealed this
pact by piercing our thumbs and pressing them together – but
it had seemed real to me. *An oath is an oath, damn it!* When
she turned on me, casting me out as she had done all the other
people she'd ever cared about, I felt as if she had broken a
sacred covenant.

Why did she behave as she did? Boredom, no doubt, played
a part. Julie seems to suffer from a compulsion to turn her life
upside down every ten years or so. At sixteen she'd run away
from home; at twenty-five she'd left her first husband; and now,
at thirty-six, she was abandoning Cosmo and starting a new
life with someone else. At each stage she'd burnt her bridges.
She had a scorched earth policy towards her friends and family:
once they started to bore her, she lit the blue touch paper and
stood well back. BOOM! For those of us who loved her, it was
a painful experience.

I was nervous when Graydon Carter called. How should I play
it? I desperately wanted the job but I didn't want him to think
I was some lapdog who'd come running whenever he whistled.

'How much money were you thinking of paying me?' I
ventured.

Graydon was incredulous.

'How much *money*? Who are you, Woodward fucking
Bernstein? Are you telling me you won't come over here for a
month unless I pay you a ton of money? I thought you wanted
this? Listen, I shouldn't be telling you this, but Si wants to meet
you. He doesn't ask to meet a lot of people, you know.'

Oh my God! Si Newhouse Jr wanted to meet me! What had
I said? I started back-pedalling furiously.

'Well, gosh, yes, that is an honour. I'd *love* to meet Si. I don't care what you pay me. In fact . . .'

'Look, I'll pay you $10,000, okay?'

Now it was my turn to whistle. If I managed to parlay this offer into a full-time job I'd end up being paid $120,000 a year. That was four times as much as I'd earned in 1994.

'When d'you want me to start?'

'How about July 5?'

That was four weeks away. The idea of uprooting myself from London in less than a month was, frankly, ridiculous. Apart from everything else, there was my girlfriend Syrie Johnson to consider. Syrie had a full-time job. Would she be prepared to drop everything and come to America with me? I doubted it.

'No problem,' I said.

2

LHR – JFK

I arrived at the Virgin check-in desk at Heathrow on 4 July, 1995 in a state of some excitement. After my conversation with Graydon I'd been sent a 'Premium Economy' ticket to JFK, a totally unexpected honour. I'd only ever flown in steerage before and was looking forward to a bit of pampering. In particular, I was hoping I might be upgraded to Upper Class. A few days earlier Alex had flown to Los Angeles on a Premium ticket to profile Metallica for the *Daily Mail* and had been upgraded when the section turned out to be full. According to Alex, who called to boast about this the moment he got to his hotel, the ground staff automatically categorised passengers as 'SU' (Suitable for Upgrade) or 'NSU' (Not Suitable for Upgrade) and they'd taken one look at him and decided he wouldn't look out of place in Upper Class. 'I was wearing a dinner jacket at the time,' he quipped. I assumed he was joking – about the DJ, anyway – but I wasn't taking any chances. I was wearing a heavy tweed suit and carrying a copy of *The Spectator*.

There was a long line of people waiting to check in for economy but no queue for Premium. The perks were beginning already.

I strode up to the desk, put down my suitcase and handed the woman my ticket.

'Are you a Premium Economy passenger, sir?' she asked,

30

ignoring my outstretched hand. 'This desk is reserved for Premium ticket-holders only.'

'Yes, I'm aware of that,' I said, haughtily. Then, not wanting to antagonise her, I smiled, lowered my voice and added: 'Don't worry. I'm not trying to jump the queue.'

I didn't want to endanger my chances of being upgraded.

'I'm afraid our Premium Economy section is full this afternoon, sir,' she said, taking my ticket. 'Let me see what I can do.'

As she buried her head in her computer terminal, my hopes soared. *At last! I'm going to see how the other half lives!* Just to be on the safe side, though, I fished a copy of *Brideshead Revisited* out of my jacket pocket and put it on the counter.

'The best I can offer you is an aisle seat, I'm afraid.'

'Anywhere in Upper Class is fine by me.'

She looked up from her computer terminal: 'Pardon?'

I stared at her for a few seconds until the penny finally dropped.

'You don't mean an aisle seat in economy?'

'That's right, sir.'

'You're *downgrading* me?'

'I'm sorry, sir, but Premium Economy is completely full.'

'Why not upgrade me then?'

'I'm afraid I'm not authorised to do that, sir.'

She gave me a slightly frosty look: NSU.

'Could you at least give me a voucher for the lounge?' I pleaded. 'It's the least you can do considering you're downgrading me.'

'Sorry, sir, but the lounge is reserved for our Upper Class passengers.'

It was the last straw.

'In that case, why's it called "the lounge"? Why isn't it called "the sitting room"?'

She didn't get it.

The *best* she could offer me turned out to be right at the back of the plane next to a Mormon gentleman called Bryce who insisted on telling me all about his trip to London. Apparently, it had included visits to Buckingham Palace, Madame Tussaud's and the British Museum. The only pleasant part of the seven-and-a-half hour journey was when the aircraft began its descent into JFK and Bryce pointed out the Manhattan skyline which, at that very moment, was lit up by dozens of fireworks. I had forgotten that July 4th was Independence Day.

'It's true what they say,' I murmured. 'You really are a welcoming people.'

Bryce gave me a quizzical look.

'Doncha know what's happening here?' he asked. 'We're celebrating the fact that we got rid of you people two hundred years ago.'

When we landed at JFK it became apparent that they might not be too keen to let people like me back in. Overweight immigration officers, stretching the seams of their black uniforms to breaking point, herded the disembarking passengers into pens according to whether they were American citizens or not. Suddenly, I found myself surrounded by a sea of brown faces. Landing at JFK is the modern equivalent of arriving at Ellis Island at the beginning of the twentieth century. Like my fellow travellers, I was an immigrant seeking to make a fresh start in the United States. The pen I was in was marked 'Non-US' but it might as well have been labelled 'Tired and Huddled Masses'. I had a sense, which I was to have again and again over the next five years, of being in some hackneyed Hollywood melodrama about America rather than the country itself. Life in the States often feels strangely clichéd in this way, which is a problem from a writer's point of view. 'Oh come on!' the reader is likely to think as he comes across a description of trying to book a table at a hot, Manhattan restaurant or being given a ticket by a Californian Highway Patrol Officer. 'It's not really like that.' But it is really like that.

I was in the International Arrivals Building for over an hour before I emerged into the tropical humidity of New York in

July. No one had told me about this. It was like being plunged into an overheated swimming pool, thick with chlorine. The fact that I was wearing a heavy tweed suit didn't help. As I pushed my way to the bus stop carrying a large suitcase and a computer bag I could feel little droplets of sweat rolling down my back. When I'd lain awake at night imagining a new life for myself in America this wasn't how I'd pictured my entrance.

I'd arranged to rent a room for a month from my friend Sam Pratt on 37th Street between 9th and 10th, an area of Manhattan known as Hell's Kitchen. It had the advantage of being near the Port Authority bus terminal on 42nd Street, so I didn't have to lug my suitcase very far, but beyond that it had little to recommend it. Originally an Irish neighbourhood, in the eighties it had been overrun by junkies and winos, making it one of the less salubrious parts of town. 'You'll think you've wandered on to the set of a Tarantino movie,' chuckled Sam.

Walking the few blocks to 37th Street, dressed in my tweeds and carrying a suitcase, I was convinced I was going to be mugged. I might as well have had a sign round my neck saying 'Tourist'. An acquaintance of mine had been mugged twice within twenty-four hours of arriving in Manhattan and he'd been staying on the Upper East Side. On the second occasion he'd been relieved of his shoes! I didn't fancy picking my way through the broken vials and discarded needles that littered the pavements of Hell's Kitchen in my socks.

Fortunately, I made it to 441 W37th Street unscathed. I went to bed straight away, and dreamt about Syrie.

3

THE CALL OF THE MILD

I'd lived in America once before. After graduating from Oxford I'd been given a Fulbright Award, enabling me to go to spend a year at Harvard as a 'Special Student'. This was a misleading title since, as far as I could tell, anyone could become a Special Student provided they were willing to pay the tuition fees. Still, it gave me a chance to take several post-graduate courses with some of the world's best teachers. My father was keen for me to become an academic and this was an opportunity to stick a toe in the water.

I picked a bad time to enrol at an Ivy League university. When I arrived at Harvard in September, 1987 America was in the grip of the political correctness epidemic. The entire student body seemed to be afflicted. The prevailing orthodoxy was that concepts like 'truth' and 'beauty' had no place in contemporary education. The idea that a person could transcend the influence of his race, gender, sexual orientation and socio-economic status to achieve a kind of bird's-eye view of a subject was completely false. There was no such thing as 'objectivity', merely a number of competing points of view, and universities were under an obligation to teach all of them, not just those of 'dead, white, European males'. In the Harvard humanities departments, the faculty was under pressure to jettison its core curriculum in favour of a more diverse, multi-cultural approach, something that had already occurred at Stanford where the mandatory humanities course on the 'Great Books' had been replaced with one called 'Culture, Ideas, and Values'.

I'd elected to live in a 'smoking dorm' even though I wasn't a smoker myself on the assumption that women who smoked would be more likely to 'put out'. That wasn't the case. On the contrary, they were a bunch of 'femi-nazis' who spent their entire time policing the behaviour of the male residents of the dorm for signs of sexism. Anyone hoping to have sex with these Witchfinder Generals had to follow a Byzantine code called 'the Antioch rules' whereby you had to seek the woman's formal permission at every stage in the seduction process: 'Would it be okay to feel your left breast or would you prefer it if my hands remained on your waist?' The Antioch rules probably did more to curb promiscuity on America's campuses in the eighties than the AIDS epidemic.

In order to help pay the fees – the Fulbright Award only covered my living expenses – I became a Teaching Fellow in the Graduate School of Arts and Sciences. This brought me into daily contact with plenty of pretty students but anything of a sexual nature was strictly *verboten*. According to yet another set of rules, I wasn't allowed to socialise with any of my charges outside the classroom unless there were at least three of them present *at all times*. I could just about understand the ban on seeing one of them by themselves – what white, European male could resist the chance to pounce on a defenceless American maiden? – but why not two of them? Presumably, there was a danger I might convert them to troilism.

I remember being very excited when *The Closing of the American Mind* was published shortly after I arrived. An attack on 'cultural relativism' by the University of Chicago's Allan Bloom, it was an arrow aimed straight at the heart of the political correctness movement. Bloom was an intellectual heavyweight who'd translated Plato's *Republic* and Rousseau's *Emile* and he made a persuasive case for the 'Great Books' approach to the humanities. According to Bloom, the purpose of a liberal education is to enable young people to transcend the unique circumstances of their individual lives and become rational creatures capable of thinking for themselves. Universities are not there to hold up mirrors to students, affirming their identity as women or homosexuals or African-Americans. They're there to challenge them, to teach them that these arbitrary facts about themselves are irrelevant when it comes to answering the most important question of all: how to lead a good life.

I agreed wholeheartedly with Bloom, but what particularly appalled me about political correctness wasn't the creed itself but the dogmatism of its proponents. This is hardly an original point, but after three years at Oxford, with its almost decadent atmosphere of intellectual freedom, I was shocked by how little dissent was tolerated at Harvard. Anyone who disagreed with the new orthodoxy was automatically branded a racist or a sexist or a homophobe – and the consequences of this were as serious as they had been for those branded communists during the McCarthy era. At Harvard, the most famous victim of political correctness was the historian Stephan Thernstrom who had to abandon teaching his class on the 'Peopling of America' after he was dubbed 'racially insensitive'. His crime was to refer to America's aboriginal population as 'Indians' rather than 'Native Americans'.

The upshot was that very few people disagreed with the tenets of political correctness. This was the most striking thing about Harvard: the absence of any real intellectual diversity. At Oxford, every political viewpoint had been represented, from revolutionary Marxism to out-and-out fascism. Among the ten undergraduates who'd studied Philosophy, Politics and Economics with me at Brasenose College there was a greater range of opinions than in the entire student body at Harvard. The cultural relativists may have believed in presenting students with a multiplicity of different perspectives, but in reality only one was tolerated – cultural relativism.[1] It was more like being at university in fifteenth-century Spain than in late-twentieth-century America.

---

[1] Allan Bloom writes: 'There is one thing a professor can be absolutely certain of: almost every student entering the university believes, or says he believes, that truth is relative. If this belief is put to the test, one can count on the

I was baffled by this. How could there be so little freedom of thought when freedom of speech was guaranteed in the US Constitution? It didn't compute. It wasn't until I discovered Tocqueville that I began to understand how this state of affairs had come about.

Alexis de Tocqueville was thirty when the first volume of *Democracy in America* was published in 1835. The scion of a French, noble family, Tocqueville regarded America as a fairly successful experiment in democracy and a model for the kind of society France might become. However, *Democracy in America* is shot through with a nostalgic yearning for the aristocratic societies of Europe's recent past, particularly that of Britain. He saw the arrival of democracy in Europe as inevitable, yet he was far from convinced of its superiority to the type of regime it was destined to replace. For Tocqueville, the best kind of democratic society was one that preserved the virtues of an aristocratic one, particularly the fierce, independent spirit that he regarded as the strongest bulwark against tyranny.

Unlike some of his contemporaries, Tocqueville did not equate democracy with liberty. While it was true that, in America, freedom co-existed with democracy, tyranny was an ever-present danger within any democratic society. In the case of America, Tocqueville wasn't concerned about the possibility of the government becoming too powerful since he recognised that the Constitution provides all sorts of safeguards against that. No, the danger lay with the people. The greatest threat to freedom in America was posed by 'the tyranny of the majority'.

Tocqueville regarded a love of equality as the chief hallmark of a democratic society. Indeed, the principle of democracy rests on equality – only if all men are held to be equal does the rule

---

students' reaction: they will be uncomprehending. That anyone should regard the proposition as not self-evident astonishes them, as though he were calling into question 2 + 2 = 4.' *The Closing of the American Mind* (New York: Simon & Schuster, 1987) p. 25.

of the majority makes sense. The reason a greater number of votes is superior to a lesser is because each person's opinion is given an equal weight. However, this means there's always a danger that the majority will exercise dominion over the individual. Tocqueville wasn't worried about people being oppressed *physically* in democratic societies, at least not in America. Rather, it was people's minds that were at risk. Once the majority had spoken, once it had come down in favour of one point of view as opposed to another, how could anyone disagree? According to the principle of democracy, the majority *must* be right: '[T]he majority possesses an empire so absolute and so irresistible that one must in a way renounce one's rights as a citizen and so to speak one's quality as a man when one wants to deviate from the path it has traced.' In this way, freedom of thought is extinguished; the only opinions held by anyone are herd opinions. More than this, people gradually lose the ability to act under their own steam. They become docile and listless, followers rather than leaders.

Tocqueville referred to this form of oppression as 'mild despotism', an erosion of liberty far more serious than the violent form of despotism characteristic of feudal societies:

> it covers [society]'s surface with a network of small, complicated, painstaking, uniform rules through which the most original minds and the most vigorous souls cannot clear a way to surpass the crowd; it does not break wills, but it softens them, bends them, and directs them; it rarely forces one to act, but it constantly opposes itself to one's acting; it does not destroy, it prevents things from being born; it does not tyrannize, it hinders, compromises, enervates, extinguishes, dazes, and finally reduces each nation to being nothing more than a herd of timid and industrious animals of which the government is the shepherd.

So had America succumbed to this intellectual torpor? Or had it managed to preserve the bold, masculine spirit that liberty depends on? Tocqueville's feelings about the States were mixed. He praised the American people for having devised all sorts of ingenious ways of maintaining their vitality: local self-government, the separation of church and state, a free press, indirect elections, an independent judiciary and a vast multitude of voluntary associations. Admirable though these mechanisms were, however, they weren't sufficient to preserve the autonomy of thought and conduct that true freedom requires. America's brand of democracy was preferable to most of the regimes in nineteenth-century Europe, particularly that of France under Louis Philippe. But the Americans hadn't succeeded in importing the virtues of Europe's best aristocratic societies. In a famous passage in *Democracy in America* Tocqueville writes: 'I do not know any country where, in general, less independence of mind and genuine freedom of discussion reign than in America.'

Looking around me at Harvard in the late eighties, nothing seemed to have changed. What was political correctness, with its 'racially sensitive' speech codes designed to protect the feelings of minorities, if not a kind of enforced mildness? The students were the best and the brightest America had to offer and while they were lively and engaging in all sorts of ways they seemed to be suffering from what Allan Bloom called 'an impoverishment of the soul'. They were less interested in expanding their horizons than packing their 'résumés' with career-enhancing activities. The reason they subscribed to the dogma of political correctness was because it enjoyed the support of the majority and they didn't have the will to resist anything that possessed such unimpeachable moral authority. The students were incapable of independent thought or action; they just went along with the crowd. They lacked the manliness, the moral courage, that opposing tyranny requires.

I was about to conclude that America wasn't the land of the free and home of the brave after all when, totally unexpectedly, I stumbled across exactly the kind of spirited citizens that

Tocqueville prized so highly. I'd decided to take a class on 'the Hollywood comedy of remarriage' taught by a philosophy professor called Stanley Cavell. My interest had been piqued when I'd discovered that much of the course work involved watching screwball comedies of the thirties and forties. According to Professor Cavell, in films like *Bringing Up Baby*, *The Awful Truth* and *Adam's Rib*, Hollywood had rediscovered 'the theme of remarriage' that Shakespeare had explored in his romantic comedies, particularly *The Winter's Tale*. Rather amazingly, Cavell believed that these films were as worthy of serious critical attention as Shakespeare's plays.

Stanley Cavell's two passions in life were philosophy and these black-and-white classics and, in this class, he'd found a way of combining them. It wasn't long before he'd imparted his enthusiasm for these films to his students and I sat down to watch the first one – *The Lady Eve* – with a sense of real excitement. I wasn't disappointed. Preston Sturges is probably the most gifted writer-director Hollywood has ever produced and *The Lady Eve* is his masterpiece. I wasn't convinced it was up there with Shakespeare, but it was better than anything George Farquhar had done. The seeds of *The Modern Review* had been planted.

The second film in the series was *It Happened One Night*. Directed in 1934 by Frank Capra, it was the first ever film to win Academy Awards in all five major categories. In particular, it netted a Best Actor Oscar for its male lead, Clark Gable. I don't know how I managed to live until the age of twenty-four without noticing this hugely appealing star but watching him up there on that screen in *It Happened One Night* I was completely transfixed. What a contrast he made to the milksops I was surrounded by at Harvard. With his proud, cockerel strut and direct, no-nonsense manner, he seemed to embody all the virtues that Tocqueville had been searching for. At last! Here was a man who managed to combine the fierce independence of the British nobility with the openness and informality of a true democrat. Woe betide the petty martinet who accused

Gable of political incorrectness. If America could produce men like this, perhaps the experiment wasn't such a failure after all.

No doubt one of the reasons I found Gable so appealing in *It Happened One Night* is because he plays a New York newspaperman. I may have been toying with becoming an academic at this stage, but journalism was in my blood. Between graduating from Oxford and arriving at Harvard I'd worked at *The Times* for six months and I found the idea of the reporter-as-romantic-hero very intoxicating. To my delight, this dashing figure proved to be a staple of Hollywood remarriage comedies. Over the next few weeks, I watched a string of films in which the male lead was a plucky, enterprising journalist, from James Stewart in *The Philadelphia Story* to Cary Grant in *His Girl Friday*. It seemed genuine independence of mind and freedom of action did exist in America after all. These qualities could be found among New York newspapermen. If these films were anything to go by, they were a race of supermen. Indeed, they seemed to qualify for membership of 'the natural aristocracy' that Thomas Jefferson identified as America's best hope in a famous letter to John Adams in 1813.

I soon discovered why reporters were portrayed so sympathetically in these films: they were either written by journalists or based on material – plays, novels, short stories – produced by journalists. Indeed, it's not an exaggeration to say that the screwball comedy as a genre was invented by that crowd of newspapermen and magazine writers who went West in the twenties known as 'the Algonquin-to-Hollywood group'.[1] According to the film critic Pauline Kael, this group, which comprised 'some of the most talented alcoholics this country has ever produced', were lured to Los Angeles by the promise of huge salaries and immediately set about importing

---

[1] Pauline Kael, 'Raising Kane', *The Citizen Kane Handbook* (London: Methuen, 1985).

their irreverent, wise-cracking style into the movies. Out went stodgy melodramas set in mythical, central European principalities; in came madcap, antic comedies set in New York newspaper offices.

Clearly, the fearless, happy-go-lucky reporters that these writers stuck in their screenplays were idealised versions of themselves, but the heroic qualities they gave them weren't totally fictitious. The most prolific member of the Algonquin-to-Hollywood group was Ben Hecht, co-author of *The Front Page*, who had a hand in over one hundred screenplays, including *Scarface*, *Some Like It Hot* and *Notorious*. Hecht's autobiography, *A Child of the Century*, is a 654-page tribute to the virtues of the writers and journalists he associated with in Chicago and New York, some of whom followed him to Los Angeles: 'We spoke our mind on all subjects and each of us felt more vital to the world than all its political philosophers. Our tongues were our only leaders and our wits the only architects of tomorrow.'

Ben Hecht's greatest creation was Walter Burns, the cynical newspaper editor at the centre of *The Front Page*. When *The Front Page* was first produced in 1926, *The New York Times* theatre critic Walter Kerr described the essence of Burns's appeal as his ability 'to walk into a tough situation in order to be brutally nonchalant'. This was the chief characteristic of Ben Hecht's circle, their complete lack of sentimentality. They prided themselves on being far more tough-minded than the average American. They weren't constrained by the petty strictures that governed the behaviour of ordinary people; the majority held no terror for them. After all, what is sentiment if not herd emotion? Indeed, their whole existence, with its regular bouts of drinking, gambling and whoring, was a two-fingered salute to bourgeois morality. As the *New Yorker* writer Brendan Gill puts it in the 'Introduction' to *The Collected Dorothy Parker*, Manhattan in the Roaring Twenties was Sodom: 'Drinking, smoking, sniffing cocaine, bobbing one's hair, dancing the Charleston, necking, getting "caught" – it was hard to imagine that things could go much farther before civilization itself broke down.' Even though the term didn't exist back then, the writers and journalists who chronicled the Jazz Age were profoundly politically incorrect. They weren't merely unafraid of being censured by the majority; they took a devilish delight in it. They shared the aristocrat's contempt for the middle classes – and in America that included most of the population.[1]

Of all Ben Hecht's colleagues, perhaps the most heroic was Herman J. Mankiewicz, the ex-*New York Times* journalist who wrote *Citizen Kane*. He specialised in antagonising the rich and powerful. On one occasion Mankiewicz was sitting in the dining room at Columbia when the head of the studio, Harry Cohn, strode in. After assuming his usual place at the head of the table, Cohn started sounding off about a 'lousy' film he'd seen the previous night. When one of his underlings protested that the audience he'd seen it with had loved it, Cohn silenced him with a wave of his hand. The mogul had a foolproof device for determining whether a film was any good or not: 'If my fanny squirms, it's bad. If my fanny doesn't squirm, it's good. It's as simple as that.' All the flunkies sitting at the table greeted this announcement with a suitably awe-struck air – all, that is, except one: Herman J. Mankiewicz.

'Imagine,' he said. 'The whole world wired to Harry Cohn's ass!'

Of course, the fact that Jefferson's natural aristocrats had once been alive and kicking in the American journalistic community didn't mean they still were. Was there any evidence that men like Ben Hecht and Herman J. Mankiewicz could still be found working on newspapers and magazines in New York? Towards the end of 1987, I decided to spend an afternoon combing the shelves of the newsagent in Harvard Square in the hope of discovering their modern-day equivalents.

---

[1] When Harold Ross originally conceived of *The New Yorker* in 1922, it was going to be subtitled 'Not for the little old lady from Dubergue'.

I wasn't particularly impressed. The attitude of American journalists to the rich and famous seemed to be far more deferential than that of their Fleet Street counterparts. The scrappy newspapermen idolised in those black-and-white films had evidently gone the way of linotype.

Then a magazine caught my eye. The first thing I noticed was its title: *Spy*. That was the name of the fictional magazine James Stewart is employed by in *The Philadelphia Story*. Coincidence? I pulled it off the shelf and flipped through it. Aha, I thought to myself. Now we're talking. *Spy* appeared to consist entirely of malicious gossip about various prominent public figures. On page after page, the most odious characters on the national stage were eviscerated with a muck-raking glee. It was a bit like *Private Eye*, except it had evidently been produced with far more care and attention. Indeed, with its elegantly written essays and old-fashioned typographical style, it appeared to be a self-conscious attempt to mimic the great New York magazines of the twenties and thirties. Clearly, this was exactly what I'd been looking for.

Spy became a lifeline for the remainder of my time at Harvard. It wasn't just the quality of the articles, which were far wittier and better written than anything I'd come across in Britain. It was the utter fearlessness with which *Spy* skewered the most powerful people in the land. *Spy* took no prisoners; the people who produced it were beholden to no one. Here, between the covers of this little magazine, was the distillation of that independent, aristocratic spirit that Tocqueville had eulogized. This was the clear, unpolluted air that the gods breathed on Mount Olympus.

I left Harvard in the summer of 1988 with a thoroughly romantic notion of what it would be like to work for a New York magazine. In my mind's eye, the offices of *Spy* were peopled by the contemporary equivalents of the characters played by James Stewart, Cary Grant and Clark Gable. As a journalist, there could be no finer place to be. For the next seven years, wherever I worked, my imagination was always fixed on this mythical paradise across the Atlantic. One day, I thought. One day.

Alas, by the time I got the call from Graydon Carter, *Spy* was a shadow of its former self, unloved and unread. However, that didn't matter. Working for *Vanity Fair* was the next best thing. You see, in its heyday *Spy* had been edited by two men. One of these was Kurt Andersen, a steely midwesterner who'd previously worked for *Time;* the other was Graydon Carter. As far as I was concerned Graydon was no less a figure than Walter Burns himself.

4

THE FIRST ROOM

On 5 July, 1995 I had to decide what to wear for my first day at work. At that time *Vanity Fair* was based at 350 Madison Avenue between 44th and 45th, a twenty-three-storey building a few blocks west of Grand Central station. '350,' as everyone called it, was then the headquarters of Condé Nast, the company that publishes *Vanity Fair* along with over a dozen other glossy magazines including *Vogue, The New Yorker, GQ, Architectural Digest, House & Garden, Condé Nast Traveler, Allure, Self, Mademoiselle* and *Glamour*. (Condé Nast has since moved to 4 Times Square.) Visitors to the building had to check in at the front desk and were either directed to the main lifts in the atrium or herded into 'the service elevator', a rickety, Heath-Robinson contraption reserved for messengers, delivery boys and the like. Security was tight after a group of animal-rights activists had staged a sit-in in the office of *Vogue* editor Anna Wintour on the thirteenth floor.

When I worked at *The Times* in 1986 I was told to dress as if I might be sent off to interview the Archbishop of Canterbury at any moment. The dress code at *Vanity Fair*, by contrast, had been described to me by Dana Brown, Graydon's secretary, as 'real casual', which I took to mean jeans and a T-shirt. That suited me fine because of the sweltering heat. After some deliberation I decided on a pair of vintage 501s and a Haynes XL T-shirt that reproduced a *Modern Review* cover featuring a bare-chested Keanu Reeves and the strapline: 'Young, Dumb and Full of Come'. I'd already sent Graydon one of these and thought he might get a kick out of seeing me wearing one.

I was supposed to be in his office at 10 a.m., so at 9.55 a.m. I presented myself at the front desk of 350.

'Could you direct me to *Vanity Fair* please?' I asked the security officer.

'Ninth floor,' he barked. 'Report to the supervisor.'

Supervisor? Good God, I thought. They do take their security seriously.

I entered one of the lifts – a gleaming, stainless steel cubicle – and noticed that I was only given the option of going to two floors: three or eleven. Where was nine?

I went back to the front desk and asked the security officer how to get to the ninth floor. 'Take that elevator over there,' he said, pointing towards another lift tucked away behind a couple of pillars. I followed his instructions and found myself in a steel cage that wouldn't have been out of place in a Soviet-built housing block circa 1925. An elderly black man was sitting on a stool in front of a giant, wooden lever that could be pushed or pulled into one of two positions: Start or Stop. Clearly, the security officer had taken one look at my jeans and T-shirt and assumed I was a messenger. This was the service elevator.

'What floor?' asked the lift-operator.

I decided to chance it.

'Nine please.'

The lever was pulled and the ancient machine groaned into life.

The ninth floor turned out to be the Condé Nast 'Messenger Center', a warren of corridors populated almost entirely by Hispanic young men. In London when I'd wanted to send a package somewhere urgently I'd put it on a bike, but the business district of Manhattan is so compact packages are generally delivered on foot. These young men were the delivery boys. It was a fascinating glimpse into below-stairs life at Condé Nast, one I was never to have again. The degree of segregation between the classes at 350 was far greater than any I'd encountered on Fleet Street. Not only did they use different lifts, but once you were in the Messenger Center it was virtually impossible to get out of it other than by taking the service elevator back down to the lobby. When Condé Nast editorial assistants needed to dispatch a package they'd take one of the normal lifts to the ninth floor and literally pop the package through a hatch. That was the extent of their contact with the Messenger Center.

The 'supervisor' was the guy receiving the packages on the other side of the hatch and by the time I found him I was five minutes late for my appointment. He looked at me suspiciously – I was a little too casually dressed even by delivery boy standards – and told me to wait there while he called Graydon's office.

'They been lookin' for you,' he said with a chuckle as he replaced the receiver. 'They're sendin' somebody up to fetch you.'

A few minutes later, a face appeared at the hatch.

'Dana Brown from Graydon Carter's office,' he announced. 'I believe you have a "package" for me?'

Still chuckling, the supervisor took out a huge bunch of keys and unlocked a small door. Seconds later I found myself face to face with someone who looked like a male model. In addition to being extremely handsome he was dressed immaculately in the style known as 'wise guy chic': a shiny, charcoal-grey shirt, a matching tie, black pleated trousers and black tasselled loafers. Needless to say, this was the same Dana Brown who'd told me the dress code at *Vanity Fair* was 'real casual'. Dana, I subsequently learnt, had been 'discovered' by Graydon while he was working as a busboy at 44, the restaurant on the ground floor of the Royalton Hotel known as 'the Condé Nast canteen'. 'This kid was so beautiful it almost broke your heart to see him there,' Graydon confessed. Indeed, Graydon had such a high opinion of Dana's movie-star good looks that he often joked about putting him on the cover of the magazine: 'Who'd know the difference, right?'

'You must be Toby Young,' said Dana, flashing his dazzling white teeth and pumping my hand. 'Don't worry, this happens all the time. A few years back Norman Mailer got completely lost when he took the service elevator. We had to dispatch an extraction team to rescue him from the basement. Luckily, he didn't punch anyone out.'

Dana ushered me into a lift and together we glided down to the fourth floor. He explained that certain lifts in the atrium only went to floors three and 11, but the rest were fine. 'You'll figure it out,' he said.

Vanity Fair has been described as 'the house organ of the Eurotrash' but at first sight the magazine's offices, at least the ones in 350, were nothing special. When Graydon had taken over from Tina Brown he'd complained that the offices had looked like 'a fucking *Dynasty* set', but three years into his reign they resembled those of any other magazine. As you approached them from the lift area, the first thing you saw were the words VANITY FAIR in big, bold letters and, beneath them, a kindly-looking old lady behind a desk. This was Bernice Ellis, the magazine's receptionist. The contrast couldn't have been greater. It was as if she'd been put there to remind the staff of exactly who the readers were. When the magazine was originally re-launched in 1983, a press release described it as 'a "fun" magazine for the very, very highbrow', but that's not strictly accurate. As one former employee told the *Independent*: 'The biggest misunderstanding about *Vanity Fair* is that it's read by celebrities like Claus von Bülow who sit in book-lined rooms wearing monogrammed velvet slippers. In fact, it's read by women while they have their nails manicured in shopping malls across Illinois.'[1]

---

[1]According to *Spy*, in 1990 only 33 per cent of *Vanity Fair*'s readers had graduated from college, with another 34.4 per cent never having attended one. 'Flattery will get you 10 pages . . . maybe', *Spy*, August, 1990.

Graydon's office, though, was something else. It was enormous, the second largest in the building after that of Anna Wintour, the editor of *Vogue*, and Graydon surveyed his kingdom from behind a large, custom-made desk. There were two huge picture windows – it was a corner office, naturally – and, to the left of his desk, a conference table surrounded by wooden chairs. Graydon was smoking a Camel Light and talking on the phone when I was shown in and he motioned for me to sit down. It was 10.15 a. m. by this time, not a good start.

When he eventually hung up his first words to me were: 'What the fuck are you wearing? You look like you're in a grunge band or something.'

'Your secretary told me that the dress-code was casual,' I protested.

Graydon came out from behind his desk and shut the door of his office. He was wearing a white, Jermyn Street shirt, a black tie with white polka dots and a pair of tan suit trousers. He looked anything but casual.

'First of all, we don't call 'em "secretaries" over here,' he said. 'The correct term is "personal assistant". And secondly, "casual" doesn't mean this –' He gestured at what I was wearing. 'It's a code word. It means khakis and a polo shirt. Get Dana to take you shopping at The Gap.'

'The Gap?' I repeated, incredulously. 'Can I put the clothes on expenses?'

Graydon laughed.

'How was your flight?'

I took this as a cue.

'Thanks for sending me a business class ticket,' I said, almost tugging my forelock. 'Much appreciated.'

'I did?' he replied, genuinely surprised. 'That was a mistake.'

'Well, if it's any consolation, I got downgraded.'

He laughed again.

'Well look, it's good to have you here,' he said, sitting back down behind his desk. 'Hang out for a month, come to a few meetings, see how you like it. If it works out, great, if not, no big deal.'

Rather ominously, there was no mention of the fact that Si wanted to meet me. Still, this didn't seem like the right time to bring it up.

'Listen, thank you very much for giving me this opportunity,' I said, trying to sound sincere. 'I really, really appreciate it. I can't think of anywhere I'd rather be.'

Graydon narrowed his eyes at me.

'You think you've arrived, doncha?' he said. 'I hate to break it to you but you're only in the first room.' He paused. 'It's not nothing – don't get me wrong – but it's not that great either. Believe me, there are plenty of people in this town who got to the first room and then didn't get any further. After a year or so, maybe longer, you'll discover a secret doorway at the back of the first room that leads to the second room. In time, if you're lucky, you'll discover a doorway in the back of the second room that leads to the third. There are seven rooms in total and you're in the first. Doncha forget it.'

This, I later discovered, was Graydon's 'seven rooms' speech, a pep talk he gives to all new recruits. It's the nightclub theory of career advancement. I was the wannabe in Studio 54 who'd somehow managed to get past Steve Rubell at the door but was a long way from snorting coke off Margaret Trudeau's cleavage in the VIP room. It sounded like the speech Gordon Gekko gave to Bud Fox in *Wall Street*: 'You had what it takes to get through my door. Next question: You got what it takes to stay?'

Graydon's own progress through the seven rooms had been swift. Born in 1949, the son of a Royal Canadian Air Force pilot, he was brought up in the suburbs of Ottawa and got his first magazine job editing the *Canadian Review* in 1974. He arrived in New York in 1978 and landed a job at *Time* where he stayed for seven years. He left in 1985 to set up *Spy* with Kurt Andersen, edited that for six years, then became the editor of the *New York Observer*. Finally, in 1992, he landed the top job at *Vanity Fair*.

After I'd been dismissed, Dana took me along to meet Matt Tyrnauer and Aimée Bell, the two editors who'd be my 'rabbis' on the magazine. Matt and Aimée – or 'mattandaimée', as everyone calls them, since they're completely inseparable – have been with Graydon since his *Spy* days and are closer to him than anyone else at *Vanity Fair*. They aren't a couple but they've been working together for so long they can complete each other's sentences. Like all members of Graydon's inner circle, they give the impression that they regard the *Ab Fab* atmosphere of the Condé Nast magazine world as completely absurd, a source of constant scorn and ridicule, and yet they stop short of developing this into a full-blown critique. It's more of a defence mechanism, a way of letting people know that they don't take life at Condé Nast *too* seriously. It's as if they're stuck in an episode of *The Twilight Zone* and they want you to know that, unlike most of the other cast members, they realise things are a little weird.

At that time, Matt and Aimée were the editors of a section called 'Vanities' and shared an office on the side of the building that overlooked Madison Avenue. More senior editors had their own offices, the most prestigious being those that overlooked 44th Street. These were located on the left-hand side of the main thoroughfare as you walked towards Graydon's office from the reception area, a corridor known as 'the runway' because people had a tendency to strut down it in case the boss caught sight of them. Among his many idiosyncrasies, Graydon likes his underlings to move purposefully round the magazine's offices and occasionally snaps at people who walk too slowly, telling them to 'pick it up'.

Aimée took it upon herself to introduce me to the rest of the magazine's staff, starting with Wayne Lawson who has the rather longwinded title of 'Executive Literary Editor'. Later, Graydon confided in me that if you stick the word 'executive' or 'senior' in front of a person's job title you can give them the impression they've been promoted without having to grant them any more power. Next up was Elise O'Shaughnessy, the

'Executive Editor', followed by George Hodgman and Douglas Stumpf, the 'Senior Articles Editors'. Finally, we arrived at the office of Elizabeth Saltzman, *Vanity Fair*'s legendary 'Fashion Director'. Elizabeth doesn't need a fancy job title to convince her of her own importance. After Aimée had introduced us, Elizabeth indicated a photograph on her desk of Si Newhouse cradling an infant in his arms and asked me to guess who the baby was. I studied the picture for several seconds, imagining it was some celebrity, but drew a blank.

'D'you give up?' she asked.

'Yes.'

'It's me!' she screamed, then burst out laughing. The subtext of this apparently innocent exchange was of course: 'Don't fuck with me.'

Next door to Elizabeth's office was a walk-in wardrobe known as 'the fashion closet'. Aimée explained that this had been cleared, apparently in my honour, but for the time being I'd have to share it with someone called Chris Lawrence. I couldn't believe how well I was being treated. *Wait till Syrie hears about this!*

'Is that a standard Condé Nast perk?' I asked, awestruck.

'What?'

'Being given your own personal changing room.'

'I don't think you understand,' she replied. 'This is going to be your office.'

Duh!

After Aimée had gone, I gingerly poked my head around the door. *Good God!* It wasn't the closet's size that surprised me, though it was scarcely any bigger than a broom cupboard, but the fact that it was occupied by an exact replica of Graydon Carter in miniature, right down to the black tie with white polka dots.

'Hi,' said the apparition, standing up and extending his hand. 'I'm Chris Lawrence.'

Chris was a 25-year-old researcher who'd been brought in by Matt and Aimée to help reduce their workload. He was a self-confessed 'East Coast preppy frat boy' and, to my delight, a complete Anglophile. 'Dress British, think Yiddish,' he replied when I complemented him on his outfit. He peppered me with questions about Manchester bands I'd never heard of and asked me what my favourite Bond film was. When I said *From Russia With Love*, we clicked immediately.

'The gypsy catfight scene!' he exclaimed.

'My first masturbatory fantasy,' I sighed.

After we'd finished comparing notes on the other great catfight scenes in the Bond oeuvre and I'd offered to lend him my copy of Kingsley Amis's *James Bond Companion*, he asked how I was settling in. Had Graydon given me his 'seven rooms' speech yet? I told him he had and started pumping him for more information. What other initiation rituals could I look forward to?

'Have you tried browsing through a magazine at the concession stand?'

'No. Why?'

'Go ahead and try it,' he chuckled. 'You'll see.'

Towards the end of my first day, after I'd thoroughly explored the fourth floor, I concluded that the most striking thing about entering *Vanity Fair*'s offices for the first time was how grave everyone was. As I walked down the main corridor I saw people on either side of me crouched over their computer screens as if they were devising the Marshall Plan. This atmosphere of studious intensity seemed completely at odds with the general tone of the magazine. I wanted to grab them by the lapels and say: 'Lighten up, for Christ's sake. It's just an upscale supermarket tabloid.'

Of course, *Vanity Fair* is a great deal more than this. It's the world's leading general interest magazine and its per-page editorial budget is three or four times that of its nearest rival. The cost of producing just one of its covers could have kept *The Modern Review* afloat for a year. An aura of wealth and glamour wafts up from its pages along with the smell of a dozen perfume inserts and I was as intoxicated by it as the lady in the shopping mall in Illinois.[1] But I was expecting the ambience in the offices to be more . . . *theatrical* somehow. 'I don't run a magazine,' was Graydon's first thought when he took over the editorship. 'I run an opera company.' It struck me as being more like an accountancy firm.

At around 6.30 p.m. I left the offices with Chris and decided to see what would happen if I flicked through a magazine at the concession stand. Among editors of small magazines this stand was legendary. If you wanted to get your publication noticed in the New York media it had to be on sale here. Unfortunately, the stand was privately owned by a hard-nosed German couple called Margit and Helmut Larsen and they weren't impressed by titles like *The Modern Review*. I'd done everything I could to get them to stock it, including sending Helmut a box of cigars, all to no avail.

When I set eyes on them behind the counter I immediately realised my mistake. Helmut was a thin, slightly stooped figure with a pained expression on his face whereas Margit was built like a sumo wrestler. I'd schmoozed the wrong Larsen. Clearly, Margit was the one who wore the trousers – or, rather, the giant underpants.

I gingerly picked up a copy of *The New Yorker* and turned to the contents page.

'Excuse me,' said Margit in a thick German accent, 'but are you going to buy dat magazine?'

'I'm not sure,' I replied, winking at Chris. 'I want to see what's in it first.'

'IF YOU VONT TO SEE VOT'S IN IT, LOOK AT DE COVER,' she bellowed. 'DIS IS NOT A LIBRARY.'

---

[1] 'The success of any general-interest magazine depends on an accidental nimbus of authority, a lucky aura.' Martin Amis, *The Moronic Inferno and Other Visits to America* (London: Penguin, 1987) p. 131.

I couldn't believe the ferocity of her response. I heard laughter coming from behind me and turned to see Chris wagging his finger.

'Jesus Christ,' I said to him, putting *The New Yorker* back on the rack, 'I see what you mean.'

'Welcome to Condé Nast,' he replied.

5

THE BEAST

Hell's Kitchen wasn't a bit like I expected. Sam Pratt had made it sound like I'd have to brave a gauntlet of knife-wielding crack addicts every night but this turned out to be a typical bit of New York bravado. New Yorkers, I discovered, pride themselves on their city's image as a lawless wilderness and like nothing more than reading about naive greenhorns being relieved of all their possessions within fifteen minutes of arriving. Listening to their war stories, it's as though they were talking about living in Beirut.

In fact, 'Soup Kitchen' would have been a better name for the area. The impoverished locals sat in their doorways, playing cards and nodding benignly to me as I walked past, looking more like extras in a Budweiser commercial than *Reservoir Dogs*. By nightfall they were all blissed out in their rocking chairs, dead to the world. Shepherd's Bush was a seething cauldron of criminality by comparison.

Manhattan suffered a terrible blow to its *amour-propre* shortly after I arrived when the Police Commissioner announced that the city's murder, robbery and burglary rates had fallen to their lowest levels in twenty-five years, making it one of the safest cities in America. It couldn't be worse if the Japanese had bought the Statue of Liberty.

Various experts were wheeled out to explain where it had all gone wrong. Some blamed the Police Commissioner's new policy

57

of 'zero tolerance' whereby the mildest disturbance on a New York street corner was met with an instant and often lethal response. Another theory was that the murderous adolescents responsible for the city's most violent crime had killed each other off in the ferocious gang wars that had erupted in the eighties. But the most plausible explanation was that crack had been replaced by heroin as that season's drug of choice among the city's criminal population. Heroin, according to the experts, is the Prozac of the underclass, transforming potential psychopaths into happy-go-lucky zombies.

One consequence of this was that parts of Manhattan that had previously been classed as no-go areas suddenly became fashionable. This is how I found myself being dragged off to the ominous-sounding 'meatpacking district' one night shortly after arriving.

My host for the evening was the legendary British journalist the Honourable Anthony Haden-Guest. Anthony is the illegitimate son of an English Lord and the half-brother of Christopher Guest, the Los Angeles-based filmmaker married to Jamie Lee Curtis.[1] When he first arrived in New York in 1976 Anthony was thought to have a brilliant future ahead of him, having already made a name for himself on Fleet Street, and was taken up by a string of influential patrons including Tom Wolfe. However, one by one he fell out with these benefactors and, even though he makes a good living as a freelance, his dazzling journalistic career never really materialized. This isn't for want of talent. On the contrary, Anthony possesses the three essential virtues of a journalist: a plausible manner, rat-like cunning and a little literary ability.[2] However, he also suffers from the journalist's vice: he drinks. By itself, this wouldn't matter. Christopher Hitchens, another British

---

[1] According to Anthony, her legal name is Lady Jamie Lee Curtis-Haden-Guest.

[2] These were the three qualities singled out by Nicholas Tomalin, the British foreign correspondent killed in Israel in 1973.

import, is also a big drinker, but it hasn't hurt his career in the slightest. On the contrary, Hitch's drinking is an integral part of his licentious, devil-may-care persona. But unlike Hitch, who seems to become more brilliant the more he drinks, Anthony is a *bad* drunk. In the course of an evening he goes from being a genial, donnish companion, full of witty remarks and erudite observations, to being a kind of football hooligan, challenging everyone who crosses his path to a fight. His transformation can be charted by the four names he's generally known by. When he first arrives at a party he's 'Haden-Guest'; after several glasses of wine he's 'Uninvited-Guest'; then, after a bottle or two, he's 'Haden-Beast'; until, finally, having started in on the vodka, he's simply 'the Beast'. Wolfe was among the first to cut him adrift, immortalizing him as Peter Fallow, the dissolute English hack in *Bonfire of the Vanities*.

Anthony's other main vice, from a career point of view, is that he can't resist a good party. Indeed, he can't resist a bad one either provided there's some free booze and canapés to be had. Not only would he go to the opening of an envelope, he'd hang around for several hours afterwards in the hope of picking up some free stamps. *Spy* held an annual competition called 'the Iron Man Decathlon' to discover who went to the most parties in Manhattan. There were several strong competitors, including Taki, Jay McInerney and Morgan Entrekin, the owner of Grove-Atlantic, but Anthony always won.

My night out with Anthony was fairly routine by his standards, but for someone fresh off the boat like me it was a real eye-opener. He invited me to accompany him to a tribute to Leigh Bowery, the London-based performance artist who'd died of AIDS the previous year. The first indication that this wasn't going to be a conventional evening was when I spotted two attractive women walking down the street in what appeared to be flesh-coloured body stockings.

'Look,' I said, nudging Anthony. 'From a distance those two women look completely naked.'

He glanced over at them and, with enviable *sang-froid*, said: 'They are naked.'

It was only 8.30 p.m. and it was still light but as they drew nearer it became clear that Anthony was right: they were, indeed, naked. We were in a queue to buy tickets and the next thing we knew they were standing right behind us. I was so consumed with embarrassment I could barely speak – *they're naked!* – but no one else seemed to bat an eyelid. They might as well have been two nuns in full habit for all the salacious looks they attracted.

The venue, an art gallery on West 13th Street, was packed to the rafters but, surprisingly, the entire front row was empty. I assumed it was reserved for the press and squeezed through the crowd, dragging Anthony behind me. As a veteran of these events, he was reluctant to sit in the front row, sensing that there must be a good reason why it was unoccupied. Nevertheless, he decided to humour me.

First on the bill was a performer who was famous for being HIV-positive and mutilating himself on stage. His naked body was covered from head to toe in duct tape and his 'act' consisted of having it cut off at breakneck speed by two assistants with garden shears. As this routine progressed, and the shears kept nicking his flesh, it occurred to me that Anthony's suspicions might be well-founded.

Next up was a man in an insect costume who attempted to balance on a rickety old stool. After falling over several times he left the stage and returned a few seconds later with an axe, whereupon he started attacking the stool with enormous gusto. Indeed, he worked himself into such a frenzy that the axe-head flew off and landed, with a tremendous thud, a few inches from where we were sitting. Anthony and I looked at each other with mounting alarm.

The third act, a drag artist called 'Lady Bunny', began by reminiscing about Leigh Bowery. With tears of laughter in his eyes, he recalled how Bowery had once had an enema just before appearing on stage and then sprayed the entire front row with effluent.

'As a tribute to the man we have come here to honour tonight,' he said, 'I have decided to repeat this legendary piece of performance art.'

The audience roared its approval. Anthony and I gulped nervously.

Lady Bunny then turned his back to the audience and began to pull his skirt up his thighs, inch by inch. This was the moment everyone had been waiting for. As the seconds ticked by, and the skirt was lifted higher and higher, the spotlight fell on the two suckers who happened to be sitting in the front row. Someone behind us then started counting off the seconds and the entire audience joined in: 'Ten, nine, eight . . .'

By the time they'd reached 'one', Anthony and I had broken the world record for the hundred-yard dash.

6

IN THE COURT OF THE SUN KING

Back in London I'd heard Condé Nast referred to as 'condescending and nasty' but my initial impression was that beneath its glamorous façade it was just like any other magazine publishing company. It wasn't long before I realised my mistake. Oddly enough, it was in one of the lifts in the atrium that I experienced the infamous Condé Nast hauteur for the first time. In the course of trying to work out which lift would take me to the fourth floor, I'd discovered that the doors of all the lifts at 350 were dangerously unpredictable. Sometimes if you stuck an arm or a foot out they would re-open, while at others they would simply shut. I was waiting in a lift one morning about a week after I'd arrived when a beautiful woman, probably on her way up to *Vogue*, stuck a hand out to prevent it from closing. She was trying to hold it for a friend but it snapped shut, almost trapping her hand in its jaws.

'It's fashion sensitive,' I joked. 'If you're not wearing Prada or Gucci it'll take your arm off.'

Instead of laughing she looked at me as if I was a messenger who'd neglected to take the service elevator.

'But I *am* wearing Prada,' she sniffed.

Condescending and nasty.

I subsequently learnt that Condé Nast etiquette dictates that people aren't supposed to talk to each other in the lifts. Indeed, it is an unwritten rule that Anna Wintour doesn't share a lift with anyone. If you were waiting for one and Anna appeared you were expected to let her go first and take the next one. Chris Lawrence joked that he was planning to hide behind a pillar in the lobby with a bunch of his frat buddies so that when Anna got into a lift they could leap out and pile in with her. 'We would all eat a ton of beans the night before and drink three pints of Guinness,' he chuckled.

Scarcely a day passed during my first few weeks at *Vanity Fair* without some incident occurring that illustrated just how different the Condé Nasties were from my ink-stained colleagues back home. For instance, shortly after arriving I discovered that a woman in 'photo' – the photographic department – lived on the Upper West Side just above Hell's Kitchen. I'd been having trouble working out the quickest way to get to 350 on the subway and since she'd been working at the magazine for several years I thought she'd know. I asked her if she could give me any tips.

It was as if I'd asked directions to the nearest lap-dancing club.

'I have absolutely no idea,' she snorted.

The reason she didn't have a clue was because she'd never taken the subway to work. For the three years that she had been there, she'd taken a Lincoln Town Car both to and from the Condé Nast building every day. Needless to say, she didn't offer me a lift.

For staff of a certain rank, Lincoln Town Cars are one of the perks of the job. If you left 350 at any time between 5 p.m. and 7 p.m. on a weekday, the street outside would be jammed with Lincolns. The company that had the account was Big Apple Cars and the controller, a man who looked exactly like Gert Fröbe, was always standing on the pavement outside the building barking orders into a walkie-talkie out of one side of his mouth and chewing a cigar with the other. Naturally, Chris Lawrence and I dubbed him 'Goldfinger'. We waited in vain for him to say into his walkie-talkie: 'Choose your next witticism carefully, Mr Bond. It may be your last.'

Before I got there, Condé Nast CEO Steve Florio had

announced that he was clamping down on expenses but there was scant evidence of this in 1995.[1] Si Newhouse – or 'His Royal Si-ness' as he was sometimes called – was regarded as a munificent king who was happy to indulge the appetites of his subjects, however extravagant. After half a dozen trips to 44, where a modest lunch for two could cost in excess of $100, I discovered that the Condé Nast catchphrase is 'Let Si get this'. One senior Condé Nast editor, on remembering she'd forgotten to return a videotape, sent a company messenger round to her flat to retrieve the tape and take it back to the video shop. Saving to the editor: $1.50. Cost to the company: $20. Florio's efforts to cut costs weren't helped by the fact that *Forbes* placed the Newhouse family fourth in its list of the 400 richest people in America in 1995. Their combined wealth, apparently, was $9 billion.

Florio also faced a formidable opponent in the form of Alexander Liberman, a flamboyant White Russian who had been Condé Nast's editorial director until 1994. 'I believe in waste,' he once announced. 'Waste is very important in creativity.' This message was not lost on one notorious member of the Condé Nast glossy posse. He persuaded the company to rent him a flat in Paris all year round but refused to stay in it when he travelled to Paris to view the spring and autumn collections, insisting on being put up at the Ritz instead. He'd originally worked at *Vogue*, but had been demoted to a lesser magazine when he'd been caught flying his boyfriend to Paris on Concorde and claiming it on expenses.

The 'fashionistas' – the *monstres sacrés* who work in the fashion departments of *Vogue*, *Vanity Fair*, *Glamour*, *Allure*, *Self* and *Mademoiselle* – are the most over-indulged of all Si's courtiers. For instance, whenever they go on a trip, work-related or not, they Fed Ex their luggage ahead so it's waiting for them

---

[1] Florio used to joke that he was so unpopular at Condé Nast he employed a full-time food-taster. It was rumoured that his driver carried a gun 'for security purposes'.

when they get there. 'So much simpler than taking it there yourself, dahling!' If they feel like a haircut they jump the waiting list at Frédéric Fekkai – the most expensive hair salon in New York – and reimburse themselves out of petty cash. The same applies to facials, manicures and pedicures – as popular with the men as they are with the women. Among the fashionistas this practice is known as 'scouting', as if it's a justifiable expense run up in the course of conducting editorial research.

When it comes to clothes they can furnish themselves with entire wardrobes without setting foot outside the building. If they need an outfit for the evening they simply 'call it in', i.e., ring up the designer and have him or her messenger it round. Sometimes they return it the following day, sometimes they don't. This is quite apart from the clothes they're sent every day as a form of tribute. One member of *Allure's* fashion department was given so many designer outfits she held a 'sample sale' in her flat and made several thousand dollars.

In the course of 'styling' photo shoots, the fashionistas run up huge bills for all sorts of goodies they claim are absolutely essential if the story in question is to 'work'. A fashion editor at *Vogue* managed to furnish her summer house with items purchased in this way. Among the 'Voguettes', this home-away-from-home was known as 'Petty Cash Junction'.

Elizabeth Saltzman, the thirty-year-old fashion director of *Vanity Fair*, was so powerful she didn't need to solicit gifts – they simply materialized outside her office every day. On one occasion I found a fax lying on the floor that began: 'Dear Elizabeth, A while back, the Diamond Information Center presented you with a diamond solitaire necklace . . .' My office was next door to Elizabeth's and whenever I had trouble getting into some glamorous party she was always happy to help. For instance, on 16 November, 1995 I asked her if she could get me some tickets to the premiere of *GoldenEye*, the first Bond film in six years. Chris Lawrence and I had been trying all day and hadn't had any luck. She immediately dialled the publicist in charge and put the call on speaker phone.

Elizabeth [Purring]: Hi. It's Elizabeth Saltzman. I wondered if I could get some tickets for tonight's event.

Publicist: Gee, Elizabeth, it's kind of tough. How many d'you need?

Elizabeth looked at me and I held up three fingers. I thought I'd ask her if she wanted to join us.

Elizabeth: Three.

Publicist: Who are they for?

Elizabeth [Incredulous]: Who are they for? What d'you mean, who are they for? ME, MYSELF AND I, OKAY?

Publicist: Okay, okay, no problem. I'll messenger them right over.

I was no slouch myself in the freeloading department. Shortly after I arrived Aimée Bell initiated me into the black art of blagging free theatre tickets. Apparently, you didn't simply call up the theatre's press agent and ask for a complimentary ticket – any rube with a press card could do that. Rather, you called him up, identified yourself as an editor at *Vanity Fair*, and asked to 'purchase' house seats. The press agent would be so impressed by your willingness to pay, not only would he immediately offer you two free seats, they would be the best seats in the house. It went without saying that no *Vanity Fair* editor should be expected to sit in anything less.

At the very top of the tree, Si's elite corps of editors-in-chief live like Pashas. In addition to their huge salaries – Graydon was paid $775,000 in 1995 – Si buys them the cars of their choice and pays for chauffeurs to ferry them about. He also gives them interest-free loans so they can purchase the kind of homes they need now that they're Condé Nast '*machers*'.[1] It's almost as if Si is an old-fashioned monarch rewarding his favourite courtiers with Baronial estates. When Graydon was appointed editor of *Vanity Fair* in 1992, Si loaned him $450,000 so he could afford to renovate his house in Connecticut and live in a flat in the Dakota – the same

---

[1] 'Macher' is a Yiddish term for a big shot.

building on the Upper West Side that had housed John Lennon. Art Cooper, the editor of *GQ*, borrowed a cool million to purchase his country house.

The Queen Bee at Condé Nast is Anna Wintour. In 1996 her salary hit the $1 million mark, making her the highest-paid editor in the world. Born in 1949 into an upper-middle-class English family – her father, Sir Charles Wintour, was at one time the editor of the *Evening Standard* – Anna's first job was in the fashion department of *Harpers & Queen* aged twenty. After five years she crossed the Atlantic to work for a succession of fashion magazines before becoming the creative director of *Vogue* in 1983. She moved back to London in 1986 to take the helm of British *Vogue* then returned to New York in 1987 to edit *House & Garden*.[1] She eventually landed the top job at the Condé Nast flagship in 1988.

Stories of Anna's notorious *froideur* are legion. Take the case of the *Vogue* department head who got her sixteen-year-old daughter a job as an intern in the summer of 1994. The teenager was ambling along a corridor one afternoon, minding her own business, when she saw Anna powering her way towards her. Now this, I can tell you from experience, is a frightening sight. After the girl had overcome her initial shock, she picked a spot somewhere over Anna's left shoulder and, by concentrating on that, hoped to get through the next thirty seconds. Suddenly, just as they were drawing level, the heel of one of Anna's Manolos snapped and she was sent sprawling to the ground, landing at the intern's feet. The girl's first impulse was to ask Anna if she was alright but then she remembered what her mother had told her: that under no circumstances was she to speak to 'Ms Wintour' – *ever*.' Consequently, she gingerly stepped over Anna's prostrate form and carried on down the corridor. As soon as she turned the corner, she sprinted to her mother's office and explained what had happened. Had she

---

[1] One of Anna's innovations was to rename the magazine *HG*. She filled it with so many celebrities it became known at Condé Nast as *Vanity Chair*.

done the right thing? Yes, her mother assured her. She'd done exactly the right thing.

I lapped up these gossipy tales. Here, at last, was Patsy from *Absolutely Fabulous* in the flesh. Or was Anna emulating Diana Vreeland, *Vogue*'s most celebrated editor? According to a Voguette I befriended, Anna often sends her assistant into the men's lavatories to hunt down male members of her staff who are late for meetings. She's also notoriously squeamish about the smell of food and it was a rule on the thirteenth floor that no one was allowed to eat at their desks until Anna had left the building. Tights, too, were *verboten*. Her extravagance – at the expense of the company – is legendary. As the editor of British *Vogue*, Anna had continued to 'live' in New York, commuting back and forth on Concorde. In her current job, she's said to employ an interior decorator to rearrange the photographs on the wall of her office every few months.

Perhaps the most persistent rumour of all is that Anna's trademark Chanel dark glasses never leave her face. (I can confirm this. I once spotted her sitting in the dark in the front row of a New York cinema with her sunglasses on.) It is as if she's taken Diana Vreeland's maxim to heart: 'Never fear being vulgar – just boring, middle class or dull.'

Of course, the privileged lifestyle of the Condé Nasties has its downside. It is customary for the staff at *Vanity Fair* to complain about the enervating effect of all this luxury, referring to the magazine as 'the velvet coffin'. Condé Nast editors have developed a whole vocabulary to convey their bitchy, slightly camp worldview. An inadequately decorated restaurant, for instance, is an 'airport lounge' or, worse, a 'McDonald's', while an overcrowded club or party is a 'rat fuck' or a 'cluster fuck'. A person who's less than drop-dead gorgeous is 'scary looking' and anyone who calls twice in one day, no matter how urgent their business, is a 'stalker'. It's as if they're celebrities having to contend with troublesome fans. The worst epithet that can be applied to anyone is that he or she is 'over'.

During my first few weeks at *Vanity Fair* I was shocked by

how openly contemptuous people were of those lower down the food chain than them. On the British magazines I'd worked for, any member of the officer class who sneered at the lower ranks would have immediately been branded a 'toffee-nosed wanker'. Snobbery of any kind was completely taboo. Not so at *Vanity Fair*, where no effort is made to camouflage the rigid office hierarchy. On the contrary, people are never really allowed to forget their place in the pecking order. The senior editorial staff treat the fact-checkers like jumped-up housemaids.

The lowest form of life in the *Vanity Fair* universe are free-lances who've sent in unsolicited articles. Even the fact-checkers look down on them and it's left to the editorial assistants to send them boilerplate rejection letters.[1] I remember one occasion, not long after I arrived, when Aimée Bell showed me a 'hilarious' spoof that purported to be the diary of a grubbing freelance hack called 'Josh Freelantzovitz'. Did I think it would make a good column in Vanities? I read it through and told her I didn't think it would. It was unseemly, I argued, to poke fun at people who were struggling to obtain the professional status that *Vanity Fair*'s contributors had achieved. Satire was supposed to be a weapon with which the disenfranchised attacked the Establishment, not the other way round. This author of this piece, I said, holding up the offending article, is a snob, wanting to kick away the ladder that he himself has climbed so no one else can follow.

After I'd delivered this little sermon, Aimée patiently explained that Josh Freelantzovitz was in fact her husband, David Kamp, a staff writer on *GQ*. Needless to say, 'The Diary

---

[1] This is an example of a rejection letter sent on 25 June, 1997 by Beth Altschull, a features associate: 'Dear Ms Browne, Thank you so much for your interest in *Vanity Fair*. I do wish that we could review your non-fiction book, *That Old Black Magic: Essays, Images & Verse on the Joys of Loving Black Men,* for our magazine. Unfortunately, we will be unable to do so. Once again, we thank you for thinking of *Vanity Fair*. We wish you luck on your book release, and please feel free to contact us with any story ideas in the future.'

of Josh Freelantzovitz' soon became a regular column in Vanities. Indeed, when David heard about my objections he penned another spoof called 'The Diary of Jeremy Feckless-Expat' which implied that British hacks in New York are lazy, good-for-nothing alcoholics. (*How dare he!*) That, too, appeared in Vanities.

7

THE TRIAL

About a fortnight after I arrived, Syrie flew over for a 'trial weekend'. She had never been to New York before and she wanted to see the place before making up her mind about whether to move over. I pretended that it was no big deal and if it didn't work out we could always have a long-distance relationship but I was worried she would dump me if she decided to stay in London. I was keeping my fingers crossed. I wasn't in love with Syrie, but I was completely, head-over-heels in lust with her.

I first set eyes on her in 1989 in the dining hall of Trinity College, Cambridge. After Harvard, I'd gone on to Cambridge and was attempting to get a PhD in Philosophy. It was the first day of the new academic year and, in keeping with College tradition, me and several other 'mature' students were checking out the latest batch of 'freshettes'. Not that we had any hope of getting into their knickers: in the Cambridge student hierarchy, post-grads are on a par with 'natscis' (natural scientists). Lusting after first years, and knowing that it would never be reciprocated, was just another exercise in self-flagellation, a favourite post-grad pastime.

Syrie stood out immediately – and not just because of her long brown hair and flashing green eyes. It was also the way she held herself: proud and erect, like a flamenco dancer. She threw her head back defiantly as she entered the dining hall and kept her eyes fixed firmly in front of her, almost as if she was expecting to cause a stir and was determined to rise above it. As she passed the post-grad table, she didn't so much as glance in our direction even though it was perfectly obvious we were all gawping at her. Everything about her radiated contempt, which suited our masochistic mood to a T. This arrogant, full-lipped beauty embodied all that was forbidden to sad losers like us. My misery was compounded when she chose a seat directly opposite mine in the College library, making it impossible for me to concentrate on my philosophy books. For the remainder of that academic year, until I abandoned my PhD altogether, I tortured myself by imagining what her nubile, 18-year-old body would look like in the nude. I was 100 per cent certain I'd never find out.

Syrie resurfaced in my life in 1994 when, as a 23-year-old researcher for an independent television production company, she called me out of the blue and invited me to lunch. Aha, I thought. This could be interesting. Instead of an impoverished student living in a hall of residence I was now a fully fledged media brat and a member of the Groucho Club. I assumed that she remembered me from Cambridge and wanted some career advice – maybe even a job! Perhaps I would get to see her naked after all.

My hopes were soon dashed. She confessed that she'd been ordered to take me out to lunch by her boss so that she could 'steal' any ideas I might have for television programmes. I'd been expecting a wide-eyed ingénue who'd hang on my every word and instead found myself sitting opposite an intelligent, confident young woman. After graduating from Cambridge with a First in English she had worked in publishing for a while and, the previous year, had helped organise the Hay-on-Wye Literary Festival. That was where she'd met her current boyfriend, the novelist Will Self. Had I heard of him? I had, as a matter of fact. *He was only the most famous young novelist in the country!*

The low point came when I told her I had been to Cambridge.

Syrie: Oh really? When were you there?

Me: 1988 to '90.

Syrie: But that's when I was there! What college were you at?

Me: Trinity.

Syrie: No! But I was at Trinity.

Pause.

Me: Yes. I know.

I'd sat opposite her almost every day for a year and failed to make any impression. I think I would have preferred it if she'd remembered me as a creepy, starey-eyed post-grad – anything would have been better than not making any impact at all. I had been completely invisible to her. What could be more humiliating? All the lust I'd felt five years earlier came flooding back, but this time I was determined to do something about it.

I called her a few days later and invited her out for a drink at the Groucho. I didn't want her to think of it as a 'date' so I asked a few other people along, including Tom Shone, the literary editor of *The Modern Review*. Big mistake! In addition to being extremely bright, Tom is a world-class swordsman, hence his nickname 'Shagger Shone'. As soon as he saw Syrie, he got that predatory look in his eye that I'd seen a thousand times before and when Syrie announced that she and Will Self had broken up he practically started salivating. (*It's the wool-uf, it's the wool-uf!*) I knew from bitter experience that there was no point in competing with Shagger when he was in one of these moods. No one could match his concentration and willpower. The bastard ended up snogging her that night.

Fortunately, their relationship never went beyond the kissing stage and once again I took up the chase. I decided that my best strategy was to be completely upfront: I told her I found her incredibly attractive and would do absolutely anything – *anything!* – to go out with her. Unlike Shagger, it took me eight weeks of hard labour just to persuade her to snog me. Night after night, we'd end up in some seedy, after-hours club in Soho and, just when I was drunk enough to make a pass, she'd jump in a mini-cab and return to her flat in Marble Arch. I'd never been made to work so hard for a girl in my life. Her surrender, when it finally came, was one of the sweetest moments of my life.

Having sex with Syrie was like being granted a wish by a fairy godmother. It was an opportunity to turn back the clock and do what I'd longed to do at the time but hadn't had the balls for. In a sense she stood for all the unattainable girls I'd lusted after throughout my life. This well of unrequited desire had left a deep psychic wound and here, at last, was my chance to heal it. By the time I moved to New York I'd been sleeping with her for about nine months but the damage was by no means completely repaired. Of course, the humiliation caused by sexual rejection can never be fully expunged, but that wasn't going to stop me from trying – again and again and again. I had no intention of abandoning my 'therapy' in mid-stream.

Syrie had heard all the usual horror stories about Manhattan but I assured her it wasn't like that any more. According to the latest crime statistics, it now had a lower murder rate than Dallas. Unfortunately, on this particular weekend, New York decided it had had enough of going straight. It was time for a spot of recidivism.

Our first bad experience happened on the way back from JFK. I met Syrie off the plane in a Lincoln Town Car and we were waiting at some traffic lights on the Van Wyck Expressway when a yellow cab slammed into the back of us. Both drivers jumped out to inspect their vehicles and quickly established that the Lincoln had borne the brunt of the damage. Indeed, the taxi was almost completely unscathed. At this point the lights changed and we were instantly deafened by the sound of dozens of car horns being pressed simultaneously. Deciding there was nothing to be gained from hanging around, the cab driver leapt back into his taxi and sped off.

Our driver immediately gave chase and suddenly we found ourselves re-enacting a scene from *The French Connection*.

Syrie clutched my arm in terror: 'Tell him to stop.'

I leant forward.

'Er, excuse me, sir, but would you mind slowing down a bit? You're frightening my girlfriend.'

Naturally, he ignored me.

I peered over his shoulder and looked at the speedometer: 95mph.

We were about fifty yards behind the taxi and gaining when I spotted another set of lights just ahead of us. Here's the other driver's chance, I thought. If the lights change at exactly the right moment, he'll be able to get away while we'll be forced to wait.

Unfortunately for him, by the time he got to the intersection the lights had already changed and he had to stop, giving us plenty of time catch up. Then, just as we were pulling up behind him, the cab driver suddenly slammed his foot down and, with a screech of burning rubber, raced through the lights, sending speeding traffic in every direction.

'*Aaaaaaaaaah!*' screamed Syrie, convinced that our driver was about to follow suit.

'P-p-p-please don't,' I stammered. 'It's n-n-n-not worth it.'

'Don't worry,' said our driver, turning round and grinning at us. 'I got his license plate.'

After she'd calmed down, Syrie shook her head in sorrow.

'Those poor people,' she sighed.

'What people?' I asked.

I hadn't noticed, but apparently there had been two passengers in the back of the yellow cab. Syrie announced that as long as she lived she'd never get in a New York taxi.

Luckily, I'd booked us into the Paramount, a fashionable, Midtown hotel, rather than run the risk of taking her back to Hell's Kitchen so the rest of the evening passed without incident. However, the following morning we were queuing up to buy a subway token in Times Square when New York ambushed us again. I'd decided to take Syrie to Coney Island, New York's equivalent of Disneyland, and since she refused to get a cab the only way to get there was on the subway. Out of the blue, a woman barged in front of us.

'There's a person on the platform who looks dead,' she said to the man in the token booth. When he looked sceptical she added: 'I'm serious. I'm a medical.'

It soon became clear that the man wasn't about to leave his post so Syrie and I offered to go with the woman to investigate. When we arrived on the platform she indicated an elderly black woman who was lying on a few squares of cardboard. Her face was the colour of newspaper pulp, her eyes were shut and she was completely motionless. There was no doubt about it. She looked dead.

Syrie squatted down in front of her.

'Are you okay? Would you like us to call a doctor?'

When she didn't respond Syrie gently took her wrist and felt for a pulse.

At that moment the woman snatched her arm away and sat bolt upright.

'CAN'T YOU SEE I'M TRYING TO GET SOME SLEEP HERE?' she screamed. 'GET OUTTA MY FACE.'

It was an inauspicious start to the day.

Coney Island is a seaside amusement park just outside Manhattan that was first established in 1887. According to all the guide books, its quirky side shows and classic funfair rides are a charming reminder of a bygone era, but when we finally got there it struck me as being more like the set of a horror film. To say it has seen better days doesn't begin to do justice to the atmosphere of almost nuclear desolation. Wizened old men, straining to be heard above the din of pre-First World War machinery, hawked the attractions of two-headed dogs and giant killer rats, while pock-marked Haitians bartered furiously with ten-year-old crack salesmen down on the boardwalk.

The first ride Syrie and I went on was the Cyclone, Coney Island's pride and joy. This roller coaster was probably considered state of the art when it opened in 1927 but for anyone familiar with what Alton Towers has to offer today it's far from impressive. It looks as if it's been built almost entirely out of matchsticks and rubber bands. Rather alarmingly, as we clambered into the rickety old car, I spotted what looked like 'mole people' skulking around at the base of the wooden structure.[1] Were they technicians of some kind?

We were sitting in the last carriage and as soon as it reached the top of the first incline we realised what a terrible mistake we'd made. We were flipped over the top with such force that the wheels of our carriage left the track and we found ourselves plummeting vertically downwards in what felt like zero gravity. We hit the bottom with a horrible, bone-crunching thud and were then yanked vertically upwards at ninety miles per hour sending the contents of Syrie's handbag flying. Hundreds of feet below I could just make out people scrabbling in the dirt like wild animals fighting for scraps of food. So that's what the mole people did.

As soon as we set foot back on *terra firma* Syrie wanted to go back to Manhattan, but I couldn't face the prospect of another ninety-minute subway journey without going on at least one more ride. We eventually settled on the Jumbo Jet, reasoning that with a name like that it must have been built after the Second World War. The same could not be said of the Rocket Ship, the Jungle Cat or the Titanic. When we sat down – Syrie had a window seat and I had an aisle – I noticed that the two Hispanic young men sitting behind us were smoking.

'Excuse me, but there's no smoking on this aircraft,' I quipped, flashing them a huge smile so they'd know I was joking. 'Would you mind extinguishing your cigarettes?'

---

[1] 'Mole people' is the name given to the tramps who live in the New York subway system.

Instead of laughing, they glared at me with undisguised contempt.

'Fug you,' said the smaller of the two and kicked the back of my seat as hard as he could.

Syrie and I fastened our seatbelts and prepared for a bumpy ride.

The Jumbo Jet didn't quite reach speeds of 550 miles per hour but the turbulence was far worse than any I've experienced over the Atlantic. It spun round with such extraordinary velocity I thought I was going to pass out. Talk about G-Force! *So this is what it must be like to go into space.* The highpoint came when the operator pretended he'd lost control of the ride and all his friends, masquerading as customers, started flying off in every direction.

Syrie's screams could be heard all the way back to Manhattan.

After the excitement of the previous day, Syrie and I decided that a pleasant way to spend Sunday afternoon would be to take the Circle Line tour of Manhattan. This involves sitting in a ferry that completely circumnavigates the island, eventually bringing you back to where you started. How dangerous could it be?

There were about 120 of us on the boat and the tour guide began by asking us to take our seats. We could either sit in 'the State Room', a covered area about the size of a ping-pong table, or on one of the plastic benches on deck, but once we had made our choice we must to stick to it. We were told that the boat had capsized once after all the passengers had rushed from one side to the other in order to photograph a group of boys mooning them from the shore.

As soon as we got going it became clear that one person had no intention of obeying the stay-in-your-seat rule: a German tourist in his early forties called Klaus. Klaus was straight from central casting. He was wearing a white T-shirt tucked into a tiny pair of khaki shorts, a Sony camcorder was hanging from his neck and he was clutching something that looked suspiciously like a handbag. The reason I knew his name was because every time he leapt up to capture some local monument on videotape his wife would start screaming '*nein*, Klaus, *nein*' and urge him to sit back down.

He should have listened.

Klaus got his comeuppance just as we were passing underneath the George Washington Bridge. He was leaning over the guardrail, pointing his camcorder at a flotilla of sailboats, when suddenly he let out a tremendous yelp and fell to the ground clutching his right shoulder.

'SCHEISSE!' he cried.

His wife immediately started screaming, but, oddly, didn't go over to help him. Nothing, it seemed, could get her to leave her seat, not even the sight of her husband writhing in agony a few feet away. Fortunately, the tour guide was soon by his side trying to find out what had happened. Was he a diabetic? Had he had a heart attack? Perhaps he was an epileptic.

As Klaus was struggling to make himself understood, a rumour suddenly swept around that he'd been shot by a sniper on Washington bridge.

People started bolting for the State Room. In less than a minute, all 120 passengers, with the exception of Klaus and his wife, who was still rooted to her seat, were crowded into an area that had been designed to accommodate no more than ten people. Needless to say, we didn't move from there until the ferry had returned to its embarkation point some forty-five minutes later. Luckily for Klaus, a water ambulance appeared within five minutes and sped him away to hospital, but only after four paramedics had prised his wife from her seat.

It would be wrong to describe this episode as the last straw – I think Syrie had probably made up her mind not to move to New York before coming out – but it was the end of the beast with two backs. In less than forty-eight hours she'd been screamed at by a corpse, robbed by mole people and a man standing less than twenty feet away from her had keeled over. When I dropped her off at JFK that evening it was clear to both of us she wouldn't be coming back any time soon. The prognosis for our relationship didn't look good.

8

VANITIES

I flattered myself that one of the reasons Graydon had brought me over was because he thought I was a funny writer and I started bombarding him with ideas for humour pieces. For instance, on 24 July I sent him the following:

Dear Graydon,
    Would you be interested in a profile of Jay McInerney in which I treat the ubiquitous partygoer as if he's a notorious literary recluse in the same vein as J.D. Salinger and Thomas Pynchon? Cover line: 'Who is the elusive Jay McInerney and why is he so publicity-shy?'[1]
    Or how about submitting one of Tina Brown's old *Tatler* articles to *The New Yorker*, pretending to be a freelance? We could print an extract from the piece together with the boilerplate rejection letter under-neath: 'Dear Ms Brown, Thank you so much for sending us "Lift-Off: The Fabulous Life and Times of the Baron and Baroness di Portanova" . . .

---

[1] This wasn't my idea. It was suggested to me by James Wolcott who at the time was a staff writer at *The New Yorker*. He later became a contributing editor at *Vanity Fair*.

At first, Graydon's response to these ideas was quite polite: 'That's great, Toby, but it's *first room stuff*.' Within a short space of time this became abbreviated to 'first room stuff' until he was eventually reduced to just mouthing the words 'first room' as he shooed me out of his office. The implication was clear: these suggestions were hopelessly naïve, the equivalent of an American pitching an article to a British editor about this fascinating new watering-hole he'd discovered called the Soho House. I'd have to come up with something a lot better than *that* if it was to stand a chance of getting into *Vanity Fair*.

In the meantime, Matt Tyrnauer and Aimée Bell were saddled with the task of finding me something to do and it wasn't long before they came up with a suitably undemanding task.[1] Vanities, the section they edited, is supposed to be a guide to whatever's hip and happening in New York, Los Angeles and London but it's used by the rest of *Vanity Fair*'s staff as a kind of all-purpose dumping ground for stuff they've promised to stick in the magazine in return for services rendered. For instance, if Jane Sarkin, *Vanity Fair*'s chief celebrity wrangler, wants to get an A-list star to pose for the cover, she might say to that star's publicist: 'Look, if you can persuade Tom/Brad/Russell to do this, I'll make sure we give some coverage to one of your up-and-comers in Vanities.' Some months later a picture of some unknown starlet will appear on the front page of the section, a slot referred to by those forced to write about these no-hopers as 'blonde bimbos on the horizon'.

My first 'assignment' was to write 175 words to accompany a picture of Wade Dominguez, a 29-year-old actor with a small part in *Dangerous Minds*. To my astonishment, before I set to work on this I was given a list of words and terms that Graydon had banned from appearing in the magazine. They were:

---

[1] 'Light lifting' they called it.

aka
bed-sitter (for apartment)
boasted (as in had or featured)
boîte (for restaurant)
chortled (for said)
chuckled (for said)
cough up (as in to spend)
doff
donned (as in put on)
eatery (for restaurant)
executive-produced and such like
flat (for apartment)
flick
freebie
freeloader
fuck (okay for exclamation, not for having sex)
funky
garner
glitz
golfer
graduate (v)
honcho
hooker
joked (for said)
moniker
opine (in any form)
paucity
pen (used as a verb)
plethora
quipped
row (meaning to fight)
sleaze
titles of books, movies, plays, etc.: no diminutives – i.e.,
    not *Prince* for *The Prince of Tides*
tome (for book)
wanna
weird

Naturally, my first impulse was to turn in a piece that broke as many of these rules as possible: '"I couldn't believe it," chuckled the six foot two honcho on the phone from his funky bed-sitter in West Hollywood . . .' In the end, though, I handed in a standard bit of puffery. Under Tina Brown, *Vanity Fair* writers had perfected the art of 'the snide puff piece', whereby they'd slobber all over some Hollywood star while leaving the reader in no doubt about what they really thought of him or her. In a sense, this was typical of the whole tone of the magazine during Tina's reign which was simultaneously fawning *and* superior, a barbed Valentine to America's fashionable elite. Under Graydon, by contrast, writers are expected to keep their reservations to themselves, at least when it comes to celebrities. Snide remarks are confined to the inter-office email system.

Aimée and Matt were so pleased with my first effort – or they pretended to be – they immediately put me in charge of 'VF Camera', a page of party pictures that appears in Vanities each month. Back in his *Spy* days Graydon had floated the idea of starting a whole magazine devoted to party photos on the grounds that they were the only things in any magazine anyone ever looked at. It had never got off the ground but Graydon insists on including at least one page of party pictures in *Vanity Fair*. He selects the photos himself and my job was to work out who the people were. I was delighted with this 'promotion', as I saw it. Once word got round that I was responsible for VF Camera it wouldn't be long before the biggest publicists in New York started asking me to A-list events. I could call myself *Vanity Fair*'s 'social editor' and in no time I'd have invitations coming out of my ears!

I soon realised why I'd been given this job – no one else wanted it. The first set of photos I was asked to identify had been taken at a Ross Bleckner opening at Mary Boone's gallery. Mary Boone, I was told, was one of the central figures in the New York art world and Ross Bleckner, a celebrated abstract painter, was her most important client. I asked to speak to her assistant but as soon as her girl Friday discovered it was *Vanity Fair* on the line she insisted on putting me straight through to her boss.

'This is Mary Boone,' a stentorian voice announced. 'How can I help you?'

I introduced myself and explained what I was doing. I decided to get the guest of honour out the way first.

'Ross Bleckner,' I asked. 'Man or woman?'

I genuinely didn't know.

'I'm sorry?'

'Is Ross Bleckner a man or a woman?'

There was a pause on the other end of the line.

'Are you really calling from *Vanity Fair*?'

'Yes, I really am.'

'Tell me, Tony,' she said, a note of strain sounding in her voice, 'why have they given you this assignment if you don't know who anyone is?'

'I'm not exactly sure,' I replied hesitantly.

'He's a man,' she snapped.

'Okay,' I said. 'Is he an old man?'

Again there was a pause.

'He's an *older* man, yes,' she said impatiently.

'Good looking?'

Pause.

'You do realize that Graydon Carter is one of my oldest friends?'

Now it was my turn to hesitate. What did that have to do with anything?

'What's that got to do with anything?'

'Right, that's it,' she replied. 'I'm calling him right now.'

Click. Dial-tone.

I probably would have been relieved of my responsibility for VF Camera there and then but, luckily, Hugh Grant came to my rescue. His brief encounter with Divine Brown on Sunset Boulevard at 1.45 a.m. prompted Dafydd Jones, one of *Vanity Fair*'s party photographers, to root around in his archive for some compromising pictures of Hugh and his then girlfriend Elizabeth Hurley. He came up with some humdingers. They were of Hugh and Elizabeth disporting themselves at a series of parties in the eighties given by the Piers Gaveston, a notoriously debauched Oxford undergraduate society. Matt and Aimée decided to make these pictures the subject of the following month's VF Camera and I was given the job of writing a thousand-word essay to accompany them. At last I was on familiar ground.

9

EARLY ALARM CALL

I was woken up by Sam Pratt. He didn't look happy.

'Phone call,' he grunted.

I looked at my watch: 7.15 a.m. It must be Syrie! She hadn't returned any of my calls since our disastrous weekend and I feared the worst. However, the fact that she was calling was a good sign. Maybe she didn't want to break up with me after all.

Me: Sweetpea, is that you?

Caller: Yeah it's me, babycakes.

It was Alex de Silva. When I'd last spoken to him he'd informed me that he'd applied to the USC screenwriting programme. That was a tad ambitious on his part. USC receives 20,000 applications a year for a total of twenty-three places on the screenwriting programme, giving him a one in 870 chance. He stood more chance of getting in to Harvard Law School.

Me: Alex? For fuck's sake. D'you have any idea what time it is?

Alex: I got in, dude! I'm now officially enrolled in the USC screenwriting programme. [Pause] Hello? Hello? What was that noise?

Me [Picking up the phone]: You bastard! You absolute fucking bastard! I can't believe it.

Alex [Laughing]: I know, I know. D'you have any idea how difficult it is to get in? They get 40,000 applications a year! It's harder to get into than—

87

Me [Interrupting]: 20,000 actually.

Alex: . . . Harvard Law School.

Me: Yes, well, congratulations. I'm really happy for you.

How on earth had he done it? Alex isn't exactly what you'd call 'academically bright'. Born in 1964 in Paris, he was the son of bohemian intellectuals, the kind that didn't saddle their children with 'bourgeois' expectations. After graduating from Trinity College, Dublin in 1986 he'd drifted into rock 'n' roll, ending up as the bassist for a band called The Dicemen. He also became a world-class junkie. He didn't decide to get clean until 1992 after he was thrown out of the band for passing out in the middle of a concert. By the time I met him a year later he was scraping a living as a freelance journalist in London but it was clear his heart wasn't in it. I think the thing that convinced him he was destined for greater things was the success of The Dicemen after they'd replaced him with a more reliable bassist. By this time they'd renamed themselves —.

Me: So when are you heading to LA?

Alex: As soon as I've sorted out my flat. The fall semester starts at the end of September.

Me: What are you going to live on?

Alex: Oh, yeah, I forgot to tell you. They're giving me a scholarship. *Hello?*

Me [Picking up the phone – *again*.]: Jesus fucking Christ. Is there anything else you've forgotten to tell me?

Alex: Like what?

Me: I don't know. Did you win the pools? Fuck a supermodel?

Alex: Not a supermodel, no, but I did get laid last night.

Pause.

Me: I think I know what's going on here. You've sold your soul to the devil haven't you?

Alex: I did that a long time ago, man.

Me: It's the only possible explanation.

Alex: By the way, I was sorry to hear about Syrie.

Me: What?

Alex: Haven't you heard?
My stomach turned over.
Me: No.
Alex: She's got a new boyfriend.
Me: You're kidding?
Alex: D'you want the good news or the bad news?
Me: You're loving this, aren't you?
Alex: The good news is he's incredibly poor, poorer even than you.
Me: He won't last long then. What's the bad news.
Alex: The bad news is he's a Viscount. His nickname's 'the discount Viscount'.
Me: Fuck, fuck, fuck.
Alex: Sorry to have to be the one to tell you.
Me: Yeah, right.
Alex: Anyway, dude, we're both going to be living in America, you in New York me in L.A. That's kinda cool, no?
Me: Yeah, but you're going to make it *because you've sold your soul to the devil.*
Alex [Laughing]: Hey, we're both gonna make it, dude. Have a little faith.

10

THE TOTAL BETTY

The discovery that Syrie had a new boyfriend was a bit of a blow, but I was in the perfect place to recuperate. There were so many beautiful girls at 350 it was sometimes called the 'Palace of Pulchritude'. I'd even heard the two men's clothing shops that flanked the building on either side – Brooks Brothers and Paul Stewart – referred to as 'sentinels at the Temple of Aphrodite'. It was like working in a modelling agency.

Needless to say, any attempt to chat up the goddesses at Condé Nast is completely taboo. I discovered this shortly after I arrived when I made the mistake of cracking a faintly risqué joke during a tour of Condé Nast's headquarters by a woman from 'human resources'. I was thrown in with a bunch of other new recruits and, at the conclusion of the tour, I asked her what we should do if we ever got lost.

'You could always consult the model in the lobby,' she suggested.

'Which one?' I quipped.

Nobody laughed.

The following morning I found a memo on my desk headed 'Policy on Harassment'. Who was it from? There was no clue. It began: 'It has long been the policy of Condé Nast to maintain a professional working environment for all employees, free of any form of discrimination or harassment.' The next bit was underlined in red, felt-tip pen: 'A joke considered amusing by one may be offensive to another.' (The word 'offensive' had been underlined twice.) It went on to list various forms of conduct that would 'result in disciplinary action up to and including dismissal'. They were:

- Sexual remarks, advances, propositions
- Touching or other physical contact
- Repeated requests for dates or other social engagements
- Comments about an individual's body

I was flabbergasted. I pointed out to Chris Lawrence that if Romeo had stuck to these rules he never would have ended up with Juliet. The contrast with the ribald, bawdy atmosphere of Fleet Street, with its constantly replenished stock of nubile hackettes, couldn't have been greater. How were we supposed to get 'dates' with the women at 350 if not by flirting with them and asking them out?

'It's all bullshit,' Chris explained. 'They just don't wanna be hit on by dweebs like us.'

It's true. With their $3,000 handbags and mink collars, the fashion plates at Condé Nast can hardly be described as politically correct. The company's policy on sexual harassment isn't a concession to the feminist sensibilities of its female employees; it's designed to protect them from men who earn less than $500,000 a year. They don't spend all those hours getting their bikini lines waxed by Brazilian beauticians just so they can go out with *journalists*. They want to date movie producers, club owners and investment bankers.[1]

The upshot was that 350 was almost entirely free of sexual

---

[1] A male Condé Nast employee was quoted, anonymously, in *The New York Times* as follows: 'Technically, a straight guy has great odds here. But if a woman is really devoted to high fashion, if her life depends on buying the shoe of the moment, how can she afford to marry a journalist who works in the building? Her habit requires an investment banker.' John Tierney, 'Masochism Central', *The New York Times*, 16 July, 1996.

tension. On one occasion, a frustrated fact-checker told me it was all to do with the fact that Condé Nast magazines are about creating needs rather than satisfying them. The reason luxury goods companies pay enormous sums of money to advertise in them is because they're staffed by women who are experts on manufacturing desire. It involves being elusive and unobtainable and cultivating an air of mystique. They aren't about to change the habits of a lifetime for a quick romp by the photocopier.

However, this explanation was a little too flattering to the men at 350. It implied that the women had *considered* going out with us but had *decided* against it, when in fact we simply didn't show up on their radar screens. As they rode up in the lifts every morning, they sized each other up with the cold-blooded hostility of professional athletes. Indeed, if they saw what they regarded as a fashion disaster, they weren't above pointing it out. Disapproving comments ranged from the fairly mild – 'Aggressive choice!' – to the outright rude – 'It ain't working, honey.' But men were completely ignored. If a very good-looking man happened to be in the lift with them, they automatically dismissed him as 'a fag'.

For heterosexual men, this atmosphere was very emasculating and Chris and I did our best to compensate by adopting these exaggeratedly laddish personae: he was the 'Frat Boy' and I was the 'Toadmeister'. (I should make it clear that this was strictly in the privacy of our office.) We communicated almost entirely in what Chris described as 'East Coast preppy frat boy slang', a vocabulary I soon picked up from listening to him chatting on the phone with his friends. An attractive girl was a 'Betty' or, if she had 'a huge rack' and 'a great set of wheels', a 'total Betty'. Betties were attracted to ''tants' (short for 'mutants'), a term that referred to muscle-bound, hockey-playing types, also known as 'buzzards', 'steak heads' and 'meat people'. They weren't interested in 'three pump chumps' like us. If, after 'flinging woo' at 'some beave' all night, you ended up 'mugging' or 'sucking face' – highly unlikely – you were entitled to do the 'stride of pride'; but if, as nearly always happened, you got 'shut down', you had to do the 'walk of shame'.

As someone who'd spent his youth watching *Porkies* and *Animal House*, I couldn't get enough of this stuff. A typical conversation between the Frat Boy and the Toadmeister after 'scoping out the Betties' went something like this:

Frat Boy: Did you see that Shermetta by the Xerox machine? She had her high beams on.

Toadmeister: I bet she can really roll. I bet she throws a mean cat.

Frat Boy: Oh yeah. I'd like to knock boots with her.[1]

There was one girl in particular we obsessed over. She was called Pippi and, in Chris's words, she had 'a kickin' system'. Blonde hair, blue eyes, button nose, skinny but with big tits, she was the kind of girl other women referred to as 'your basic nightmare'. To Chris and I, though, she was the ultimate total Betty.

Pippi was also – and this is what convinced us we had a chance – extremely dimwitted. She was Elizabeth Saltzman's assistant and on one famous occasion she was supposed to have had the following telephone conversation with Si Newhouse, the owner of Condé Nast:

Pippi: Elizabeth Saltzman's office.

Newhouse: Hi, it's Si. Can I speak to Elizabeth?

Pippi: I'm sorry, sir, I didn't catch your name.

Newhouse: Si, Si Newhouse.

Pippi: Come again?

Newhouse [Exasperated]: Just put Elizabeth on the phone.

Pippi [Chirpy]: Can I tell her what it's concerning?

Click. Dial-tone.

Naturally, the Frat Boy and the Toadmeister decided to hold

---

[1] This translates as: Chris: Did you see that beautiful girl by the Xerox machine? You could see her nipples through her T-shirt. Me: I bet she's good in bed. She looks like she really knows what to do. Chris: You're right about that. I'd like to sleep with her.

a contest to see who could 'drop the hammer' with Pippi first. Chris's strategy was to pretend to be a 'snag' (Sensitive New Age Guy) in the hope of appealing to her alternative side. As a 25-year-old who liked listening to Phish, Pippi was what Chris called 'a Starbucks bohemian' and his plan was to impress her with his hippyish credentials. These weren't totally false. He may have bought his suits from 'the Brethren' (Brooks Brothers), but he'd been known to wear the occasional Grateful Dead T-shirt.

My strategy, hardly any more honest, was to pretend to be a small-dog lover. In the summer of 1995, small dogs were 'in' and the *Vanity Fair* fashion department was absolutely teeming with them. Elizabeth's dog, a long-haired Chihuahua, was called Cuba because it was the colour and size of a Cuban cigar; Pippi's dog, also a long-haired Chihuahua, was called Picolina because . . . well, because Pippi thought that was a cute name. In addition, there were Miniature Dachshunds, Yorkshire Terriers, Shih-Tzus – a whole menagerie of different breeds, all yapping away like mad.

Of course, it was strictly against company rules to allow dogs in the building but Graydon tolerated them because Elizabeth was, as Chris put it, 'connected up the wazoo'. I was in Graydon's office once, pitching some hopeless story idea, when Dana poked his head round the door and said, 'It's Elizabeth calling from the plane.' 'Oh, she *always* does that,' sighed Graydon. He explained that whenever Elizabeth was flying 'non-commercial' she liked to call him in midair to let him know which billionaire's private jet she was on.[1] He referred to Cuba as 'the rat'.

Elizabeth, I should point out, didn't take the rat *that* seriously. I once asked her if Cuba was going to be attending a fund-raiser being staged by a charity called 'Powars' (Pet Owners With Aids) at which small dogs would be modelling a

---

[1] *Vanity Fair* is sometimes referred to as 'the in-flight magazine of the GulfStream jet set'.

selection of different designer outfits. 'He'd love to,' she said sadly, 'but he's already committed himself to going sailing in the Hamptons that weekend.' On another occasion I was playing with Cuba in her office, trying to get him to roll over, when Elizabeth said: 'He doesn't understand "roll over". He thinks it means croissant.'

Pippi displayed no such levity when it came to Picolina. At one point, according to Pippi, the pressure of being surrounded by so many other small dogs, all of them impeccably groomed, became too much for Picolina and she developed 'an eating disorder'. Picolina also had a number of other 'issues', including 'fear of abandonment', 'separation anxiety' and 'intimacy problems'. Naturally, everyone assumed Pippi was talking about herself.

My first opportunity to impress Pippi came on the opening day of Fashion Week when Elizabeth and the rest of the department were about to decamp to Bryant Park to watch the shows. All the other girls were taking their small dogs with them – they were fashion accessories, after all – but Pippi didn't think Picolina was 'ready' for that kind of excitement. She was intending to shut her in Elizabeth's office for the day and was worried about leaving her alone. Did I think she'd be okay?

'Would you like me to look in on her from time to time to make sure she's alright?' I offered.

'Would you?' squealed Pippi, clutching my arm. 'That would be *so* sweet.'

'It'd be a pleasure,' I assured her.

She wrinkled her nose and gave me an adoring smile.

This is it, Frat Boy, I thought. It won't be long before the Toadmeister is 'hobbling' the total Betty.

I checked up on Picolina at about 2.30 p.m. and everything appeared to be okay. She had a dog biscuit to chew on and a little bowl of water and if she wanted to 'do anything', as Pippi put it, there was a litter box in the corner.

At 3.45 p.m. I noticed it was getting a little stuffy in

Elizabeth's office so I replenished Picolina's water supply and cracked open a window above the desk. Apart from that, she seemed fine.

When I next looked in again at about 5 p.m. I almost had a heart attack. The window had blown right open, there was a tiny little dog turd on Elizabeth's desk and Picolina was nowhere to be seen. The implication was clear: she'd somehow climbed up on to the desk and jumped out of the window. She'd gone from being 'in' to being 'out'.

I bolted down the emergency stairs and ran out on to 44th Street to see if I could see any sign of her.

Nothing.

I walked up and down the street calling out her name: 'Picoleeena? Picoleeeeeena? *Picoleeeeeeeeeena!*'

Again nothing.

Jesus Christ! What am I going to tell Pippi?

At that moment, a Lincoln Town Car drew up outside 350 and out popped Elizabeth and her posse. Pippi immediately spotted me.

'Hi, Toby,' she said, skipping over and giving me a kiss. 'How's Picolina?'

She could tell from the look on my face that something was wrong.

'What's happened?' she asked, grabbing me by the shoulders. 'TELL ME.'

'It's p-p-probably nothing,' I stammered.

'Where is she?'

'That's just it. I'm not exactly sure.'

'You didn't leave the door open, did you?'

'No, no, not the door.'

'So how could she have gotten out?'

I glanced up at the window. Pippi followed the direction of my gaze.

'No!' she said. '*Tell me you're kidding.*'

I held out my hands, palms upwards, as if to say, 'What can I tell you?'

Pippi rushed into 350 and jumped into a lift. I did my best to keep up. When we got to the fourth floor she ran to Elizabeth's office and threw open the door. The scene was exactly as I'd left it.

'Toby,' she whimpered, looking beseechingly into my eyes. 'Where is she?'

I stood there feeling completely useless. I'd been entrusted with the care of Pippi's precious little baby and somehow I'd managed to kill her. It was a total disaster.

'Is this what you're looking for?'

I wheeled round to see Chris standing in the doorway. He was holding Picolina.

'I found her running around in the corridor,' he explained.

Pippi rushed up and clutched Picolina to her bosom. She burst into tears.

'Thank you, thank you, thank you,' she sniffed.

'No problem,' he said smugly and winked at me.

Clearly, Chris had kidnapped Picolina and carefully placed the turd on Elizabeth's desk to make it look as though she'd jumped out of the window. To use one of his favourite words, he'd 'schmageled' me.

So everything's fair in love and war, eh, Frat Boy? Well, two can play at that game.

A chance to get my revenge came shortly afterwards when Chris announced that it was his birthday. I decided on the perfect present: a strippergram. Once Pippi saw him being entertained in this traditional, frat-house style, she'd soon realise he wasn't the sophisticated, caring man he pretended to be. He'd be exposed as the knuckle-dragging Neanderthal he was!

Having read the company guidelines on sexual harassment, I knew that hiring a stripper to come to 350 would be considered completely inappropriate but somehow I managed to convince myself I could smuggle her in and out of the building without being detected.

Some hope.

I looked up 'Strippergrams' in the yellow pages and, after calling half a dozen numbers, found exactly what I was looking for: a stripper called Picolina.

Would it be possible for her to come to 350 Madison Avenue that afternoon?

'350 Maddy? You got it,' said the goombah who answered the phone. 'She'll be there in an hour.'

'When she turns up at the front desk, could she tell security she's from "corporate services"?'

'Corporate services? No problemo.'

'And could she dress as normally as possible? I don't want my colleagues suspecting anything.'

'Donchoo worry, sir. We're very discreet.'

At 3 p.m. I got a call from security to tell me that a 'Miss Picolina from corporate services' was there to see me. I could tell from the sceptical tone of his voice that she looked anything but 'normal' and when I reached the lobby she wasn't exactly hard to spot: she was dressed from head-to-toe in stonewashed denim and clutching a ghetto blaster. I debated whether to take her up in the service elevator but decided better of it. I'd just have to brazen it out.

She caused a sensation in the lift. The two women we happened to be sharing with made no attempt to conceal their disdain. 'That's *brave*!' said one. The other agreed: 'It's kinda *matchy*, doncha think?' Luckily Picolina, who was from the Czech Republic, spoke very little English.

I'd persuaded Elizabeth to let me use her office for the festivities and I ushered Picolina in with as little fuss as possible. I could tell from the general murmur of excitement in the fashion department that Elizabeth had brought everyone up to speed. Everyone except Pippi, that is, who smiled at Picolina as if she was just another senior executive who'd come to meet with her boss. It was all going to plan.

As soon as I got the 'Okay' sign from Elizabeth, I told Chris she wanted to see him about something. I followed behind to make sure he didn't try and back out once he realised was what going on. The door to Elizabeth's office was opened by Picolina wearing a nurse's uniform.

'Halpy bir-day, Christophe,' she said in a halting Czech accent.

'You guys!' said Chris, but made no attempt to escape.

Showtime!

Picolina sat Chris down in a chair in the centre of the room, switched on her boogie box and began her routine accompanied by Michael Jackson's 'Beat It'. It was quite a performance. As each article of clothing came off, Elizabeth took a photograph of the proceedings with a Polaroid camera and every time the bulb flashed her posse shrieked with delight. It wasn't long before the Frat Boy started getting quite 'stoked', at one point exclaiming: 'Now that's what I call a spectacular rack!' Pippi looked on in horror, holding her long-haired Chihuahua in one hand and shielding the dog's eyes with the other.

Everything was going swimmingly until we heard a faint knocking sound on Elizabeth's door followed by a plaintive, little girl's voice asking if she could come in. Who was that? Elizabeth immediately shut off the music, told us all to be quiet and cracked open the door. We were all terrified, not least because at that moment Chris had Picolina's knickers stretched over his face.

It was Bronwen, Graydon Carter's three-year-old daughter.

'Hi, Bronwen,' cooed Elizabeth. 'How are you?'

'Can I come in?' Bronwen asked.

'Not right now, honey,' Elizabeth said. 'Could you come back in fifteen minutes?'

There was a long pause during which we all held our breath.

'Oh-kay,' said Bronwen reluctantly.

As soon as she'd gone, Elizabeth closed the door and turned the music back on, but a few seconds later there was another knock on the door. Once again we all froze.

'Yes?' asked Elizabeth.

This time it was *three* little girls and they, too, wanted to come in. Elizabeth shooed them away, but a minute later another group of little girls appeared, followed by another, then another. What the fuck was going on?

It turned out that in my wisdom I'd arranged for a strip-pergram to come to the office on 'Take Our Daughters to Work Day'. Apparently, Take Our Daughters to Work Day is an annual American institution whereby employees, particularly female employees, can bring their little girls into the office so they can see exactly what Mummy and Daddy get up to all day. Needless to say, on this occasion the only bit of *Vanity Fair* the little girls were interested in seeing was the fashion department.

We had to wind up the entertainment pretty quickly after that.

I expected Chris to be amused by my little stunt – after all, I'd never complained about him dropping me in it with Pippi – but he was furious.

'You chump!' he exclaimed. 'What the fuck were you thinking?'

'Come on, Frat Boy, lighten up. It was just a bit of fun. No one will hold it against me.'

'Are you kidding? Hiring a stripper at Condé Nast? That's a capital offence round here. They're gonna *crucify* you.'

'Well,' I said, trying to make light of it. 'We'll just have to hope no one hears about it.'

'Yeah, right,' he said. 'This is Condé Nast, remember?'

Chris was right. In less than twenty-four hours I was known throughout 350 as 'the British guy who hired a strippergram on Take Our Daughters to Work Day'.

He was wrong about the reaction to it, though. Luckily, what I'd done was so off the charts in terms of what was and wasn't acceptable, so *galactically* inappropriate, people didn't quite know what to make of it. If I'd done something straightfor-wardly sexist, like put a Pirelli Calendar up in my office, I would have been severely reprimanded, possibly even fired. But the fact that I'd brought a stripper into the building on Take Our Daughters to Work Day . . . it was almost baffling. *How could anyone be that dumb?* I wasn't classed as a male chau-vinist pig so much as a complete and utter moron. In any case,

I wasn't someone worth worrying about because I clearly wouldn't be around for much longer.

Pippi, I regret to say, never showed much interest in either Chris or me after this and any chance of either of us 'hooking up' with her completely vanished. However, I did get something out of it. The following morning I came into work to find a large present on my desk from Aimée Bell. I unwrapped it and discovered a book entitled *Letitia Baldrige's New Complete Guide to Executive Manners*. Inside was a message: 'Toby, do not leave your office until you've read this book from cover to cover. I mean it.' The words 'I mean it' had been underlined in red, felt-tip pen.

11

LIBERTÉ, EGALITÉ, PUBLICITÉ

As autumn approached, I was worried about what Graydon would think of my 'sophomoric hi-jinks', as Chris Lawrence called them. I had been at *Vanity Fair* for over a month at this point and the subject of my future hadn't come up. Would he conclude that I wasn't first room material after all? The prospect of returning to London after so brief a period wasn't appealing. What would I tell my friends? In addition, I'd just been appointed the *Evening Standard*'s New York columnist and I didn't want to give that up so soon after getting it.

Fortunately, Graydon was prepared to overlook the stripper incident as a beginner's error but counselled me not to 'pull another stunt like that'.

'Women in the New York media don't have a sense of humour about that kind of thing,' he warned. 'Maybe on Wall Street you could get away with it, but not at Condé Nast.'

Surely, I protested, no one would take it seriously? Didn't they know that I was a decent, upright young man who'd never dream of hiring a stripper for sexual purposes? (I debated whether to wink at him at this point.) I told him about Britain's lad mags and the culture of 'ironic sexism' that has grown up around them whereby it's socially acceptable for middle class men to engage in the kind of practices that would have got them tarred and feathered in the eighties. Wasn't there a comparable phenomenon in New York?

'*Ironic* sexism?' he repeated. 'Listen, Toby, I don't know about London but in New York there's no such thing as ironic sexism.' He stared at me to make sure I was getting the message. 'That's like ironic anti-Semitism or something. In this town, you can get *unironically* lynched for stuff like that.'

Instead of lynching me, though, he offered to put me on the masthead as a 'contributing editor' and said that if I managed to stay out of trouble for the next few months I could sit in Aimée Bell's chair when she went on maternity leave. (She was pregnant with her first child.) I'd take over her responsibilities as the co-editor of Vanities and when she came back, who knows what might happen. The implication was clear: if I played my cards right I could look forward to a permanent editorial position at the magazine.

However, there was one bit of bad news. He couldn't continue paying me $10,000 a month. 'It's too much,' he said. 'I mean, what do you do all day, apart from hiring strippers?' Instead, he'd pay me $5,000 and put me on a six-month contract. It would be renewed on a rolling basis, provided I didn't 'fuck up'.

Once again, he'd failed to bring up the fact that Si wanted to meet me, but nevertheless I was cock-a-hoop. Together, *Vanity Fair* and the *Evening Standard* would be paying me two salaries and, just as important, I'd have two expense accounts. According to my 1994–95 tax return, my net profit for the previous year had been £19,964.10. At a stroke I'd more than quadrupled my income. My favourite part was that I was now issued with all the accoutrements of a fully fledged member of staff: a press card, a business card and some headed notepaper with my name and title printed at the top. I immediately set about writing to all my friends.

When I got over my initial euphoria – a *contributing editor*! – I decided it was time to really get stuck in to New York. What with my *Vanity Fair* press card and my name on the masthead, I'd effectively been handed the keys to the city; it was now just a matter of working out how to use them. The secret of social success in Manhattan, I'd discovered, was to be 'on the list'. This hadn't taken much detective work. In the autumn of 1995 the hardest place in the city to get into was Bowery Bar, a watering hole on East 4th Street, and in spite of numerous attempts I'd yet to get past the clipboard Nazis. To give you some idea of the clientele, one disgruntled neighbour had put up a homemade neon sign in his front window that listed the following groups above an enormous arrow pointing towards the entrance: 'Neo-Trash', 'Boring Yuppies', 'Pseudo Models', 'Limo Pimps' and 'Black-Leather Conformists'.

None of the techniques I'd perfected for getting into clubs in London seemed to work at Bowery Bar. One of my favourites was to march up to the front of the queue with a girl in tow, turn round so my back was to the bouncers and boldly announce that I was with 'this person', indicating the girl, but not with 'this person' or 'that person', pointing at a couple of no-hopers waiting in line. The bouncers were so used to the club's regular patrons behaving like this they usually let us in without a murmur.

Another foolproof method was to pretend to be in the throes of a full-scale, nuclear row with my date as we approached the venue. The natural human impulse not to get involved in a 'domestic' meant the doormen would often usher us past the velvet rope as speedily as possible.

But the clipboard Nazis at Bowery Bar were made of sterner stuff. I'd seen grown women reduced to desperate measures to try and gain admittance. On one occasion I witnessed an attractive women in her late twenties – a Pseudo Model, no doubt – telling one of the doormen that she was sleeping with the owner.

'Sorry, lady,' he replied. 'You and half the other broads in this city.'

No, the only way to get into Bowery Bar was to be among the names that the hostess – a Boring Yuppie – kept by the door. In club jargon, it was a 'list only' establishment – no invitations, no flyers, no 'plus ones'. The question was: how to get on the list?

The answer was to butter up the publicist who had the Bowery Bar account. If you're a single, thirtysomething journalist looking to have a good time in New York you have to be on the right lists and the only way to get on them is to 'make nice' with the right PRs.[1] They're the guardians of what Anthony Haden-Guest, a twenty-year veteran of the New York party scene, calls 'night-world'. A handful of these flaks control access to all the city's best clubs and restaurants, not to mention shop openings, product launches and movie premieres, and if they don't have your name in their Palm Pilots you don't get invited to anything.

It was ever thus. In 1892 *The New York Times* published 'the 400', a supposedly definitive list of the members of New York society assembled by Ward McAllister, an early prototype of the modern PR man. McAllister had married into money and the purpose of his list was to redefine 'Society' as a mixture of 'Nobs' – the Wasp old guard – and 'Swells' – nouveau riche types like himself. The reason his list was limited to 400 was because that was the number that could be squeezed into Mrs John Jacob Astor's ballroom.

The equivalent today is 'the PMK 400', a list drawn up by the publicist Pat Kingsley whose clients include Tom Cruise, Sharon Stone, Arnold Schwarzenegger, Demi Moore, Al Pacino and Jodie Foster. All the most successful PRs have computerised databases of VIPs ranked according to how socially desirable they are and updated 'every ten minutes', as they put it. They rarely use such crude terms as 'A-list', 'B-list' and 'C-list' just in case a celebrity gets wind of the fact that they're not in the top tier and throws a 'hissy fit'. Jeffrey Jah, for instance, who describes himself as a 'club promoter'[2] has a database of 8,000 names divided into 'AAAAs' ('top models, rock stars, movie stars, editors-in-chief'), 'AAAs' ('the best of the best people you

---

[1] Never referred to as 'PRs' in New York – that stands for Puerto Ricans.
[2] People in the New York public relations industry never describe themselves as 'flaks' or 'publicists'. Rather, they're 'promoters', 'event producers' or 'image consultants'. The PR industry, it seems, has a PR problem.

know'), 'AAs' ('good but not the best') and 'As' ('if you need to fill a stadium').[1] That's a bit like dividing condom sizes into 'Giant', 'Extra Large' and – for the seriously under-endowed – 'Large'. Sometimes the PRs adopt a classification system that's scrupulously non-hierarchical. Lizzie Grubman, a publicist who's frequently referred to as 'the reigning queen of New York nightlife',[2] divides her database into 'Model', 'Celebrity', 'Fashion', 'Junior', 'Editor-in-Chief' and 'Clubbers', which sounds suspiciously like Neo-Trash, Boring Yuppies, Pseudo Models, Limo Pimps and Black-Leather Conformists.[3]

The most influential PR woman on the East Coast in Peggy Siegal, the flak who organizes all the most glamorous film premieres, but if you want to get past the clipboard Nazis of New York's hippest bars and clubs the most important publicists to know are a group of predominantly Jewish women in their mid-twenties whose most powerful members are known as 'the Seven Sisters' although there are a lot more of them than that. So how do you gain admittance into their charmed circle? One way is to *literally* get into bed with them. According to Bobby Zarem, a grizzled veteran of the PR industry, this coterie of über-flaks are just in it 'to get laid'. The trouble with this, though, is that the moment you stop sleeping with them you're struck off their lists – *for ever*. New York is full of washed-up swordsmen who made the mistake of cutting a swathe through the city's army of female publicists when they first arrived, only to find themselves unable to get in anywhere six months later. In any case, I'm not exactly what these women would call a 'babe'.

Unfortunately, if you're a balding British hack the only way to get on their lists is to plug their clients in print at regular

---

[1] Quoted in 'Social Life in a Blender', Michael Gross, *New York,* 2 February, 1998.

[2] This was before she reversed her Mercedes SOV into a crowd of people outside a nightclub in the Hamptons in the summer of 2001.

[3] Quoted in 'Welcome to the Dollhouse', Vanessa Grigoriadis, *New York*, 7 December, 1998.

intervals; you have to be what they call 'plantable'.[1] Now, I don't consider myself a beacon of journalistic integrity, but I balked slightly at this *quid pro quo*. As the editor of *The Modern Review*, I'd regarded PRs as the enemy. Their job was to try and persuade my writers to look favourably on whatever it was they were promoting and my job was to ensure that the staff remained aloof. If we ever received a press release it went straight in 'the circular file', i.e., the bin. Indeed, throughout Fleet Street PRs are regarded with a good deal of disdain. They're the agents of commercial interests and even those on the lowest rung of the professional ladder – even diarists – are expected to resist their blandishments. We all accept 'freebies', of course, but it's considered bad form to write something gushing and complimentary in return. As far as most of us are concerned, the relationship between hacks and flaks is essentially adversarial.[2]

In New York, by contrast, they're as thick as thieves. As Elizabeth Harrison, one of the Seven Sisters, puts it: 'Journalists are no longer covering the scene – they're part of the scene.' This is odd because in most other respects American reporters are much more scrupulous than their British counterparts. When it comes to factual accuracy, for instance, their standards are far above ours. Even my 175-word article about Wade Dominguez went through a rigorous fact-checking procedure; I spent longer talking to the 'checker' than I did to Dominguez. They're painstakingly even-handed too, always making sure that both parties to a dispute are given a chance to air their views. Even in right-wing papers like the Murdoch-owned *New York Post* political ideology is confined to the editorial page; it doesn't really influence the reporting. On the whole, American

---

[1] In the early days of the public relations industry, the firms would empoy 'planters' to place stories about their clients in gossip columns. Pat Kingsley's first job in PR was as a planter for Rogers & Cowan.

[2] Admittedly, I've occasionally said something nice in return for a MASSIVE bribe, but at least I've felt guilty about it. Really, *really* guilty.

journalists take their responsibilities as members of the fourth estate much more seriously than we do.

Why, then, are they so willing to climb into the pockets of publicists?[1] This isn't just true of the fairly low-grade reporters covering the New York party scene. It goes all the way up the ladder. In his book *Nobrow: The Culture of Marketing – the Marketing of Culture*, John Seabrook talks about the routine compromises he had to make as a contributor to *The New Yorker* under Tina Brown: 'If you wrote about a pop star, or a designer, or an athlete, you were necessarily borrowing some of your subject's celebrity and using it to sell your story. And if you thought you could get away with that – with taking their Buzz and not giving up some of your creative independence in return – well, brother, you were kidding yourself. There was always a transaction involved.'

That goes double for *Vanity Fair*. During the autumn of 1996, when the magazine's offices were being redecorated, I was temporarily housed in a cubicle next door to Krista Smith, the magazine's West Coast editor, whose principal job is to liaise with the Hollywood publicity machine. One afternoon I overheard her discussing Quentin Tarantino with another woman whose voice I didn't recognise. At the time Tarantino was suffering from enormous over-exposure and I didn't think the magazine should give him any more publicity. I burst into Krista's cubicle and launched into an anti-Tarantino rant, focusing on the arrogance that led him to cast himself in his own movies even though he couldn't act. 'You don't see Graydon putting himself on the cover of *Vanity Fair*,' I fumed.

After I'd finally run out of steam, Krista fixed me with a look that let me know I'd made a total prat of myself. 'Have

---

[1] This hasn't always been the case. For instance, in *The Sweet Smell of Success* J.J. Hunsecker is a far more powerful figure than Sydney Falco. If the film was remade today, the power relationship would have to be reversed.

you met Bumble Ward?' she asked, indicating the woman she'd been talking to. 'She's Quentin Tarantino's publicist.'

At least *Vanity Fair* stops short of granting celebrities copy approval; less prestigious magazines are only too happy to surrender their editorial independence altogether. In all my time at *Vanity Fair*, the worst instance of kow-towing to a public relations firm I heard about was when a researcher had to walk over a photograph of Carrie Fisher, Penny Marshall and Meryl Streep to the New York offices of PMK so Pat Kingsley herself could indicate where the picture needed to be airbrushed.[1]

One of the reasons so many American journalists are such quislings is because they're simply bought off. Lara Shriftman, the most powerful of the Seven Sisters, numbers among her clients Gucci, Motorola and Mercedes-Benz and it isn't hard to spot the reporters that are her 'favourite friends' – they're the ones wearing Gucci watches, carrying StarTacs and driving SLK roadsters.[2]

'They seduce you,' one editor told *New York* magazine. 'Every day, they send you this endless stream of free stuff, cell phones and facials and a month with a Mercedes, and all they want back is a tiny little item. Eventually, your whole social life starts to revolve around them. Let's face it: Most journalists are neither

---

[1] The researcher writes: 'David Harris [*Vanity Fair*'s art director] sent me over to PMK with an already retouched photo of Carrie Fisher, Penny Marshall and Meryl Streep. I think that David thought the work was already adequate and that it would merely be a matter of some "mid-level flak" signing off on the shot. Instead, I was ushered into a meeting with Pat Kingsley herself at which she pulled out a grease pencil and began attacking turkey necks and crow's feet . . . What was funny about it was that she was discussing it with me as though I were some important, skilled person from the art department and that I would be making the changes. It was too good not to play along with and we were soon in a philosophical/aesthetic discussion about aging and beauty – very surreal. I remember that we pointedly didn't discuss "truth in advertising" or "journalistic ethics".'

[2] In the New York media such bribes are referred to as 'tchotchkes'.

rich nor cool, and to sit at a table with an heiress on one side and a movie star on another – it's hard not to fall for that.'

Further up the chain, the reason the editors-in-chief of glossy magazines are so quiescent is because the PRs have them by the short and curlies. In order to sell their magazines on the newsstands, the editors need to get A-list stars to pose for their covers and the only way to do that is to agree to whatever terms their publicists dictate. In a business that depends on a constant infusion of showbiz glamour, the celebrities – and their publicists – hold all the cards.

This was the unhappy conclusion of Lynn Barber, the British journalist who worked for *Vanity Fair* from 1992–94. 'Any magazine that relies on having a big star on the cover every month and whose newsstand sales depend to some extent on the appeal of that star, has already sold the pass to the PRs,' she writes in the Introduction to *Demon Barber*, a collection of her interviews. 'When you have a virtual monopoly position, as you do now with Pat Kingsley in Hollywood, editors are pretty well powerless.'[1]

I occasionally tackled my *Vanity Fair* colleagues about this, accusing them of having become collaborators in the war between hacks and flaks. Their defence was that sacrificing their independence in these areas doesn't really matter in the grand scheme of things. It's not as if they're covering national politics. In any case, the people who buy the magazine don't want to read 'hit' pieces about movie stars. The vast majority of them are avid fans. My co-workers didn't come right out and say it, but the implication was that *Vanity Fair* is basically just *People* magazine for those who can read without moving their lips.

Whenever I brought this subject up with Graydon he refused to accept that the magazine was enmeshed with the PR industry

---

[1] Pat Kingsley's monopoly was consolidated in May, 2001 when PMK merged with Huvane Baum Halls, a rival PR firm with a roster of movie star clients including Russell Crowe, Gwyneth Paltrow, Jennifer Aniston, Liv Tyler and Jude Law. This means that the whole of the Hollywood A-list is now represented by just one company under the control of Pat Kingsley.

and, to be fair to him, he makes more of an effort than most to maintain the separation between church and state. Nevertheless, the impression I got is that he doesn't set much store by the celebrity profiles, having more or less concluded they'll have to be puff pieces, and instead devotes his energies to the rest of the magazine. His track record there is pretty good, too. For instance, in September 1995 *Vanity Fair* published an extremely critical piece about Mohamed Al Fayed by Maureen Orth that resulted in him bringing a libel suit against the magazine. Graydon stood his ground and the case was eventually dropped.[1] Later, he ran a long piece by Marie Brenner on the tobacco whistleblower Jeffrey Wigand even though Brown & Williamson, the company Wigand had worked for, threatened to withdraw millions of dollars worth of advertising if the story was published. The article became the basis for the film *The Insider*.

It's difficult to avoid the conclusion that the reason publicists exercise such power over the New York media is because American journalists, particularly those who work for glossies, just aren't as pugnacious as their British equivalents. This was

---

[1] According to someone closely involved in the case: 'Al Fayed sued very shortly after publication having been persuaded by arguments from his staff that he would gain a quick retraction. The slow pace of the initial legal exchanges meant that nine months passed before the company began to defend the action in earnest. Fayed claimed defamation in four main areas of the article which meant that the magazine had to work very hard to defend the original story, but also that Fayed was more exposed than if he had gone for a rifle shot suit in a single area where he could make a strong case. Libel plaintiffs often mistakenly believe a wide-ranging complaint that alleges numerous inaccuracies stands a greater chance of success; in fact, the opposite is true because it leaves the plaintiff vulnerable to investigation. Three years later Fayed backed off when he saw the case the magazine had built to support Maureen Orth's original story. The magazine was always confident because of the rigorous fact-checking that preceded publication. No damages were paid to Fayed. No apology or retraction or clarification was made by the magazine. Fayed absorbed his own costs, as did the magazine which was insured. The insurers paid up.'

bitterly disappointing to me. Where were the scrappy rebels that I'd first glimpsed in Hollywood's black-and-white newspaper pictures? I'd been looking forward to meeting the hardscrabble reporters Ben Hecht pays tribute to in *A Child of the Century*: 'Scores of them return vaguely to my mind. But there is nothing vague in my memory of their combined quality. They sat, grown and abuzz, outside an adult civilization, intent on breaking windows.' I was expecting their contemporary equivalents to adopt a them-and-us attitude towards celebrities and their handlers, ridiculing and lampooning them at every turn. In fact, they behaved like flunkies at the court of Louis XIV, snapping to attention whenever a boldface name so much as glanced in their direction.

This is in stark contrast to Fleet Street where the attitude of most hacks towards the glitterati is epitomised by the *Sun*'s unofficial slogan: 'Everybody hates us and we don't care.' With a few notable exceptions, hacks aren't part of the scene they're covering; they stick to their trusted watering holes. Those who do get caught up in it are branded 'social climbers' and tend to be mistrusted by their colleagues. In some vague, undefined way, to get too chummy with the kind of people who appear in *Hello!* is regarded as a betrayal of the hack's warrior code.

The upshot of all this is that in New York the publicists tend to look down on the journalists. To them, we're just another bunch of wannabes clamouring to be let into the VIP section. 'I have no respect for writers,' Peggy Siegal told *New York* magazine. 'They never make money. They're like poor people looking in the windows.'

Of course, in the autumn of 1995 I was absolutely desperate to be on the other side of that window. In Fleet Street terms, I was one of the social climbers. But while I was willing to go to almost any lengths to achieve fame, I was a bit reluctant to sell my soul just for the honour of *hanging out* with famous people. What kind of Faustian bargain is that? In the end, I decided the best solution was to promise the flaks the earth, but deliver them nothing. I reasoned that it was perfectly okay to let the Seven Sisters think I was going to write something nice about their clients as long as I had ABSOLUTELY NO INTENTION of doing so. As Cicero said, there's nothing wrong with accepting a bribe if you don't let it influence your behaviour. Of course, such a policy could only buy me access for a few months, but by the time the PRs realised I wasn't plantable I'd be bored by the whole scene anyway. At least, that was my hope.

With this rather flimsy rationalisation in place, I set out to conquer nightworld.

12

ON THE LIST

It didn't take me long to find out who the publicist was that drew up the list at Bowery Bar: it was Nadine Johnson, an attractive Belgian woman in her early forties. Although not one of the Seven Sisters, Nadine has a formidable secret weapon: she's married to Richard Johnson, the editor of Page Six. Page Six is the most influential of the *New York Post*'s four daily gossip columns, the thing most New Yorkers turn to when they sit down for their first bagel of the day. The movers and shakers who fill the column may not like what's written about them, but the fact that they're being written about at all means that at least they're on the radar screen. Bowery Bar owed its pre-eminence in the autumn of 1995 to the fact that it appeared in Page Six almost every day.[1]

I was introduced to Nadine by Matt and Aimée who dragged me along to one of the Johnsons' regular soirées at their West Village townhouse. It was without doubt the best party I'd been to so far. Up until this point, the few social events I'd crashed – I still hadn't received a single invitation – were a far cry from the shindigs I was used to back home. In London parties had been noisy, bacchanalian affairs where all class distinctions were quickly forgotten; in New York they were stiff, rather formal

---

[1] One rival publicist complained: 'In a city that runs on questionable relationships, [Richard and Nadine's] probably is the most conspicuous.'

occasions in which differences in status were, if anything, even more pronounced. I blamed this on the fact that not nearly enough alcohol was consumed. America is currently undergoing one of those periodic bouts of repression that punctuate its history. All the pleasures I was expecting to find in Manhattan – illicit sex, the perfect dry Martini, Bolivian marching powder – have been completely pathologised and anyone caught enjoying them is immediately press-ganged into joining a twelve-step programme. It's miserable.

Richard and Nadine's get together was different. It was like an oasis at which all the party animals from the previous decade had assembled to . . . well, drink, for starters. It was the first time I'd seen people actually getting shit-faced (apart from Anthony Haden-Guest, of course). They were also misbehaving. At one point it was rumoured that two people were actually having sex in one of the children's bedrooms upstairs. (The children weren't present at the time.) Jay McInerney and Bret Easton Ellis were there, as was Candace Bushnell, who at that time was still writing the column in the *New York Observer* that would become *Sex and the City*. I knew she was no ordinary journalist when I was introduced to a man who identified himself as her 'manager'. It wasn't unheard of for a journalist to have an agent – even, in Hunter S. Thompson's case, an attorney – but a *manager*? I asked him what he did but he declined to say.

The person I was most excited about meeting was Richard Johnson. Richard is a legend among New York hacks, a throwback to an earlier era when gossip columnists weren't so easily bought. In spite of being married to Nadine, he has a much healthier attitude to publicists than most of his colleagues: he hates them.[1] Tall and athletic-looking, he has a macho swagger that lets the world know he isn't a typical member of his trade. He's less like J.J. Hunsecker, the duplicitous hatchet-wielder

---

[1] 'Nobody can berate a publicist like he can,' his second-in-command, Jared Paul Stern, once told me. 'I mean, listening to him, it's just hilarious.'

played by Burt Lancaster in *The Sweet Smell of Success*, than 'Swede', the charismatic psychopath also played by Lancaster in *The Killers*. Since being put in charge of Page Six in 1985, Richard has been policing the nocturnal habits of the rich and famous with a diligence that would put J. Edgar Hoover to shame. (He's the Elliot Ness of the journalistic vice squad.) He prides himself on not kow-towing to celebrities and, as a result, is always embroiled in feuds with them. For instance, in 1991 Mickey Rourke, one of Richard's favourite targets, gave an interview to *The Fort Lauderdale Sun-Sentinel* in which he accused the six foot three columnist of hiding behind his type-writer. 'He wouldn't have the balls to come up and say, "Mickey, I think you're a douchebag" or "Mickey, I think your acting sucks",' fumed the star of *Nine-and-a-half Weeks*.

In his reply Richard didn't mince words: 'Memo to Mickey Rourke: Any time, any place.'

When the party started winding down, I attached myself to a group of people heading over to Bowery Bar – here, at last, was my chance to get in. The group included the infamous *Vanity Fair* columnist George Wayne, a flamboyant, Jamaican homosexual. Among his many idiosyncrasies, George has the celebrity's habit of always referring to himself in the third person. I'd never met a black homosexual before and, sitting next to him in the cab on the way to East 4th Street, I was slightly intimidated.

'So, George,' I asked, trying to break the ice, 'how long have you been a hack?'

'A *hack*?' he replied in horror. 'GW is not a *hack*. He's a belletrist, darling. A FUCKING BELLETRIST!'

I decided to keep my trap shut after that.

When we arrived at Bowery Bar George marched straight to the head of the queue and stood impatiently in front of the velvet rope. He gave the bouncer a look as if to say: 'Come on, come on, I haven't got all day.'

'Step away from the door, please, sir,' growled the clipboard Nazi.

'Why should I?' retorted George.

'You may notta noticed, sir, but there's line.'

'I'm on the list.'

'All those people are on the list,' said the bouncer indicating the crowd behind George. 'If you go to the back a the line, I'm sure you'll be accommodated in doo course.'

George shot a contemptuous glance over his shoulder.

'GW doesn't wait in line,' he announced grandly. He then stuck out his chin and folded his arms: he wasn't going anywhere.

'Okay,' sighed the bouncer. 'How many you wid?'

I was astonished. I'd assumed that if you talked to a clipboard Nazi in this way, not only would he not let you in, you'd go straight to the top of his shit list. Throughout the altercation I'd been backing away, hoping the bouncer wouldn't catch a glimpse of me over George's shoulder. But it had worked!

Once inside, George was recognised by the hostess who immediately fell on him like Basil Fawlty greeting a food inspector.

'George! How *are* you? You look fantastic! Oh my God, it's so great to see you.'

'You should tell that fucking gorilla on the door to treat GW with a little more respect,' George harrumphed.

'Did you have a problem?' she asked. Her tone was one of utter amazement. Did you, the great George Wayne, have difficulty getting in? It couldn't be!

'Yes, I had a *problem*,' he snapped. 'That man didn't recognise GW. He's an ignoramus. A FUCKING IGNORAMUS!'

Instead of apologising, the hostess took George by the hand and whisked him back outside. This was clearly something that would have to be dealt with immediately.

'Hey, Sal,' she said, addressing the clipboard Nazi, 'this is George Wayne, okay? *The* George Wayne?' She stood behind George and placed both hands on his shoulders. 'George is a *really* good friend of mine. He's, like, my best friend. Never make him wait on line again, understand?'

She stared at Sal until he grunted his assent and moments later we were back inside, teleported into one of Bowery Bar's famous 'booths'. The hostess made it clear to our waiter that we were to be her 'guests' for the evening.

So *that* was the 'VIP treatment'. I wondered if the hostess would ever stand behind me, arms on my shoulders, saying, 'This is Toby Young, okay? *The* Toby Young?' I fantasised about jabbing the clipboard Nazi in the ribs: 'Never. Make. Me. Wait. On. Line. Again. *Unnerstand*?'

'What are you smiling about?' asked George.

'Er, nothing,' I replied. 'I'm just happy to be here I suppose.'

'*Here*?' he said, looking round contemptuously. 'This is a fucking McDonald's.'

The booths were where the 'heavy hitters' sat, four 'high-visibility' tables where people like George could see and be seen. Indeed, being *seen* appeared to be more important than *seeing* since the occupants of these tables showed absolutely no interest in the rest of the bar's patrons. This wasn't altogether surprising. As far as I could tell, the disgruntled neighbour's summing up of Bowery Bar's clientele seemed about right.

Seated opposite us in our booth was the rock star Dave Lee Roth. His date for the evening was a Brazilian dancer called Sabrina and every time Roth embarked upon some interminable anecdote she rolled her eyes. Formerly the lead singer of Van Halen, one of the great 'big hair bands' of the eighties, Roth's star was in the descendant at this point. In a humiliating episode not long before, he'd been busted for attempting to buy marijuana off a cop in Washington Square Park. That was the kind of elementary error that only NYU freshmen and bridge-and-tunnel people made.

'Did I ever tell you about the time I played Rio de Janeiro?' Dave asked no one in particular. 'Now *that* was a gig.'

Sabrina's eyes shot heavenward.

'GW can't stand it,' George whispered, extracting himself from the booth. 'He's too boring.'

I called it a night shortly afterwards, but before I left I folded a $20 bill into my palm and on my way out stopped to talk to the clipboard Nazi.

'Hey, Sal, no hard feelings,' I said. 'I know you were just doing your job.'

'It's a fucking zoo out here,' he complained. 'How am I s'posed to know who everybody is?'

'I'm Toby Young,' I said, offering him my hand. 'I've just been appointed the social editor of *Vanity Fair*.'

He took my outstretched paw and I made sure the bill passed from my hand to his.

'You're alright,' he said, shoving it into his breast pocket. 'Any time you have a problem, just ask for Sal, okay?'

'Thank you,' I replied. 'I'll do that.'

Finally! I was on the list.

13

NIGHTWORLD

For New Yorkers, the fall social season starts on Labour Day when the leases on their 'summer rentals' expire. For the next three months, until the social elite departs for the Caribbean for Christmas, there are half a dozen parties every night peaking in Fashion Week, a seven-day orgy of non-stop revelry. Shortly after being appointed a contributing editor I began assiduously cultivating all the PRs in the city – writing to them on my headed notepaper, pestering them with phone calls, energetically pumping their hands when I finally met them – and the invitations gradually started coming in. Among the events I attended in that hectic period were the launch of *Time Out New York*, an exhibition opening hosted by Claus von Bülow, the premiere of *Casino*, Candace Bushnell's birthday party and the Metropolitan Museum's Costume Institute ball.

The most striking thing about these A-list parties was how much more glamorous they were than the equivalent events in London. Typically, as I approached the entrance there were crowds of people standing behind metal barriers on either side of a red carpet, much like there had been at the *Vanity Fair* Oscar party. Once inside I was struck by how much care had been taken to get everything right, from the lighting to the canapés. I was often staggered by the amount of money that had been spent. At the opening of Calvin Klein's 'flagship store' on Madison Avenue, for instance, I found myself standing next to a series of trestle tables supporting nothing but these huge great ice cylinders full of Beluga caviar. They were literally the size of buckets. It was like an all-you-can eat restaurant for members of the Jet Set. In the course of the evening I must have ploughed my way through £10,000 worth.

Yet, paradoxically, the more lavish the soirée, the less atmosphere it had. To the publicists who organised them, these dos were known as 'positioning events' and the fact that they had such an overtly commercial purpose made it difficult to have any fun. They weren't great parties that just happened to coincide with the opening of a film or a shop or an exhibition; they were organised solely for publicity purposes. The gossip columnists dutifully wrote about them the following day, as if they had had some news value, when in fact they'd been organized precisely in order to produce this sort of coverage. They had no real point other than to generate column inches yet in order to serve that purpose everyone had to pretend they were dazzling social occasions. They were the social equivalent of Potemkin Villages, photo opportunities with nothing beneath the surface.

Sometimes this was painfully obvious. For instance, at the world premiere of *GoldenEye* Pierce Brosnan appeared on stage just before the curtain went up and invited the audience to applaud the revival of 'this amazing franchise'. It was as if we were there to celebrate the opening of a new branch of Kentucky Fried Chicken rather than the reappearance of Britain's most glamorous popular icon. Brosnan was followed by the director of the film, Martin Campbell, who told everyone how pleased he was to be in New York. 'There couldn't be a greater city in which to have this premiere,' he gushed.

'Oh yeah?' whispered Chris Lawrence, who was sitting next to me. 'How about London, you clown?'

Needless to say, all of these events were studded with celebrities, but judging from the looks on their faces they weren't enjoying themselves very much. They were usually there on sufferance, at the request of their agents, managers or publicists, or as the date of some billionaire like Donald Trump.

Their sole purpose was to be photographed when arriving in order to make sure the events received some coverage. At movie premieres they rarely stayed to watch the films, invariably sneaking out the back just before they started. They would return for the after-parties where they lingered for a few minutes in specially cordoned-off areas, scowling at the looky-loos, before being whisked off again by their handlers.

One of the reasons the celebs were so ill tempered is because they were often absolutely starving. A-list stars, I discovered, don't dare eat anything in public in case they're photographed in the act of stuffing their faces. To an image-conscious VIP, that's about as welcome as being snapped on the lavatory. One of the more amusing sights I witnessed in Los Angeles on Oscar night in 1996 was the long line of limousines waiting outside a drive-in McDonald's on the way back from the Dorothy Chandler Pavilion. Behind the tinted glass some of the biggest names in Hollywood were inhaling Big Macs. I suggested to Graydon that *Vanity Fair* should station a photographer in this branch of McDonald's the following year to capture this spectacle on film, but, not surprisingly, he didn't go for it.

The attitude of the Manhattan press corps to the stars in their midst was, predictably enough, one of fawning deference. I could always tell when a celebrity had entered my airspace at one of these parties because the person I was talking to would suddenly become all glassy-eyed and wouldn't hear a word I was saying. Interestingly, though, they'd never look over my shoulder. Among New York hacks it's considered so 'trailer park' to gawk at celebs that whenever one comes near they look anywhere but straight at them. Consequently, when Matt Dillon was standing right next to me the pretty young entertainment reporter I was talking to would look me directly in the eye for the first time that evening.

Then she'd go home with Matt Dillon.

I couldn't help feeling that if I'd arrived in New York at almost any other time in the twentieth century I would have had more fun. Seasoned observers of the party scene claim it has become more meritocratic in the last decade or two, but while this is true in the sense that admission into New York's charmed circle isn't limited to the wellborn, the people I encountered rarely possessed any actual *merit*. On the contrary, they tended to be fairly disreputable. They usually claimed to have some vague-sounding profession – 'financiers', 'stylists' or 'interior decorators' – but most of them were just standard rent-a-crowd types. They were liggers, blag artists, hangers-on, self-promoters and friends-of-friends rather than people who'd achieved anything in their own right. In short, they were no different from me.

One event in particular epitomised everything that's wrong with the New York social scene. It was an 'Extravaganza' to celebrate the birthday of Michael Musto, the gay gossip columnist of the *Village Voice*, hosted by Divine Brown, the LA prostitute made famous by her encounter with Hugh Grant. The occasion was like a parody of celebrity culture. Resplendent in a brown leather Versace outfit, Divine held court in the centre of the room surrounded by forelock-tugging journalists while lesser celebrities queued up to pay hommage. What was striking was how like every other famous person she seemed, how effortlessly she'd stepped into her new role.

This wasn't what I'd had in mind when I'd fantasised about being a magazine writer in New York. I was looking forward to meeting the contemporary equivalents of members of the Algonquin Round Table, men like Alexander Woollcott who 'animated a room like a scandal'.[1] Instead, I found myself in a world that seemed as if it had been dreamt up by members of that circle on a particularly drunken night. More often than not, I found myself being cast as the rube in this world, the out-of-town patsy who's always the butt of the joke. I'd set out wanting to be Cary Grant and ended up as Ralph Bellamy.

Take my experience at the premiere of *Strange Days* on 7 October, 1995. Even by New York standards this was a fairly

---

[1] Ben Hecht, *A Child of the Century* (New York: Simon & Schuster, 1957) p. 395.

opulent affair – the after-party was at the Radio City Music Hall – and it wasn't long before I'd drunk a little too much champagne. In my befuddled state I got it into my head that I simply must meet Ralph Fiennes, the star of the film. An old friend of mine called Tamara Harvey had told me she was the first girl he'd ever snogged and I decided this was the perfect opportunity to find out whether this was true. I'd simply ask him.

Getting to Fiennes was no easy task. He was in the VIP section while I was in the main auditorium and the velvet rope separating the immortals from the *hoi polloi* was being guarded by a ferocious-looking clipboard Nazi. Still, I had a trump card. The party was being thrown by 20th Century Fox and I'd been invited to the premiere by Lewis Canfield, a friend who worked for Fox. If anyone could get me in, he could.

We approached the clipboard Nazi who Lewis recognised as a member of the Fox publicity department called Penny.

'Hey, Penny,' Lewis said. 'Is there any chance we can go through?'

'Why?' she asked.

'It's a wager,' said Lewis. 'My friend here bet me $20 I wouldn't be able to get him in.'

'Sorry, Lewis,' she snapped. 'You lost.'

Lewis looked at her beseechingly.

'Come on, Penny. Please?'

'I'll tell you what,' she replied, appearing to weaken, 'I can take a couple of steps back so you and your friend can each put one foot in this area. That way, technically, you'll be able to *say* you were in the VIP section. That's the best I can do.'

We declined to take her up on her offer.

Lewis took this in his stride – he was used to being treated this way by Fox's publicists – but I worked myself up into an alcohol-fuelled rage on his behalf. How dare she humiliate one of her colleagues like that? I tried to persuade him to get the head of his department to overrule the officious cow but, quite sensibly, he declined.

However, all was not lost. I chatted up one of the waitresses and asked her if there was another way in. There was, apparently. She sweetly allowed me to follow her into the kitchen and pointed to a passageway that led to the VIP section. Seconds later I was hobnobbing with the stars of the film.

Even in the VIP section, Fiennes was well protected. In order to speak to him, you had to join a receiving line and, when your turn arrived, a lady-in-waiting figure would present you to him with a little curtsy. You only got about thirty seconds but it was long enough for my purposes. In a few minutes I'd know once and for all whether Tamara was telling the truth.

I joined the queue and was immediately approached by the lady-in-waiting. She wanted to know exactly who everyone was before she introduced them to her liege.

'Are you a friend of Ralph's?' she asked.

'*Ralph's*,' I corrected, pronouncing it so it rhymed with 'chafe'. 'Yes, I am, as a matter of fact.'

She nodded her head disbelievingly and then looked over my shoulder for instructions about what to do. Should she present me to Fiennes? I glanced behind me to see who she was deferring to and immediately my heart sank: it was Penny, the clipboard Nazi who'd barred my entrance a few minutes earlier. Penny gave me a brief look and shook her head emphatically: No way, no *fucking* way. She then started barking orders into her walkie-talkie and seconds later I was being escorted out of the VIP section by two burly security guards.

As I was being manhandled towards the exit I made one last desperate bid to communicate with Fiennes.

'Hey, Ralph,' I screamed at the top of my voice. He stopped talking to the person in front of him and turned his head in my direction. The security guards picked up the pace, determined to get me out of there as fast as they could now that I was making a scene.

'I'm a friend of Tamara Harvey's,' I shouted as I was propelled towards the exit at warp speed. 'She said to say hello if I saw you. First snog, right?'

He nodded politely but clearly didn't have a clue what I was talking about and a few seconds later I found myself back on the wrong side of the velvet rope.

14

UPTOWN GIRLS

Before I was tossed off Mount Olympus at the *Strange Days* party I managed to strike up a conversation with a 22-year-old goddess called Zoe Kohlmayer. She was exactly the kind of girl you'd expect to find in the VIP section at a New York movie premiere: half-Russian and half-Swiss, she was dressed from head to toe in Chanel and accompanied by a stern-looking matron who was intent on protecting her from people like me. The dragon turned out to be her mother and as I hopped from foot to foot trying to engage Zoe in conversation she looked as though she'd like to dispatch me with a well-aimed ball of fire. I wasn't bold enough to ask for Zoe's number – not under the fierce glare of her chaperone – but she let slip that she and her mother lived in an apartment at The Carlyle. That struck home. The Carlyle is New York's smartest hotel and before this the only person I'd heard of who actually *lived* there was Jackie O. I'd stumbled on a grown-up version of Eloise.

The following day I called The Carlyle and asked to be put through to 'Miss Kohlmayer'. I placed as much emphasis as I could on the word 'Miss'. I didn't want to end up speaking to the mother.

The conversation didn't go well. I'd just signed a lease on a flat in the West Village and when I got through to Zoe I asked her if she'd like to come over and help me move in. Admittedly, it wasn't much of a date but I thought she might like to give me some advice on how to arrange my furniture and what pictures to hang on the walls. It was just the kind of invitation my women friends in London would have thought of as 'sweet'.

'Help you *move in*?' queried Zoe. 'What am I, your maid?' Click. Dial-tone.

Clearly, the women on the New York party circuit were very different from the ones I'd been hanging out with back home. In London, the girls in my peer group didn't behave that differently from the boys. They drank in the same pubs, laughed at the same jokes and had a similarly relaxed attitude to sex. They enjoyed being looked at and admired but they weren't in any sense ornamental. It rarely took them more than fifteen minutes to get ready.

Women in Manhattan, by contrast, behaved more like courtesans – at least, the ones I met did. They existed in a completely different world from their male counterparts, often spending the whole day preparing for an evening out. A typical New York party girl would start the day with a visit to her dermatologist, followed by a trip to an expensive hair salon, then go shopping for a designer outfit on Madison Avenue and, finally, summon a make-up artist to her boudoir to apply the finishing touches.

Whenever my women friends from back home asked me what the difference was between them and their New York counterparts, I would say: 'I can sum it up in one word: stairmaster.' The was partly intended to provoke, but there was also an element of truth in it. On a visit to New York in 1999 to promote *Bridget Jones's Diary*, Helen Fielding said that the main distinction between her fictional creation and Ally McBeal was that the latter was 'quite a lot thinner'.

To a certain extent, these differences are attributable to the fact that I wasn't comparing like with like. The women I knew in London were mainly middle-class professionals – journalists, lawyers, television producers – whereas the kind I was bumping into on the A-list merry-go-round were 'Park Avenue Princesses'. Our nearest equivalent, I suppose, are 'It Girls', except that in New York there are tens of thousands of these show ponies.

The level of personal grooming that only a handful of women in London can be bothered with is almost the norm in Manhattan. Even women who have jobs that require them to be in the office from 9 a.m. to 7 p.m. spend an extraordinary amount of time beautifying themselves.

To get a sense of how different your average New York woman is from your average Londoner, compare the cast of *Friends* with the cast of *EastEnders*. On American television, the only time you see women like Natalie Cassidy – the actress who plays Sonia – is as some hapless guinea pig in an informercial for the latest gizmo designed to tighten abs, hips and thighs.

In terms of relations between the sexes, Manhattan is like a throwback to the nineteenth century. At the 'hot boîtes' of the moment the men slouch at tables in chinos and button-down shirts while the women parade past them like peacocks, fanning out their tail feathers for all the world to see. Sitting in the audience at the premiere of *Sense and Sensibility* on 13 December, 1995 it suddenly struck me that the reason for the glut of Jane Austen adaptations – *Clueless* and *Persuasion* had been released earlier that year and *Emma* would soon follow – was because of the overwhelming similarity between early-nineteenth-century rural England and late-twentieth-century urban America.

Contrary to popular belief, the reason Austen adaptations struck such a chord with American audiences wasn't due to the usual nostalgic yearning for a kinder, gentler era in which everyone wore top hats and lived in stately homes. It was because they recognised their own society up there on the big screen. Austen's novels may appear to be light, pastoral comedies about romantic love, but whisk the tea cosy aside and the cruel mechanics of nineteenth-century English society are laid bare. To quote W.H. Auden:

> You could not shock her more than she shocks me;
> Beside her Joyce seems innocent as grass.
> It makes me most uncomfortable to see
> An English spinster of the middle-class

Describe the amorous effects of 'brass',
Reveal so frankly and with such sobriety
The economic basis of society.

There was plenty of evidence of 'the amorous effects of brass' in New York in the mid-nineties. Take the case of Ron Perelman, the richest man in the city. In 1995 he was married to Patricia Duff, a gorgeous blonde trophy wife, having divorced Claudia Cohen, a middle-aged glamour puss, a year earlier. After Perelman separated from Duff in 1996 he was linked with a string of beauties, including the actress Ellen Barkin. Given Perelmen's physical appearance, it seems unlikely that he would have gotten all these women if he'd been, say, a plumber.[1]

The world Austen depicts – a world in which ambitious young women compete with each other to attract the attention of rich, eligible men – is uncannily like contemporary Manhattan. Both societies are rigidly hierarchical, with power concentrated in the hands of a plutocratic elite, and the swiftest route to the top is through marriage. The cavernous waterfront mansions that New York's ruling class retreat to every summer in the Hamptons are the equivalent of Pemberley, Darcy's estate in Derbyshire.

In Manhattan, of course, the most sought-after bachelors aren't wellborn landowners but celebrities. I remember a conversation with Candace Bushnell late one evening when we were both in our cups in which she confessed that she was 'a real snob' about who she'd go out with. (I think she may have sensed I was on the verge of making a pass at her and wanted to head me off.)

---

[1] Kurt Andersen made this point in an email exchange with Nora Ephron in *Slate* on 13 September, 1999: 'Regarding Ron Perelman (and the Ron Perelmans of the world): At what level of consciousness do you suppose he knows or cares that if he weren't rich he wouldn't get to sleep with women like Patricia Duff and Ellen Barkin? And, even more coarsely, how tightly do you think the Patricia Duffs and Ellen Barkins of the world have to close their eyes and think of $$$ as they're being ravished by unattractive billionaires?'

'I wanna go out with someone who's really successful,' she explained. 'I feel like I'm successful, I'm gonna be more successful . . . I wanna be with somebody who's like maybe *famous*, you know? I wanna be with somebody who's like me. I sort of feel like I've earned that.'

The willingness of New York women to enter what is essentially a nineteenth-century marriage market is surprising. After all, the cause of women's emancipation is more advanced in Manhattan than in any other city in the world. They might not describe themselves as 'feminists', but if these women experience any form of discrimination they're straight on the phone to their attorneys. They're more ambitious, better educated and less oppressed than any previous generation of women and yet they're prepared to go to any lengths, however demeaning, to secure a husband. Why?[1]

The short answer is in order to impress other women. As anyone who's read Edith Wharton will know, it's long been a fact of life in Manhattan, particularly among the social elite of the Upper East Side, that women judge each other according to who they can ensnare. Status is valued more highly than any other commodity in New York and marrying well is still the fastest way to get it. At *Vanity Fair* legend has it that when one female contributing editor finally landed her trophy husband the first person she called was not her mother but the gossip columnist Liz Smith. Only after Liz had promised to announce the engagement in her column did the contributor deign to tell her family.

But why is a prominent husband still considered such a desirable asset? A hundred years ago women's status was largely

---

[1] Katie Roiphe wrote an article for *Esquire* in which she discussed this paradox: 'Seen from the outside, my life is the model of modern female independence . . . But it sometimes seems like my independence is in part an elaborately constructed facade that hides a more traditional feminine desire to be protected and provided for.' 'The Independent Woman (and Other Lies)', *Esquire*, February 1999.

dependent on who their husbands were but today they're perfectly capable of acquiring it in their own right. So why don't they? The answer is they do, but on the whole they prefer to do it with a ring on their finger. Part of the reason is that New York is such a Darwinian place. In this fundamentally hostile environment, full of ruthless predators who'll stop at nothing to get to the top, people are constantly forming alliances for their own protection and a husband is the most dependable ally a woman can have. Yet it's also because, in terms of sheer status wattage, women shine more brightly if they're married to a powerful man, particularly successful women. The ideal is to become the female half of a 'power couple'. In Manhattan, the highest tier of society is occupied by these all-conquering husband-and-wife teams: Diane von Furstenberg and Barry Diller, Diane Sawyer and Mike Nichols, Gail Sheehy and Clay Felker, Binky Urban and Ken Auletta, Tina Brown and Harold Evans – the list is endless. For the city's most ambitious women, this is the ultimate goal.

After Zoe Kohlmayer had given me the brush off it became clear that I'd have to smarten up my act if I was to stand a chance with these Upper East Side debutantes. Given their interest in bagging an elephant, what hope did a penniless, thirtysomething hack like me have? I was hardly the modern-day equivalent of Darcy. More like some snaggle-toothed farm labourer.

I decided it was time to start using my title.

Let me quickly point out that I'm not a member of the aristocracy – far from it. My father is a socialist intellectual and his father was an Australian impresario who at one stage was the music editor of the *Daily Express*.[1] Nevertheless, I'm technically an 'Honourable' because my father was ennobled by

---

[1] My father told me that he was walking down Fleet Street with my grandfather one day when the old hack spotted hundreds of rats scurrying towards the Strand. He immediately nipped into a phone box, called up the *Evening Standard* and sold the story to the *Londoner*. This is *exactly* what I would do in the same circumstances.

James Callaghan, the former Labour Prime Minister. In Britain, being the son of a life peer, as opposed to an hereditary one, carries about as much social cachet as being the son of Sir Caspar Weinberger, but in America such distinctions are lost on all but the most die-hard Anglophiles. (Chris Lawrence knew the difference of course.) Needless to say, pretending to be a nob in order to bamboozle unsuspecting socialites into bed is hardly a new trick – New York is teeming with fake aristos – but at least my scam had the advantage of not requiring me to lie.

The first problem I faced was how to let people know I was an 'Hon'. I couldn't very well just announce it since no genuine toff would ever dream of doing anything so vulgar. So I hit upon the idea of applying for an American Express in the name of 'Hon Toby Young'. After all, the only people I wanted to impress with my bogus credentials were women and I'd be able to flash my new Amex card, complete with fancy-sounding title, when taking them out to dinner.

A few weeks later a letter arrived from American Express addressed to 'Hon Toby Young'. I squeezed the envelope to check whether it contained a card – it did! I tore it open and read the letter.

'Dear Hon,' it began, 'We are pleased to inform you . . .'

Wait a minute. American Express were evidently under the impression that Hon was my first name. I checked the piece of plastic and, sure enough, the name on the card, was 'Hon Young'. That was no good. My glamorous dining companions would assume I'd stolen the card from some poor Korean student.

I called up American Express's headquarters and explained their mistake.

'You say "Hon" is your title?' a sceptical administrator inquired. 'What are you, some kind of judge?'

'No, no,' I said, 'it's a British title. My father's a Lord.'

'Does that mean you're going to be a Lord?'

'Well, no, actually, it doesn't.'

'So how come you've got a title?'

This was proving more taxing than I'd anticipated.

'Look,' I said, lowering my voice to a whisper, 'I shouldn't be telling you this, but my father's a member of the Royal Family.'

Pause.

'Yeah, whatever,' he replied, clearly not believing a word of it. 'I'm afraid we can't change the name on the card once it's been issued. You're gonna have to apply for a new card – and it's gonna have to be from a different address.'

In my second application I put down 350 Madison Avenue as my address and about a week later I received another card, this one in the correct name. It was time to put my new identity to use.

To that end, I enlisted the help of Candace Bushnell who by this stage had become a friend. After meeting her at Richard and Nadine Johnson's party, I started bumping into her wherever I went and we often ended up getting 'loaded' together – her word for it – in some late-night dive. She was thirty-seven but at her birthday party she told everyone she was thirty-two and they believed it. She was extremely pretty, with long, straight, blonde hair and a cute, button nose. Her manager called her 'the Sharon Stone of journalism' but I preferred to think of her as a grown-up version of the character played by Alicia Silverstone in *Clueless*. She was tough and mercenary, but she was also funny and smart. Her 'Sex and the City' column in the *New York Observer*, which she'd started writing in 1994, was a huge hit. There was a kernel of sweetness in her that nineteen years of living in Manhattan hadn't eradicated. She was no Dorothy Parker, but she was the closest I'd come to the sassy, wisecracking broads I'd fantasised about meeting in New York.

When Candace heard about my title, she sweetly offered to spread the rumour that I was the scion of a landed Scottish family on the look out for a wife to take back home. With great fanfare, she introduced me to a string of aging party girls as 'the Honourable Toby Young' and then stood back and watched as the dollar signs danced in their eyes. Unfortunately, on the few occasions that I managed to entice any of these women back to my flat their expectations were soon dashed. What illusions they had about living happily ever after in a castle in the Highlands were immediately shattered when they set eyes on my furniture. They were usually out of the door before I could unscrew a bottle of wine.

However, there was one exception. She was a Chilean bombshell who, for legal reasons, I don't think I dare name. She was in her mid-thirties and, in spite of being a twenty-year veteran of the London-New York-LA party circuit, was still breathtakingly beautiful. According to Candace, she'd had her breasts 'done' by the finest plastic surgeon in Miami – it had cost her $20,000 – and the rest of her had been nipped and tucked to perfection. She had a list of celebrity conquests more dazzling, and longer, than the PMK 400 and was rumoured to be the first woman Mick Jagger called whenever he was in town. Her nickname, inevitably, was the Red Hot Chilli Pepper.

Towards the end of my first date with _____, after I'd shamelessly waved my Amex card under her nose, she surprised me by asking if she could borrow $250. I was a little taken aback but she explained that if she didn't pay that week's rent she and her five-year-old daughter would be thrown out on the street. Was there any way I could help?

Naturally, I trotted along to the nearest cashpoint and withdrew the money.

She was suitably grateful and suggested we go back to my flat for an after-dinner drink. Aha, I thought. I'm finally going to get laid! We were just rounding the corner of my street when a shady looking character approached us and asked if we'd like to buy any drugs. I shook my head but _____'s eyes lit up.

'Tell me, señor,' she said, taking him to one side, 'how much cocaína can I ge' for two hunret and fifty dollar?'

After a brief negotiation _____ told me to go back to the flat while she concluded the transaction. She'd be along in a minute. This was at 12.30 a.m.

I was slightly irritated that the money she'd so desperately needed half an hour earlier was now to be spent on nose candy, but I decided not to kick up a fuss. _____ was so damn sexy, she was easily worth $250. In any case, she was such a live wire under normal circumstances, my mind boggled at the thought of her on Bolivian marching powder. I turned the lights down low, stuck on a Frank Sinatra CD and sat down on the sofa to wait for her. *Oh boy! I'm going to see my first Brazilian bikini line!* I was so excited I could barely catch my breath.

After ninety minutes had passed, and still no sign of her, I reluctantly concluded she wasn't coming. At that point I really did begin to mind about the $250. The bitch had ripped me off! I went to bed in a smouldering rage.

I was woken up by my doorbell at 5.15 a.m. It was _____, though the person who tottered into my flat was almost unrecognisable as the Red Hot Chilli Pepper I'd been out with the night before. Her dress was covered in patches of horrible brown gunk and traces of blood were visible beneath each of her nostrils. Her hair looked like she'd spent the last four hours and forty-five minutes standing on the deck of a Channel ferry.

'Oh, Toe'ee,' she cried, 'that fu'ing bastar', he reep me off. He sol' me washeen power.' She indicated the dried blood beneath her nostrils. 'But I know a guy who live roun' the corner where we can get some really goo' sheet.' She assumed a coquettish pose. 'Can you gi' me anu'er two hunret and fifty dollar?'

I never went out on another date with _____.

15

THE 600LB GORILLA

All this socialising wasn't doing my reputation at *Vanity Fair* much good. The majority of the magazine's staff are either married or settled in long-term relationships and take little interest in the social whirl of Manhattan. Indeed, they regard people who go out every night as slightly suspect. After all, who but the most superficial social butterflies fritter away their lives going to A-list parties? Once you've been to one, you've been to them all, right?

An additional problem was that I could never remember anyone's name. Shortly after I'd arrived, Aimée Bell had impressed upon me how important it was to get to know all my colleagues. She told me about a famous occasion on which *60 Minutes* had filmed a segment on Tina Brown. Apparently, Tina had taken the presenter on a tour of the magazine's offices and, for the first time ever, greeted every member of her staff by name. Needless to say, she got several of them wrong.

As I rolled in every day at around 11 a.m., reeking of alcohol and nursing a dreadful hangover, I would have to run a gauntlet of bright-eyed staff members all of whom would welcome me with a cry of 'Hey, Toby'. The correct response was to reciprocate with 'Hey _____', depending on who it was, but I never dared risk it in case I got the person's name wrong. Consequently, I'd just mumble 'Hey' in the hope that this left the question open of whether I knew their names or not. In fact, I'm sure that they all guessed – correctly – that I didn't.

Matt Tyrnauer didn't help by always greeting me with the words 'Lord Young'. When I'd reapplied for my American Express card I'd given 350 Madison Avenue as my address and as a result my monthly statements now started arriving at *Vanity Fair*'s offices. It wasn't long before Matt intercepted one and demanded to know why it was in the name of 'Hon Toby Young'. When I told him it was because my father was a Lord he was flabbergasted – he had me down as middle class – and from that day forward addressed me either as 'Lord Young', 'Little Lord Fauntleroy' or 'Your Lordship'. I tried to explain that I was merely the son of a life peer, that I was in fact every bit as middle class as he imagined, but it made no difference. He continued to call me 'Lord Young' for the remainder of my time at the magazine, occasionally even bowing his head in mock-deference. Somehow, I don't think it enhanced my professional standing around the office.

Fortunately, *Vanity Fair* wasn't a democracy and it didn't much matter if my colleagues thought I was an upper class buffoon so long as the editor-in-chief liked having me around. The important thing was to stay on the right side of the 600lb gorilla in the corner office. As both Matt and Aimée repeatedly drummed in to me, I'd be fine as long as I didn't antagonise Graydon.

I should have listened.

The chain of events that led to the souring of my relationship with Graydon began when he spotted me at the Calvin Klein show during Fashion Week. Needless to say, the big issue for me at that year's spring collections[1] wasn't what was 'in' at each show but how to get *in* to each show. I turned to Elizabeth Saltzman for advice.

---

[1] Rather confusingly, the spring collections are held in the autumn.

'To begin with, the only one you should bother with is Calvin,' she told me. 'Believe me, you really don't want to go to more than one unless you absolutely have to.'

That sounded sensible. But how should I go about getting a ticket?

'Forget the front row,' she said, dismissing the collective wisdom of an entire industry. 'The place to be is backstage. I mean, you wanna see naked girls, right?'

Absofuckinglutely!

She promised to get me an 'access-all-areas' pass and, in the meantime, gave me a crash course in the fashionista food chain. After backstage, apparently, the front row comes a distant second, but only if there isn't an army of photographers blocking your view. The next best place to sit is not the second row but the third. The view in the second row is often obscured by the headgear of the people in front of you, but the third row is on a raised dais. Then comes an aisle seat and finally – a humiliation only to be endured as an absolute last resort – standing.

The following day I arrived to find a white envelope on my desk with 'Tobi' written on it in pink, felt-tip pen. Aha, I thought. It must have been addressed by Pippi which means . . . it must be from Elizabeth. *It's my access-all-areas pass to the Calvin Klein show!* I tore it open but, alas, all that fell out was a common-or-garden ticket. At the top, in big, black letters, was printed the word 'standing'.

'Sorry, kid,' explained Elizabeth, popping her head round the door. 'It's the best I could do.'

Well, it was better than nothing and on the day in question I stood patiently in line with the other bottom feeders outside the Calvin Klein venue while *tout le monde* filed past, all kitted out in battle dress. There was George Wayne in his purple velvet suit; there was Anna Wintour in her mandatory Chanel dark glasses; there was Donald Trump wearing his 'cufflinks' – a blonde on each arm. It was a fashion show in its own right.

Finally, the standing-room-only ticket holders were herded in and we took our places in a kind of pen behind a metal barrier at the back.

Elizabeth was smack bang in the centre of the front row and, I couldn't help noticing, the seat on her immediate left was empty. So was the one at the end of the row on her right. I didn't dare take the seat next to Elizabeth – that was probably earmarked for Graydon – but what about the one at the end? It looked awfully inviting. Admittedly, it did have a 'RESERVED' sticker sellotaped to it, but as far as I could tell no one had claimed it. When it still hadn't been taken a few seconds before the show was about to start I took one last look around at the miserable faces in the standing section and decided to go for it. I ducked under the barrier and started pushing my way towards the front. The place was teeming with clipboard Nazis but I thought if I could just project the right air of authority I might get away with it. *Aren't half these people bluffers anyway?* After a nerve-shattering tightrope walk down through the rows, all the while looking into the middle distance and smiling benignly, I got to the front without being button-holed. I'd made it!

Almost as soon as I sat down, Graydon marched in. He cut quite a figure, striding purposively towards the front row. If there's one thing Graydon knows how to do, it's walk. 'I like how he moves,' Jay Leno once told *New York* magazine. 'He's a breed of New York-Connecticut Yankee patrician you didn't know still existed.' I sat there watching him in awe. Next time you approach some clipboard Nazi, I told myself, this is the way to do it. *God damn it, he should be up there on the catwalk!*

Suddenly, he caught sight of me and a look of faint irritation crossed his brow. *What's he doing here?* He stopped directly in front of me.

'Toby, you can't sit in the front row,' he whispered. 'You're still in the first room.'

I thought he was joking.

'Don't worry,' I whispered back. 'Elizabeth's saving a seat for you right over there.'

'I don't care,' he said, raising his voice. 'Get the fuck outta here.'

I flushed crimson. *Why's he doing this?* Feeling totally humiliated, I got up and in front of what felt like the whole of New York slowly made my way back to Siberia. My walk, as I shuffled along, head bowed in shame, was the exact opposite of Graydon's. I felt as if I had a 'Kick Me' sticker attached to my bum.

In retrospect, the sensible thing to do would have been to just brush this off. Such ritual humiliation is a standard initiation rite at Condé Nast and the correct response is to grab your ankles and say: 'Please, sir, can I have another?' However, I'd yet to master the art of pride-swallowing.[1] Until a few months earlier I'd been the captain of my own ship, for God's sake. I vowed to take revenge.

The opportunity presented itself a couple of days later when I came across an article Graydon had written for *GQ* some years earlier about a trip he'd made to London. He told of how he'd gone to a *Private Eye* lunch one day, a *Spectator* lunch the next, and – incredibly – some of the same people were at both lunches. He'd then gone to Malcolm Muggeridge's memorial service and – would you believe it? – some of the people who'd been at both lunches were also at the memorial service! Graydon concluded that British society was actually rather small and you kept bumping into the same people wherever you went, just like in *A Dance to the Music of Time*.

I photocopied the article and slid it under his door accompanied by a note:

---

[1] In *Jerry Maguire*, Tom Cruise describes the life of a junior sports agent as a 'pride-swallowing siege'. When I saw the film – at a special *Vanity Fair* screening in 1996 – that phrase really struck home. Afterwards, Chris Lawrence and I walked back to the office along Madison Avenue screaming 'a pride-swallowing siege' at the tops of our voices.

Dear Graydon,

Glad to see you got as far as <u>the first room</u> on your trip to London. Better luck next time.

Regards,

Toby.

As soon as he saw it, he summoned me to his office. Judging from his scarlet countenance, he'd gone completely thermo-nuclear.

'Frankly, you're just not a good enough friend to make that kind of crack,' he said, anger pulsing through his face like an electrical current. 'You British people come to New York, you take our money, you look down your noses at us . . . What you don't realise is, we could wipe your country out in twenty minutes! There wouldn't be a chip store left standing! GODDAMNIT, IF IT WASN'T FOR US, YOU'D BE SPEAKING GERMAN!'

Wait a minute, I thought. Aren't you Canadian? It took an almost superhuman effort of will not to say, 'Actually, Graydon, if it wasn't for us, you'd be speaking French.'

This time, though, I managed to swallow my pride.

By anyone's reckoning, I'd made a colossal blunder. I was expecting him to be mildly irritated, not to fly into an eye-popping, heart-attack-inducing rage.[1] God knows, I'd written enough embarrassing articles in my time and no one had been shy about drawing my attention to them. I didn't like it any more than Graydon, of course, but I'd learnt to suck it up. What I'd failed to grasp is just how rigid the pecking order is at *Vanity Fair*. While it was perfectly okay for Graydon to be as rude as he liked to me, paying him back in his own coin was completely taboo. In Aimée Bell's words, I'd 'crossed the

---

[1] Chris Lawrence's term for a heart attack was 'a gripper', since heart attack victims often grip their hearts as they keel over. He would often joke that he thought I was going to give Graydon a gripper, grabbing his heart and making a croaking sound as he said it.

line'. Suddenly, my future at the magazine looked bleak.

I'd naively assumed that because Graydon is so apparently down-to-earth, always poking fun at the excesses of the rich and fabulous, he wouldn't object to a bit of mild teasing himself. His whole wise-cracking persona seems designed to convey the message that he may be *in* the world that *Vanity Fair* chronicles, but he's not *of* it. This is certainly the subtext of all his advice about how to succeed in the New York media. 'You know what the secret of success in this business is?' he once asked me. 'The three "f"s: faxes, flattery and flowers.'[1] The implication of these little gobbets of wisdom is that while he's something of a Jedi Master when it comes to playing the media game – surveying the field of play from his picture window in the seventh room – he doesn't take it all that seriously. He might be a Big Swinging Dick but, beneath all the bullshit, he's still just a regular guy. He certainly doesn't give the impression that you need to employ 'the three "f"s' – or any other Jedi mind tricks – in order to get on *his* good side.

But the better I got to know him, the clearer it became that this is all rhetoric. When it comes to those lower down the food chain than him Graydon expects to be treated with the same fawning reverence as any other *macher*. Naked obeisance to power is the rule in Manhattan, irrespective of how 'normal' the person appears to be. I remember one occasion at the beginning of 1996 when I had dinner with Graydon at Le Cirque, New York's most famous power restaurant.[2] The Italian owner, Sirio Maccioni, greeted Graydon in a suitably deferential manner, bowing so low I thought his toupee was going to fall off, then turned to his staff and clicked his fingers. Within seconds, two flunkies came scuttling out of the wings carrying

---

[1] Graydon has dozens of these rules: 'You can edit with a typewriter or a calculator, but not both'; 'Don't make the mistake of thinking the advertiser is the customer; he's not the customer, the reader's the customer'; 'It's not who you put in the magazine that's important, it's who you leave out'.

[2] It metamorphosed into Le Cirque 2000 at the turn of the century.

a table and set it down in the middle of the restaurant. Clearly, no existing table was good enough for such a distinguished personage. Before long, a team of waiters started making their way towards us from the kitchen bearing trays of expensive delicacies, a perk that's only extended to the grandest of grandees. 'Oh God,' Graydon said, rolling his eyes. 'Here it comes.' Yeah, right, I thought. Such abject brownnosing may be absurd, but woe-betide the restaurateur who treats you like any other paying customer.

This is fundamentally different to the way powerful people are treated in London. Anyone expecting their social inferiors to prostrate themselves before them, like Michael Winner, is regarded as pathetically insecure. Indeed, any public display of flattery is considered bad form. The correct way to behave towards a superior is to be ever so slightly insolent, thereby paying them the compliment that they're confident enough to take a bit of public ribbing.[1] Of course, in private you suck up to them like crazy. Indeed, it's often said that the difference between London and New York is that in London people are rude to your face but loyal behind your back, whereas in New York they're polite to your face but rude behind your back.

Obviously, the way powerful people in London behave towards those beneath them has a lot to do with notions of good breeding that are bound up with the English class system and it was naive of me to assume that the same rules would apply in Manhattan. Nevertheless, Graydon gives the impression that he has a fairly relaxed, 'British' attitude towards the trappings of success. My mistake was to take Graydon's Wasp persona at face value.

To illustrate just how thin-skinned Graydon can be, take the following story. Towards the end of my time at *Vanity Fair*, a young man appeared in the office next door to Chris and mine's

---

[1] This may be wishful thinking. The only staff position I've ever had on a British newspaper was as a news trainee on *The Times*. I was fired after six months.

called Morgan Murphy. After Chris and I heard his Southern drawl we started referring to him as 'Forrest Gump', but he was a nice enough guy, always eager to ingratiate himself with whoever crossed his path. Like the simpleton played by Tom Hanks, he was completely guileless. One day Morgan bumped into Graydon in the lift and, without thinking, said he hadn't seen him around much lately. Instead of replying, Graydon scowled at him and the following day Morgan was summoned to Aimée Bell's office for a dressing down. 'Here's a piece of advice,' she said, adopting her most matronly manner. 'In future, don't tell the hardest-working editor at Condé Nast that you haven't seen him around the office much, *okay*?'

This is precisely the kind of dotty, megalomaniacal behaviour that *Spy* would have gone to town on in its heyday. It's one of the ironies of Graydon's character, frequently remarked upon by his friends, that if *Spy* was around today he'd almost certainly be included in 'the *Spy* 100', the magazine's annual list of 'the most Annoying, Alarming and Appalling People, Places and Things in New York and the Nation'. Indeed, virtually every newspaper and magazine in Manhattan has, at one time or another, given Graydon the *Spy* treatment, uncovering all sorts of embarrassing facts about him.

For instance, according to a 1989 article in *New York* magazine, the business plan for *Spy*, which Graydon circulated in the winter of 1985, was accompanied by a CV that contained some rather dubious 'facts'. Among other things, Graydon claimed to have worked as a speechwriter in the office of Pierre Trudeau, the former Canadian Prime Minister, and attended Carleton University in Ottawa. The reporter was unable to substantiate either of these claims, though Graydon has always maintained that they are both true. (And, for what it's worth, I believe him.)

In another, more recent *New York* magazine piece it was revealed that Graydon spent at least several years between leaving school and starting university doing a series of menial

jobs. On one of these – working on the Canadian railways –
he told colleagues that he was Jewish.

Clearly, the Graydon Carter of that era was very different
from the Graydon Carter of today. With his ramshackle West
Village townhouse, his collection of wood-panelled station
wagons and his raffish, silver hair he's the very picture of a
Wasp gentleman. Indeed, he regularly makes an appearance on
New York's official 'Best Dressed' list. But it's difficult to get
too worked up about Graydon's transformation from a Royal
Canadian Air Force brat into a 'Yankee patrician'. Beyond
pointing out that his well-bred manner is only skin deep, what
else is there to say? Manhattan is the world capital of résumé-
embellishers and Graydon is no more Gatsby-like than the vast
majority of the city's elite. Not that this stops people frowning
on his bogus Wasp credentials. I remember having a conversation with Anthony Haden-Guest in which the English blueblood
complained that Graydon is 'completely self-invented'.

'But isn't everyone in this city?' I replied.

'Yes,' said Anthony, 'but the problem with Graydon is he left
too much out.'

I was reminded of this exchange years later when I came
across the following passage in Saul Bellow's novel *Ravelstein*:
'The challenge of modern freedom, or the combination of isola-
tion and freedom which confronts you, is to make yourself up.
The danger is that you may emerge from the process as a not-
entirely-human creature.'

A more serious charge is that Graydon has failed to live up
to the expectations that *Spy* gave rise to, particularly in the
breasts of New York's dwindling population of radical journalists. From being a ferocious attack-dog, ridiculing everyone
from Donald Trump ('a short-fingered vulgarian') to Si
Newhouse ('a slightly rumpled, earth-tone-clad magnate'),
Graydon has turned into a pillar of the Establishment, or 'the
New Establishment', as *Vanity Fair* calls it in its annual eulogy
to 'the titans of the information age'. *Spy* once threw a party
to which it invited every single one of its subscribers; today,

only a tiny fraction of *Vanity Fair*'s staff are invited to the magazine's positioning events. To describe Graydon as a poacher-turned-gamekeeper is something of an understatement. He now owns the land he used to poach on.

The extent to which this makes him a hypocrite depends on how seriously you took *Spy*. If, as Graydon now maintains, it was just a bit of fun, a superior gossip magazine and nothing more, then his current position as 'the high priest of celebrity culture'[1] isn't all that anomalous. In this light, *Spy* was just a calling card, a way for Graydon and his co-editor, Kurt Andersen, to let people like Si Newhouse know that they were talented magazine editors and, at the right price, were available for hire.

If, on the other hand, *Spy*'s stories about the greed and mendacity of New York's ruling class were prompted by moral disapproval, if its whole satirical outlook was underpinned by something more than jealousy, then Graydon's present status begins to seem a little suspect. For many people, *Spy* was a beacon of light, a brilliant, seditious magazine in the tradition of H.L. Mencken's *American Mercury*. From that standpoint, Graydon looks very much like a man who has struck a Faustian bargain, abandoned his scruples in return for worldly success.[2]

On balance, I don't think it makes much sense to accuse Graydon of hypocrisy. As the co-editor of *Spy* he may have frequently exposed the double standards of New York's high and mighty, but he never staked out the moral high ground. If a self-righteous note occasionally crept into *Spy*'s denunciation of some corrupt politician it was usually just a literary device, a way of making the scoundrel look even more venal. Satire shouldn't be confused with moral censure, even if the satirist occasionally puts on a dog collar.

---

[1] Jennifer Senior, 'Graydon rides the wave', *New York*, 11 December, 2000.
[2] This case was made very forcefully by Tim Carvell in 'The spies who shagged Manhattan', *Fortune*, July 19, 1999, pp.30–31.

No, where Graydon has changed is in becoming less spirited; he's not the fearless warrior he once was. *Vanity Fair* was a disappointment to me because it contained so little of the defiant, take-no-prisoners attitude that had made *Spy* such a great magazine. When I first became a *Spy* subscriber in 1987 its combination of exploding-cigar humour and no-holds-barred reporting struck me as the embodiment of the aristocratic-democratic ideal. It was journalism at its best: irreverent, mischievous and beholden to no one. Graydon was brilliant at pricking the pomposity of the rich and powerful; he was a thorn in the side of the media-industrial complex. As such, he'd been my role model.

He hasn't become tame, exactly, but he no longer has fire in his belly; he's mellowed. He's like a guerrilla leader who has made his peace with the old regime and been rewarded with a huge, baronial estate. Occasionally, you can see glimpses of the revolutionary he used to be, a devilish glint in his eye as he briefly considers throwing a bomb at the car of some capitalist fat cat; but the moment soon passes. He has responsibilities now and, besides, the fat cat is a neighbour of his in Connecticut.

Insofar as he does still have a desire to make trouble, it takes the form of encouraging others to do so. He was constantly urging me to start a *Spy*-like magazine, claiming that Manhattan was full of pompous arseholes just waiting to be given the custard-pie treatment: 'If I was a younger man . . .' Perhaps if he could use his muscle to help people like me get started in New York, the compromises he'd made on his way to the top wouldn't be so . . . compromising. Maybe I was flattering myself, but given how unsuited I was for the job he'd given me I couldn't think of any other reason why he'd brought me over. Graydon was looking for someone to pass the baton to before he lost his grip on it for ever.

On my last day at *Vanity Fair* in 1995, just before I was due to go home for Christmas, I came in to work to find a gift on my desk. It was a first edition of a book called *Around the*

World in New York by Konrad Bercovici. There was a note inscribed on the flyleaf: 'And on to the next room . . . Merry Christmas, Graydon.'

Thank God! He'd forgiven me.

16

THE BRITERATI

By Christmas, 1995, I had spent almost six months in New York. I didn't realize how much I'd been affected by it until I stepped off the plane at Heathrow. It was as if I was seeing England through the eyes of an American. The people, with their sallow complexions and cheap, non-designer clothes, looked so drab. They were also – and I don't think I was imagining this – ever so slightly smelly. It was like stepping off the set of *Sex and the City* and walking straight into a Mike Leigh movie.

Living in the States for six months I'd involuntarily picked up an American view of Britain. I was half-expecting to come home to a Merchant Ivory version of *ye olde country*, full of men in riding britches and ladies in corsets: 'So, Mr Darcy, what brings you to Hertfordshire?' The real Britain was so dowdy by comparison, as if everything was covered in a thick layer of dust. It all seemed so shabby after the shine and sparkle of Manhattan. I felt like holding my hands out in front of me and uttering that condescending American phrase: 'Too much reality.'

It dawned on me that this might partly explain why I hadn't been going down too well across the Atlantic. When New Yorkers imagine a British male they immediately think of a floppy-haired, Hugh Grant type, not a balding, William Hague look-a-like. Unfortunately, they weren't about to kiss me to see if I'd turn into a prince. On one occasion a beautiful girl I'd been chatting to at a party asked if she could see my teeth. After I bared my gums she called out to her friend: 'Hey, come look at this. This guy's got "English Teeth".' Judging from the state of my molars, 'English Teeth' are not something American girls ask for when they go to the dentist.

When I'd first arrived in Manhattan I'd hoped that being a 'teabag' would be a big asset. My uncle Christopher Moorsom who'd lived in New York in the fifties had assured me that my home-counties accent would charm the birds out of the trees. Society hostesses would be falling over themselves to invite me to parties and the richest men in American would be queuing up to introduce me to their daughters. In short, I was in for the time of my life.

Unfortunately, that hadn't happened. For New Yorkers weaned on a diet of BBC costume dramas, the sight of me in my Nike trainers and Levi 501s was a bit of a shock. Weren't all Englishmen supposed to be dandyish fops with impeccable manners and perfect skin? Who was this . . . *homunculus*? It just didn't compute. As Graydon said to me after the stripper-gram incident: 'Toby, you're like a British person born in New Jersey.'

In retrospect, though, I doubt I would have fared much better even if I'd looked like Rupert Everett. There are a few genuine *Brideshead Revisited*-types lounging about in Manhattan but even they've given up on trying to trade on their Britishness. I discovered this in the summer of 1996 when for a brief, heady moment I thought that having a title, even one as meaningless as mine, was about to pay huge dividends.

It started with a phone call from a woman claiming to be an editor at *Vogue*. Would I be interested in being a model in the December issue? Naturally, I assumed this was a joke being played on me by one of my friends so I tartly informed her I didn't get out of bed for less than $10,000. However, it turned out to be a serious offer. *Vogue* was putting together a fashion spread under the heading 'The 12 Days of Christmas' and she was looking for ten British aristocrats to pose as 'Ten Lords A-Leaping'.

I could scarcely believe it. In the twelve months that I'd lived in America this was the first time the 'Hon' before my name had fooled anyone. Up until that point, it had been nothing but a joke. Now, at last, it was going to result in the highest honour American society could bestow – my picture was going to be in *Vogue*!

My euphoria was short-lived. The editor called back the following day to tell me they were going to use male models instead. Apparently, all the *bona fide* British aristos she'd approached had turned her down flat because they knew what damage it would do to their reputations if it got out that they had a title. I was the only person stupid enough to say yes.

I'd suggested she get in touch with Lord _____ _____, an English toff straight out of *Masterpiece Theater,* so I called him up to find out why he'd declined to do it. 'The moment people find out who you are they don't see you as a modern man,' he explained. 'They think you're just some layabout who sits on his arse all day getting drunk.'

Being identified as an Englishman of any stripe, it seems, is a handicap in present-day New York. Fifty years ago it might have opened a few doors, but nowadays it just puts the natives on their mettle. As Tom Wolfe writes in *The Bonfire of the Vanities*: 'One had the sense of a very rich and suave secret legion that had insinuated itself into the cooperative apartment houses of Park Avenue and Fifth Avenue, from there to pounce at will upon the Yankees' fat fowl, to devour at leisure the last plump white meat on the bones of capitalism.'

Why should this be? One theory is that New Yorkers have finally woken up to the fact that we're out to fleece them of their hard-earned dough. ('I have come here to rook the Americans, to make money and to have a good time,' wrote Cecil Beaton when he first arrived in Manhattan.) This used to be something the Brits joked about among themselves at the bar of Mortimer's, the now defunct ex-pat watering hole on the Upper East Side, but were careful not to reveal to 'the Septics' (septic tank = Yank).[1] However, too many articles have appeared with titles like 'The British art of freeloading' in American magazines for this to remain a secret any longer. 'In England old money is treated like an esteemed family heirloom – a medieval sideboard, say, to be admired, occasionally dusted, but never, never used,' wrote Richard Stengel in a 1987 article in *Spy*. 'Money in America, on the other hand, is made to be spent. Indeed, Brits seem to believe that New Yorkers can spiritually launder their nouveau wealth by spending it on civilized English folk.'

The problem with this theory, though, is that the locals weren't exactly in the dark about just how 'cheap' we are before pieces like this started appearing. After all, upper class and upper-middle class Brits have been coming to Manhattan for over two hundred years and have consistently spent as little money as possible. Brian McNally, the cockney restaurateur, is fond of telling the story of how an aristocratic English couple decided to go Dutch on their wedding night in one of his establishments. 'They had a table for about twenty-six people running right down the middle of the restaurant,' he recalls, 'and when the check came the blushing bride stood up and said "Right, who had the duck? You, was it, Charles? That'll be $12.95. Okay, who had the two margaritas?" It was just incredible. *On her wedding day!*'

The Hon Anthony Haden-Guest has also done his bit to popularise the notion that we're 'tightwads'. According to Graydon, the reason he fell out with Anthony was because the Beast literally stole money from his son. The story goes that Anthony was out walking with the Carter family on Graydon's estate in Connecticut one day when Max, one of Graydon's four children, spotted a coin twinkling in a stream.

'Look, Dad,' said Max, pointing at the silver object. 'There's a quarter.'

---

[1] Mortimer's closed in 1998.

'Where?' asked Anthony, looking round excitedly.

'There,' replied Max, indicating the spot.

As soon as Anthony saw it, he darted into the river, snatched up the coin and stuffed it into his pocket.

'Aren't you going to give that to my son?' inquired Graydon.

'No fear,' replied Anthony. 'Finder's keepers.'[1]

But if the locals have always known what a bunch of 'moochers' we Brits are, why the sudden dip in our popularity? The reason, I think, is that there are just too damn many of us in Manhattan these days. While New Yorkers might have been prepared to tolerate us when we were relatively thin on the ground, now that we're lining the pavements our freeloading antics have begun to stick in their craw. According to official estimates, there are a total of 28,740 Britons resident in New York City.[2] However, the British Consulate puts the figure much higher than this, at approximately 200,000, and the number is increasing all the time. Among all the Western Europeans immigrating to New York, Britons rank second after the Irish, with about 1,200 becoming permanent US residents every year.[3] It's a second British invasion!

The West Village is awash with teabags. On an average day, as I carried out my various chores, I would bump into at least half a dozen people I'd been at either Oxford or Cambridge with. Indeed, living in Manhattan often felt like being back at university, not least because my flat was about the same size as my college digs. At Tea & Sympathy, the ex-pat greasy spoon on Greenwich Avenue, I used to see so many familiar faces I began to suspect that there was a secret passageway connecting it to 192, the fashionable bistro in Notting Hill Gate.

---

[1] In *The Last Party: Studio 54, Disco, and the Culture of the Night* Anthony writes: 'In all my many, many, many nights at Studio 54 . . . I seldom actually laid out more than a few bucks in actual folding money.' He has always maintained the story is untrue although he is a self-confessed skinflint.

[2] The United States Census of 1990.

[3] These figures come from the New York City Department of Planning.

At Condé Nast the Brits are so numerous the Immigration and Naturalisation Service is rumoured to have set up a whole department just to keep an eye on the situation. A disproportionately high number of Si Newhouse's editors-in-chief have been British, including Tina Brown, Anna Wintour, James Truman, Harold Evans, Anthea Disney and Mandy Norwood, and they've brought planeloads of their countrymen with them. It's no surprise that *Glamour,* the cash cow of the Condé Nast empire, spells itself in the British way.

The occasion that really brought home to me just how many of us there are in New York was Independence Day in 1999. I was sitting at the bar of Sunset Beach, a hotel/restaurant in the Hamptons, when it dawned on me that there were so many Brits in the place we probably outnumbered the Americans. Admittedly, Sunset Beach is on Shelter Island, a tiny plot of land that's practically a British colony, but even so. As the rockets lit up the sky celebrating Britain's defeat at the hands of the Americans, I decided to chance my arm. I began to chant: 'In-ger-lernd, In-ger-lernd, In-ger-lerrrrrrnd . . .' Thirty seconds later, so many people had joined in it was like being at Wembley Stadium during a World Cup final against the Germans.

It is not an exaggeration to say that the Brits are to New Yorkers what the Australians are to Londoners: what special place we once occupied in their hearts has long been filled by the wish that we'd simply go home. They've had it up to here with all these 'Limeys' complaining about how disgusting American chocolate is. If we don't like it, we know where we can stick it. Jumbo jets disgorge thousands of British liggers at JFK every day and most of them start complaining about the lack of Marmite and HP Sauce before they've even got through Immigration. It's not as if anyone invited them. I can't tell you the number of times I heard a local say to a Brit: 'We had to kick you guys out in 1776. Don't make us do it again.'

One corollary of all this is that New Yorkers have begun to lump us in with the French, the Italians, the Greeks, the Spanish and the Germans. Where once we enjoyed a privileged status in their eyes, towering above our Continental neighbours, we're now thought of as 'Eurotrash'. I once tried to convey to a *Vanity Fair* colleague how inappropriate this was by quoting that famous headline 'Storm In Channel – Continent Isolated'. He laughed politely then asked what the Channel was. He had no idea that Britain was separated from the rest of Europe by a stretch of water.

So has it come to this? Have the Brits fallen so low in New York that we're now indistinguishable from all the other European hustlers, with their Gucci loafers and Cartier watches? In fact, there are still plenty of teabags in Manhattan doing quite nicely, thank you very much. Every issue of *Time Out New York* contains a breathless puff piece about a DJ/club entrepreneur/record producer from the old country who's just bought a loft in TriBeCa on the strength of his or her overnight success. The editors of *Vogue, Harpers Bazaar, Elle* and *Mademoiselle* are all Brits and a season doesn't go by on Broadway without some veteran British actor like Alan Cumming being 'discovered' by the New York critics. To hear these people tell it, America is still the land of milk and honey, with plenty of opportunities for talented go-getters like them.

However, even these people acknowledge that life's become tougher for Brits in the last ten years, not least because it makes their success seem that much more remarkable. 'I'm more than happy to see the backlash against English people,' I was told by Simon Doonan, the man responsible for the celebrated window displays at Barneys, New York's chicest department store. 'I came to America in 1977 and I got away with murder because I had an English accent. It's almost the last gasp of the commonwealth, this idea that there's something intrinsically interesting about the English.'

At the conclusion of 1995, when I still hadn't advanced beyond the first room, I was a bit less sanguine about the end of our 'special' status. As far as I could tell, the Brits had become just another ethnic group battling for their slice of the American pie, no different from the Pakistanis, the Nigerians or the Albanians. It won't be long before we're driving taxis, I thought to myself. Then I remembered that my maternal grandfather, Raisley Moorsom, *had* driven a cab in Washington during the Second World War. *Christ!* Was I destined to follow suit?

17

NOT NEARLY GAY ENOUGH

After I returned to New York at the beginning of 1996 I was determined to turn over a new leaf. My six-month contract at *Vanity Fair* was coming up for renewal and since my run-in with Graydon no mention had been made of me sitting in Aimée Bell's chair during her maternity leave. As for Si's desire to meet me, that had been completely forgotten. If I was to have any sort of future at the magazine it was clear I'd need to do more than simply write photo captions.

I was still convinced that Graydon had brought me over to inject some irreverent, *Spy*-like humour into the magazine so I continued to deluge him with ideas for funny pieces. Here's an example sent on 22 January:

Dear Graydon,
How hard is it in this day and age to become a social pariah? Why don't I try and find out. The idea would be to antagonise as many people as possible by indulging in various forms of anti-social behaviour in a 24-hour period. I would begin my day by attending an 8 a.m. meeting at Perry AA – the Alcoholics Anonymous meeting place on Perry Street in the West Village – and while some poor recovering addict is regaling the assembled company with his tale of woe crack open a can of Bud. Between 9 a.m. and 10 a.m. I would go to as

many branches of Burger King as possible and ask directions to McDonald's. At 11 a.m. I would take a dog for a walk on that stretch of Madison Avenue between 55th and 65th Streets that has become the ground zero for designer shoppers and try and get it to crap all over the sidewalk. I would, of course, neglect to clean it up. Instead, I'd let the dog off the leash. I would spend the afternoon walking the length of Broadway wearing a mink coat without ever setting foot on the sidewalk. I would set up a stall on Sutton Place selling XXX-rated videos. I would take in a performance of *Death of a Salesman* and ensure that my pager, cellphone and wristwatch alarm all went off at five-minute intervals. I would have dinner at a high-visibility table in New York's most expensive health-food restaurant and fire up a Cohiba. Finally, at 7 a.m., I would repeatedly set off my car alarm in a quiet, residential neighbourhood by opening the door of my car over and over again. Naturally, I would expect *Vanity Fair* to indemnify all my legal expenses, pay my hospital bills and bail me out of jail.

Not surprisingly, he didn't go for this. I was now at the end of my tether so as a last resort I proposed profiling some Hollywood star. That may sound like a safe bet, but Graydon had got his fingers burnt when he dispatched Lynn Barber to interview Nick Nolte in 1992. She met him in his house in Malibu and, according to her, they talked quite amicably for about two hours. 'Well, it wasn't a great interview,' she thought afterwards, 'but it was okay, and I have enough background to make him sound interesting.'

The following day she was woken by a *Vanity Fair* staffer demanding to know what had happened. Apparently, Nolte was so upset he'd cancelled the photo shoot with Annie Leibovitz scheduled for that morning and announced that he didn't want anything further to do with the magazine. Nolte's publicist, Pat

Kingsley, told Graydon that Barber wouldn't be allowed anywhere near any of her clients ever again. Since they included nearly all of the top stars in America, Barber's career as a Hollywood interviewer was effectively over.

I had already tried to interview one celebrity for the magazine – Martin Amis – and it had come to nothing. I first met Amis at the 1986 British Press Awards where we both had been 'Commended' for work on the *Observer* – he in the category of 'Critic of the Year', me in the category of 'Young Journalist of the Year'. Unfortunately, so many of the *Observer*'s hacks had won prizes that year the paper had taken two separate tables and I was at the B-table while Amis was at the A-table. However, at the conclusion of the dinner I spotted an empty seat next to him, so I lit up a cigar and strolled over. I was a 22-year-old Oxford undergraduate but I didn't lack for *chutzpah*.

'Mr Amis,' I began, waving my cigar nonchalantly in the air, 'I've long been a fan of your work . . .'

'Excuse me,' said a middle-aged woman to my left, 'but would you mind putting out that cigar? The smoke's getting in my eyes.'

It was the wife of Donald Trelford, the editor of the *Observer*. Amis looked at me with an amused expression.

'Er, no,' I replied and went to extinguish it in the ashtray. 'As I was saying, Mr Amis . . .'

'You can't put it out there,' she objected. 'I'll still be able to smell it.'

Amis broke into a smile.

'No problem,' I said, and placed the cigar on the floor just beneath my left foot. 'Mr Amis . . .'

'No, don't do that. It'll burn a hole in the carpet.'

I was stumped. I couldn't continue to smoke the cigar and yet I wasn't allowed to put it out either. In other words, fuck off back to the B-table! As I returned to my seat next to the 'Sports Writer of the Year' I could hear Amis's laughter pealing away behind me.

Total humiliation.

In 1994, on the eve of the publication of *The Information*, I'd pitched Graydon with the idea of profiling the literary wunderkind. Admittedly, it was a long shot since I'd written an article in *The Sunday Times* earlier that year in which I'd said it was difficult to suppress a hint of *Schadenfreude* on hearing the news about the collapse of his marriage. My justification for making such a horrible remark was that in the Introduction to *Einstein's Monsters*, his collection of short stories about the Bomb, he ascribed his moral awakening to the fact that he was now the father of two young boys. This had given him a vested interest in the future of the planet, apparently. The question I asked in my article was: if you're really so concerned about your children's welfare how come you've left their mother for a younger, prettier woman?

After Graydon gave me the thumbs-up I fired off a fax to Amis, via Christopher Hitchens, in which I challenged him to a game of tennis. Given how crap I am at the game, I hoped for a repeat of John Self's humiliation at the hands of Fielding Goodney, one of the best set-pieces in *Money*. Not surprisingly, Amis never got back to me, but a few weeks afterwards I happened to be having lunch at 44 when I noticed that a New York journalist of my acquaintance was interviewing Amis in one of the restaurant's high-visibility booths. Even though this was a golden opportunity to ask Amis face to face if I could profile him, I wasn't about to make the same mistake I'd made eight years earlier. However, I got my answer anyway when, at the conclusion of the interview, the journalist paused at my table on his way out.

'I have a message for you from Martin Amis,' he said.

'Oh yeah?'

'I want to stress that these are his words, not mine,' he said, looking rather sheepish.

'Alright, no problem.'

'I mean, don't shoot the messenger, okay?'

'I promise.'

'The message is "Go fuck yourself".'

Graydon was aware of all this, so he was understandably reluctant to assign me another celebrity interview. Eventually, though, after I'd pestered him for several weeks, he came up with a star that he thought even I couldn't possibly alienate: the actor Nathan Lane. Nathan Lane is a funny, down-to-earth raconteur who made a name for himself playing comic roles on Broadway. As a profile subject, he was virtually idiot-proof. All I had to do was get him talking and write down what he said. Nevertheless, Graydon wasn't taking any chances. The interview was scheduled to take place *during* the photo shoot, so if anything went wrong they'd still have some pictures in the bag.

I went through the cuts beforehand and, to my surprise, discovered that no one had ever asked Nathan Lane whether he was gay. Indeed, the whole issue of his sexual orientation had never come up. That struck me as odd because he'd done the voice of Timon in *The Lion King*, Disney's first gay animated character, and . . . well, his whole persona as an actor was that of a SCREAMING HOMOSEXUAL. The reason *Vanity Fair* was running a profile of him was because he was about to appear in *The Birdcage,* a big-budget remake of *La Cage aux Folles*, playing Robin Williams's boyfriend. This seemed like the perfect opportunity to tackle him on the subject.

At the appointed hour I went along to the New York studio where the photo shoot was taking place and was met by a publicist – not Pat Kingsley, thankfully – who took me over and introduced me to the actor. He seemed pleasant enough and when there was a break between 'set ups' he came over to where I was sitting and indicated he was ready to be interviewed.

'Okay,' I said, nervously shuffling my notes. 'Am I right in thinking you're Jewish?'

There was an awkward pause. He looked at me as if I'd just asked him whether he masturbated about his mother.

'I don't see what the relevance of that is,' he snapped. 'Next question.'

Good God, I thought. If he regarded that as impertinent, how will he react to being asked whether he's gay? At this point the sensible thing would have been to steer the interview back on to safer ground but there was something about the way he'd said 'next question' that had got my goat. Once again, I had difficulty swallowing my pride.

'Nathan,' I said, 'you've often played homosexual characters and yet, looking through the clippings, I couldn't find a single reference to your sexual orientation. [Pause.] Are you gay?'

He stared at me in open-mouthed disbelief: *Was I serious?* Suddenly, a flash of anger passed across his brow and, for a second, I thought he might hit me (or slap me). Instead, he simply got up and walked away.

A few minutes later his publicist came over.

'Would you please leave?' she asked. 'You're making Mr Lane uncomfortable.'

'But I haven't interviewed him yet,' I protested.

'The interview's *over*,' she barked. 'You're going to have to leave. RIGHT NOW.'

I tried to catch the actor's eye, thinking that I might try and patch things up. Surely, we'd just got off on the wrong foot? But he just glowered at me like a wounded animal. It looked as though I really would have to leave.

When I got back to the magazine I was immediately summoned to Graydon's office. Evidently, 'Mr Lane's' publicist had already reported back.

'What were you thinking?' asked Graydon, too staggered by my ineptitude to work himself up into a proper rage. 'You can't ask Hollywood celebrities whether they're Jewish or gay. Just assume they're both Jewish and gay, okay?'

What was I thinking? I was effectively inviting Nathan Lane to 'out' himself in *Vanity Fair*, something that would have been completely unprecedented. Indeed, the very idea of a star's sexual orientation being raised in the magazine was absurd. *Vanity Fair* and the world it operates in is populated by a large number of homosexuals, yet surprisingly few of them are out. For most of them it's something that's simply never discussed, at least not in the presence of straight men. Like members of Hollywood's 'Velvet Mafia' they prefer to keep it an open secret. It's a safe bet that no gay movie star will ever be outed in a Condé Nast magazine.

Condé Nast's workforce hasn't changed much since Sam Newhouse, Si's father, bought the company in 1959. By and large, it is still made up of Wasps, Jews and a motley assortment of Europeans. There are some Italian-Americans, some Asian-Americans, even a sprinkling of African-Americans, but on the whole they have very little clout. The only really significant change of the last forty years is the ascendance of homosexuals.

Within Condé Nast the editors-in-chief tend to be straight, but the art departments, the photography departments, even the fashion departments, are gay strongholds. When it comes to questions of taste, from which clothes should be used in the fashion spreads to which photographers should shoot the covers, homosexuals rule the roost. There are magazines in America that cater explicitly to the gay community, such as *Attitude*, *Out* and *Poz*, but it's through glossy magazines, particularly Condé Nast's titles, that homosexuals exercise cultural power outside their demographic. To a large extent, they define what passes for good taste in contemporary America.

One of the best kept secrets at Condé Nast is how large the gay readership of *GQ* is. The concern is that if it got out it might put off *GQ*'s straight readers. However, even the so-called women's magazines have homosexual fans. A survey of *Glamour*'s readership carried out by Condé Nast in 1992 discovered that 18 per cent of the magazine's male readers were gay or bisexual. According to the market research company that conducted this research, one fifth of this group were cross-dressers looking for beauty and fashion tips.

Throughout my time at *Vanity Fair* I frequently put my foot in it by not realising the person I was speaking to was homosexual. For instance, on one occasion a colleague of mine asked me what readership I thought *Details* was aimed at. (*Details* is a Newhouse-owned men's fashion magazine.) 'It's for guys who like staring at pictures of naked men but haven't quite figured out why,' I quipped.[1] He glared at me with undisguised hostility. Evidently, I lacked the 'gaydar' that enables most New Yorkers to tell at a glance whether someone's gay.

This inability proved just as much of a handicap outside the office. At the beginning of 1996 I decided to host my first ever New York dinner party to which I invited five men and five women. The man sitting opposite me, a black writer for the *Village Voice*, was smoking pastel-coloured cigarettes and, towards the end of the evening, I absent-mindedly picked one up and said, 'These are so *gay*.' A hush fell over the table and all the other diners looked at him to see how he'd react. I hadn't realised it, but he was a prominent member of New York's gay community who'd made a name for himself by coming down hard on precisely this sort of casual, homophobic remark. Fortunately, he decided not to make an issue out of it. 'Smile when you say that,' he purred.

The following day one of the female guests called to chastise me about this *faux pas* and I told her I'd simply had no idea that the man in question was a homosexual.

'Toby,' she said, as if explaining something to a child, 'every man at your dinner party was gay.'

I was flabbergasted. *Really?* She thought I'd deliberately not invited any straight men in order to give myself a clear run at all the female guests.

On another occasion a fellow scribe invited me to his 'coming out party'. In addition to all his friends, every member of his

---

[1] A version of this joke was originally made by Elvis Mitchell, a *New York Times* film critic, who said: '*Details* is for men who don't understand why they like looking at pictures of other men.' *Details* is probably the only gay magazine in the world which is still in the closet. It was once outed on an episode of *The Simpsons* in which one New Yorker says to another: 'How d'you like a *Details* magazine up the wazoo?'

family was present, including his Jewish grandmother. After he'd made a speech in which he announced to the assembled company that he was, in his own words, 'a total fag', he was given three presents: a cake with the words 'Welcome Out' on it in bright, pink icing, the complete works of Barbra Streisand and a copy of *The Rules: Timetested Secrets for Capturing the Heart of Mr Right*.

It eventually dawned on me that a significant percentage of the male journalists I came across were gay – Jewish and gay, in fact. In saying this, my intention isn't to fuel the paranoid fantasies of America's conservative critics. I'm not suggesting that the New York media is run by a cabal of Jewish homosexuals – in overall terms they're still a tiny minority. But the journalists I found myself gravitating towards tended to fall into that category because they were so much smarter and funnier than everyone else. Of course, by the time I figured out most of my friends were gay I'd alienated the vast majority of them by assuming they were heterosexual and inviting them to share my lascivious thoughts about various women: 'Check out the tits on that! Is she sex on a stick or what? Eh?'

Of the two dozen or so men who came into *Vanity Fair*'s offices every day during the period I worked there, no more than four or five were straight. It was a long-standing joke between Chris Lawrence and me that we would advance far quicker through the magazine's ranks if we pretended to be homosexual. Indeed, we would often wonder whether those few staffers who were openly gay were actually straight men in disguise, a category known in New York as 'Steers' (straight queers).[1] Wouldn't it be fun to 'in' them? Reluctantly, we concluded that they were probably all as camp as Christmas.

---

[1] The most out homosexual I ever encountered in the office was Kevin Sessums, *Vanity Fair*'s celebrity-interviewer-in-chief. In the Tina Brown era he wrote a piece for *Poz* in which he discussed how it had felt to sleep with the HIV positive grandson of George Wallace, the one-time governor of

Appearing to be gay is such an all-round advantage in present-day Manhattan it's even an asset in the dating arena. *Talk* magazine ran an article in May, 2000 identifying the magic ingredient that makes Jude Law, Matt Damon and Edward Norton such heartthrobs: apparently, they're 'Just Gay Enough'. A female veteran of the New York dating scene was quoted describing her ideal man: 'You want him to be a little gay about things. You want a lover who has pride of ownership in his house, who cooks, likes to dance, loves his mother, cares about his wardrobe and his body, but who doesn't go too far in any of those pursuits. You want him to be Just Gay Enough.'

Unfortunately, for the purposes of attracting New York women, making dinner party small talk and interviewing Hollywood celebrities, I was Not Nearly Gay Enough.

Georgia who'd been such a fierce opponent of civil rights. When it appeared, Sarah Giles, a British editor, ran down the main corridor waving the magazine over her head and shouting 'omigod, omigod, omigod' at the top of her lungs.

18

CELEBRITY WRANGLING

You can tell it's Oscar season at *Vanity Fair*'s offices because you begin to overhear members of staff having the following telephone conversation as you wander down the main corridor:

'Who? Oh my God! How the hell are you? I haven't heard from you in, like, ten years, man.'

Pause.

'Gee, I'd love to help but there's really nothing I can do. I'm not even invited myself. Sorry.'

Click. Dial-tone.

One of the burdens of working for the magazine is that for the month of March you do virtually nothing other than field telephone calls from your most distant acquaintances fishing for invitations to the Oscar party. Each year 15,000 people call Graydon Carter's office begging to be invited. The total calls received by the magazine's staff must number ten times that. It's not an exaggeration to say that an invitation to the *Vanity Fair* Oscar party is more coveted than an invitation to the Academy Awards.

People go to extraordinary lengths to try and secure a place on the guest list. In 1996, about a week after the party had taken place, I remember spotting a fake Academy Award on Graydon's desk. It had been sent to him by one of that year's guests and she'd inscribed it with the words 'Best Oscar Party, 1996'.

'I guess she'll be invited again,' I quipped.

'Not necessarily,' said Graydon.

More recently, someone called up a member of the magazine's staff and offered them a bribe of $300,000 for an invitation. 'Give them my cellphone number,' Graydon joked when he heard about this, 'I have four children to educate.'

To date, the only non-celebrity to successfully gatecrash the party was a hack from *The Star* supermarket tabloid who turned up in 1996 with a pig on a leash. Claiming it was the pig from *Babe*, which was a Best Picture nominee that year, the reporter sailed past the clipboard Nazis who were apparently unaware that over a dozen pigs took turns to play the title role.

Since then the party has been made gatecrasher-proof. These days, in order to get anywhere near the entrance you have to get past a series of checkpoints manned by Los Angeles county sheriffs. If you're in a car you have to display a colour-coded 'parking pass' on the dashboard. One colour entitles you to 'valet' – meaning a flunky will park your car for you – while the other doesn't. At the third checkpoint, assuming you make it that far, you'll be greeted by 'a surgically modified brunette with a headset'[1] who'll check your name against her 'master list'. Even if you're on the list, that's no guarantee you'll get in. Tara Palmer-Tomkinson was turned back in 1998 when she arrived at 9.30 p.m. She'd been told not to get there any earlier than 11.30 p.m.

Rather surprisingly for such an exclusive party, the total number of guests has been growing steadily each year. In 1999 approximately 750 people were invited; in 2001 that number had increased to 1, 200, though in order to accommodate them Graydon had to employ his architect, Basil Walter, to pull down the back wall of Mortons and build a temporary extension. The wall was put back up the following day.

The reason for all this hoopla is simple: the harder the party is to get into, the more people will clamour to be invited. By branding the event 'the most exclusive party in the world'

---

[1] Jennifer Senior, 'Graydon rides the wave', *New York*, 11 December, 2000.

Graydon has succeeded in making it the hottest ticket of Oscar Week.

'It's not who you say "yes" to,' Graydon told me in 1996, disclosing his formula for throwing such a successful party, 'it's who you say "no" to.'

Of course, not all the guests have to beg to be allowed in. Believe it or not, some of them actually receive invitations out of the blue. For instance, all the Oscar nominees in each of the major categories are invited because that's the only way Graydon can ensure that the winners will have the necessary documentation – parking pass, stiffy, etc – to get past the various checkpoints. It has also become an annual tradition to invite the 'bimbo *de jour*'. At the 1994 party, as I discovered, it was Nancy Kerrigan; in 1998 it was Monica Lewinsky.

The most important guests at the party are those who comprise the Hollywood A-list and no stone is left unturned in persuading them to attend. These include past Academy Award winners like Tom Hanks, Gwyneth Paltrow and Martin Scorsese, moguls like Rupert Murdoch, Edgar Bronfman Jr and Summer Redstone and 'blue-haired California matrons' like Nancy Reagan, Barbara Davis and Betsy Bloomingdale. These are the people who can expect to receive a gift along with their invitations, both delivered by a Fed Ex armoured lorry. In 1997, the lucky few received a red director's chair with the words 'Vanity Fair' emblazoned on the back. In 1998, all 150 diners arrived to discover a pewter ashtray and a Zippo lighter in their place settings. This was Graydon's way of letting people know it was okay to smoke.

More resources are devoted to planning the Oscar party than to putting together the Hollywood issue of the magazine, which is saying something. To describe the degree of preparation that goes into organising the event as 'military' is an insult to Sara Marks, *Vanity Fair*'s chief party planner.[1] In 1999, she scoured Cuba looking for a sixteen-piece band to play in a marquee

---

[1] Her title on the masthead is 'Director of Special Projects'.

that Graydon had got his architect to put up in the Mortons' car park. If Sara Marks had been in charge of the Bay of Pigs it might not have been such a fiasco.

Graydon takes it all very, very seriously. When I spoke to him in the course of writing a piece about the 1999 Oscar party for the *New York Post* he said, 'Don't make it fucking snarky or I'll come and carve your heart out with a pencil. If you say anything other than it's the number one party I'll fucking kill ya.'[1] Every year, a crack team of 15–20 *Vanity Fair* staffers flies down to LA at least two weeks beforehand to make sure everything's running smoothly. Graydon himself arrives a week later to personally take command of the operation. He even has the equivalent of a staff car. In 1998, one of his assistants called John Gillies arranged for Graydon to have the use of a Mercedes S500 throughout his time in the city. John was terrified because he was only able to get his nibs a red one, not the blue one he'd requested. Fortunately, he chose to overlook this imperfection.

Why does Graydon lavish such attention on the party? In part, it's for solid business reasons. The Hollywood issue of *Vanity Fair* is so fat with advertising it could do with some liposuction. The magazine now has ad revenues in excess of $100 million a year and the April issue forms the cornerstone of its annual advertising strategy. The reason advertisers want to be in that issue is because, thanks to the party, it receives more publicity than any other. It is an 'event issue', the publishing equivalent of an 'event movie'.

The party also serves to brand the magazine as a sexy, glamorous product; it links it in the public's mind with everything that's desirable about Hollywood. Within Condé Nast, parties are positioning events, enabling each magazine to distil its 'brand essence'. *Vanity Fair* is an upmarket celebrity magazine with particularly close ties to the entertainment industry so its annual Oscar party is a perfect opportunity to consolidate its

---

[1] He also said that I couldn't quote him in the article. 'I think I'm overexposed,' he explained.

identity. Of course, it helps if something scandalous happens at the party and there are usually one or two celebs happy to oblige. In 1997, Ellen DeGeneres started fooling around with Anne Heche in full view of the other guests and in 2001 Elizabeth Hurley and Pamela Anderson did likewise. In both cases, the tabloids went nuts.

'Two kinds of people read *Vanity Fair*,' Graydon once told me. 'Trailer park white trash and everyone who matters.' The reason the former group read it, at least in part, is because they see the coverage the Oscar party gets in papers like the *National Enquirer*. The reason everyone who matters reads it is because they're invited to the party.

This goes to the heart of why Graydon attaches such importance to the event. It gives him leverage over some of the biggest players in the media-industrial complex. Graydon hasn't created this annual institution to make the job of editing the magazine easier; he edits the magazine so he can throw parties like this. For the Royal Canadian Airforce brat and former railway worker, the Oscar party is an annual reminder of just how far he's come. During the run-up to the event, he's feted by all the biggest names in town, culminating in a lunch party in his honour hosted by Barry Diller. This lunch – a subject of much speculation in *Vanity Fair*'s offices – is attended by, among others, Stephen Spielberg, David Geffen, Ronald Perelman, Jeffrey Katzenberg, Sandy Gallin, Diane Von Furstenberg, Fran Lebowitz and Edgar Bronfman Jr. One staffer who spotted him immediately afterwards in 1998, cruising back to the Beverly Hills Hotel in his Mercedes, described him as looking 'as happy as a pasha'. At moments like this, Graydon isn't simply the cat that got the cream. He's the python that swallowed the panther that *ate* the cat that got the cream.

19

'STAY THE FUCK AWAY FROM THE CELEBRITIES!'

Naturally, my sole concern in the spring of 1996 was how to get invited to the party. This was no easy task. To give you some idea of how rare it is for members of *Vanity Fair*'s staff to attend, neither Matt Tyrnauer nor Aimée Bell had been invited that year. They professed not to be bothered by this – 'It's not like a *party* party,' Aimée explained – but I found that hard to believe. What was the point of working for *Vanity Fair* if you didn't get to go to the Oscar party, for Christ's sake? For a grubbing hack like me, the rewards that could flow from a successful bit of Hollywood networking were potentially enormous. My role models in this regard were Andrew and Leslie Cockburn, two English contributors who'd recently sold the movie rights to an article of theirs that hadn't even been published.[1] I'd written dozens of unpublished articles that I thought would make great movies!

I decided my best strategy was to offer to write a piece about the party for the *Evening Standard*. This led to the following conversation:

---

[1] The article, which was about the availability of weapons-grade plutonium on the Russian black market, never appeared in the magazine, though it did form the basis of a book called *One Point Safe*. The movie, on the other hand, got made the following year. It was *The Peacemaker*.

173

Graydon: What kind of piece?

Me: The most flattering, oleaginous, sick-making piece you've ever read. You'll be *embarrassed* it'll be so sycophantic.

Graydon: I don't know, Toby. All the stuff I've read of yours has been kinda snide.

Me [Launching into a rendition of my own deathless prose]: Graydon Carter looked pityingly at the supplicant who'd prostrated himself before him. 'I'm sorry, but my hands are tied. The Los Angeles Fire Marshals have specifically said I can't let anyone else in until somebody leaves. Is there any way you could come back in half-an-hour, Mr Cruise?'

Graydon: Okay, okay, but I'm not paying your expenses. You're going to have to make your own way there.

Me: No problem.

Graydon: And stay the fuck away from the celebrities, okay? I don't want you going up to anyone and asking them whether they're gay.

Me: I'm going to assume everybody there is both Jewish *and* gay.

Graydon [Eyeballing me]: Don't make me regret this.

Me: I swear to God.

Graydon: And don't even think about getting there before 11.30pm.

The day before the party was due to take place I was met at LAX by Alex de Silva, though I barely recognised him he looked so 'LA'. In addition to a pair of 'skate shorts' that came down to his ankles, he had a serious amount of 'facial topiary',[1] not to mention an impressive array of rings and studs inserted into different parts of his anatomy. His hair, which had been cropped like mine back in London, was now corkscrewing over his shoulders and was only kept out of his eyes by a pair of sunglasses jammed on top of his head. As far as I could tell, just one aspect of his appearance

---

[1] Also known as 'chin pubes'.

remained unchanged: he still had his English teeth.

'Hey, dude!' he cried. 'What's happening?'

He went to give me a hug, but I took a step backwards.

'Listen, Alex, before you say anything else, I want to make it absolutely clear that there's no way I can get you into the *Vanity Fair* party. It's a total impossibility I'm afraid.'

'Chill, baby. I'm already on the list.'

What?

It turned out that he'd befriended a famous, Oscar-winning producer and the man had offered to act as his mentor. In addition to helping Alex out with his first script – a biopic about William Shatner – he'd offered to take him along to the *Vanity Fair* party instead of his wife. What a jammy little bastard!

Suddenly, I had a horrible thought: 'What time is you're invitation for?'

'What d'you mean?'

'You know, when will you be allowed in. What timeslot have you been allotted. Time, time, *time*.'

'10.30 p.m. I think.'

Shit, fuck, bollocks!

Alex could tell from my face that something was wrong: 'Why? What time's yours for?'

'10 p.m.' I said, a little too quickly.

'Because if it's not until 11 p.m. or something I'm sure you could come along with us.'

'Jesus Christ, Alex, I'm the one that works for *Vanity Fair*, not you. I don't need *your* help to get me into my own party, thank you very much.'

'Okay, dude. Whatever. I was just trying to help.'

We walked to the LAX car park in silence as I desperately tried to think of a way to get myself bumped up from 11.30 p.m. to 10 p.m. Even Kim Masters, the magazine's Hollywood correspondent, isn't invited that early, I thought. What the fuck am I going to do?

Luckily, the sight of his car pulled me out of my reverie. It was the oldest, most beaten-up, clapped-out VW Golf I'd ever set eyes on.

'Is that roadworthy?' I asked, beginning to cheer up.

Alex explained that the car had been lent to him by the famous producer so he could 'help him out' in various ways.

'Like what?' I asked.

'Oh, you know, just the occasional thing.'

It turned out the 'occasional thing' included fetching his groceries, picking up his dry cleaning and ferrying his kids back and forth to school. The producer's assistance didn't come without a price, it seemed. He'd agreed to be Alex's mentor and, in return, Alex had agreed to play Mr Sulu to his Captain Kirk.

I teased Alex about becoming a Kato Kaelin figure but he assured me that this was a perfectly standard way for people like him to get into the movie business. He told me the story of a boy in his class at USC called Michael who had a similar relationship with Brad Pitt. Apparently, Michael had been at a beach party in Malibu when he'd spotted Brad playing with his dogs a few yards away. Seizing this opportunity, Michael wandered over and started petting Brad's dogs, complementing him on what wonderful animals they were. This was the right thing to say, according to Alex, since Brad loves his dogs more than anything else in the world. Consequently, he invited Michael to join in the game he was playing.

Brad handed Michael a baseball bat and threw a ball up into the air for him to hit. Unfortunately, one of Brad's dogs intercepted the ball at precisely the same moment that Michael's bat connected with it and he ended up whacking the dog in the head. The dog fell to the ground, apparently lifeless, and Brad suddenly became very emotional.

'You killed my dog, you killed my dog!'

With amazing presence of mind, Michael told Brad he'd seen a similar incident on *Rescue 911*, a cheesy television programme, and he knelt down and began to massage the dog's heart. Miraculously, the animal completely recovered and was soon bounding along the beach with the other dogs. Brad looked at Michael with love in his eyes. He was so grateful he insisted on taking him out to dinner that night and the two had become inseparable ever since.

'So this screenwriter guy,' I said. 'Does he have a dog?'

'He does as a matter of fact,' Alex replied. 'A black lab.'

'And do the "occasional things" you have to do for him include trailing along behind him when he's out walking this dog with a little pooper-scooper?'

'Very funny, dude.'

At 10 p.m. on Monday, 25 March I strode up to the first police barrier outside Mortons. Back in 1996 there was only one checkpoint you had to get through before facing the surgically modified brunette with a headset, though it was hardly a piece of cake. It was manned by an overweight, Chief Wiggum look-a-like who was checking each person's credentials very carefully. I didn't have an invitation – I'd been assured I would be on the list – but I was wearing an extremely smart Giorgio Armani tuxedo that I persuaded Pippi to call in for me. My hope was that I'd look so cool he'd simply wave me through.

'Evening, officer,' I said, without breaking stride.

'Invitation?' he barked.

At this point I had two options. I could either ask him to summon Beth Kseniak on his walkie-talkie, and risk her telling him I wasn't allowed in until 11.30 p.m., or try and bluff it. I decided to go through door number two.

'I'm on the staff of the magazine,' I said. Then, breaking into a knowing chuckle, I added: 'In fact, I'm one of the people responsible for this three-ring circus.'

He continued to look at me suspiciously so I showed him my *Vanity Fair* press card: 'Can I go ahead? My boss'll kill me if I show up any later than 10 p.m.'

'I guess it's okay,' he said, examining my card. 'You work for the magazine, huh?'

'For my sins,' I said, rolling my eyes.

'Yeah, okay, you can go through.'

'Thank you, officer. You're doing an excellent job.'

One down, one to go.

Approaching the main entrance at Mortons, I was struck by the sheer number of journalists who were there to cover the party, all of them in evening dress. For entertainment reporters this area between the police barrier and the entrance was 'prime real estate', even though they weren't allowed past the velvet ropes on either side of the main gangway. That area was reserved exclusively for people who had been invited to the party.

I was terrified I'd bump into Graydon. The previous year he spent so much time standing outside Mortons greeting his guests in person that one of the magazine's journalists had dubbed him 'the maitre d' in the car park'. Fortunately he wasn't around, but that wouldn't make getting in any easier. Fanning out in front of the gangway, forming an impenetrable cordon, were members of *Vanity Fair*'s crack regiment that had flown in two weeks earlier, all wearing headsets and clutching clipboards. They weren't about to let in one of their colleagues an hour and a half early, particularly as they had to spend the entire evening standing outside the party. How the hell was I going to get past them?

Suddenly, I spotted Darryl Brantley. Darryl, who at that time, was Sara Marks's assistant, is a flamboyant black man whose main claim to fame in the *Vanity Fair* office is that he'd made a cameo appearance in the Madonna documentary *Truth or Dare*. He'd always been friendly to me so I thought he was my best bet.

'Hey, Darryl,' I said, flashing my most winning, Hugh Grant smile.

'No way, Toby,' he replied, wagging his finger at me. 'I have strict instructions not to let you in before 11.30 p.m. You're a bad, bad boy.'

'Graydon said it would be okay if I came a little early.'

'A little early?' Darryl said, looking at his watch. 'It's not even 10.05 p.m.'

'Listen, Darryl, cut me some slack. I've got to write a story about the party for the *Evening Standard* and file it by 7 a.m.

London time. That's in less than an hour. If I'm not allowed in until 11.30 p.m. I'll have to write the story without actually having *been* at the party.'

That was true. What I didn't tell him was that I'd already written the story. It was in my breast pocket.

Darryl looked furtively from side to side: 'I could get into trouble for this.'

'I won't tell if you won't.'

'If anyone asks, I haven't seen you,' whispered Darryl.

The first celebrity I spotted was Jim Carrey standing by the bar. Ever since seeing *Dumb & Dumber*, I've been a huge fan of Carrey's. He's one of those stars who broke through completely against the odds. He's not good-looking, he's never won an Oscar and you wouldn't exactly call him sex on legs, yet he's so funny audiences just love him. Indeed, a couple of hours earlier he'd done a two-minute routine at the Academy Awards that had completely stolen the show. He had hundreds of millions of people all over the world in stitches and yet here he was by himself not ten feet from where I was standing. It was too good an opportunity to miss.

'Toby Young,' I said, extending my hand. 'I work for the magazine.'

'Hey,' he said, shaking it without much enthusiasm.

'I'm sure you must have heard this a hundred times before, but if there was an Academy Award for the Best Presenter of an Academy Award you'd win it every year.'

His face brightened: 'Actually, you're the first person who's ever said that.' He pointed a finger at my chest: 'What are you drinking?'

'Er, Black Label on the rocks please. Thanks.'

He turned to the barman, ordered me a drink, then swivelled back to face me. This was turning into my most successful celebrity encounter ever!

'For what it's worth,' I added, 'I thought you should have won an Oscar for *Dumb & Dumber* as well.'

He wheeled round again: 'Better make that a double!'

After he'd placed the Scotch in my hand he launched into a story about the motivational speaker Tony Robbins visiting him on the set of *The Cable Guy* that was so funny I was physically incapable of taking a sip for the next five minutes. I couldn't believe it. Jim Carrey – *Jim fucking Carrey!* – was doing a comedy routine for an audience of one: me. It didn't get much better than this.

Suddenly, we were interrupted.

'Heyyyy! What's happening?'

It was Alex. What was he doing here? I hadn't been expecting him for at least another fifteen minutes. Of course, I was pleased that he'd spotted me talking to Jim Carrey – what could be cooler than that? – but if he thought I was going to let him muscle in on my special moment with my favourite movie star he could forget about it.

'I'm sorry, but I don't believe I know you,' I said, giving him a frosty look. 'Jim, d'you know this man?'

'Sure do,' said Carrey. 'Everybody knows Alex!'

To my astonishment, Alex and Carrey then started to shadow box like the best of friends. How the hell did they know each other? Maybe it was an AA thing. Yeah, that was probably it. I'd noticed that Carrey hadn't ordered himself a drink when he'd got me one. In fact, they probably didn't know each other at all. Phew!

'So,' said Carrey to Alex, 'how's that William Shatner script coming along?'

Rats!

'Okay,' said Alex. 'In fact, how would you feel about playing James Doohan?'

Carrey immediately launched into a flawless imitation of Scotty. 'I don't know how much more she can take, Captain.'

'Full Power, Mr Scott,' said Alex, and both he and Carrey collapsed with laughter.

Needless to say, while all this had been going on Alex had refused to acknowledge me. I'd started off pretending not to know him and now he was pretending not to know me. I suppose I only had myself to blame.

At that moment Nicholas Cage walked in clutching the Oscar he'd just won for *Leaving Las Vegas*. He held it aloft and the crowd broke into spontaneous applause. I'd actually prepared a 'zinger' about this film and here was my chance to use it. With a bit of luck, I might regain the initiative from Alex.

'I didn't get that movie,' I said, jerking my thumb in Cage's direction. 'I mean, why would anyone want to *leave* Las Vegas?'

I was expecting them to crack up but instead they both looked at me blankly.

'I thought it was an incredible piece of work,' said Alex, turning to Carrey. 'Mike Figgis should have won Best Director.'

'Absolutely,' said Carrey, nodding enthusiastically.

Wait a minute, I thought. Aren't you the guy who spent last year making the sequel to *Ace Ventura: Pet Detective*? I decided not to stick around any longer in case he said anything more to disillusion me.

As I stood off to one side, nursing my drink, I reflected that Alex was much better at talking to celebrities than me. He wasn't intimidated by them. He could look them in the eye and keep his nerve, whereas I couldn't get past the fact that I was talking to an A-list movie star. The status discrepancy between Jim Carrey and me had been too big to ignore; it coloured my whole attitude towards him. Alex had been aware of it too, I was sure, but he had the gift of being able to conceal it. He kept a poker face. In LA, to even tacitly acknowledge that the person you're talking to is famous is a complete no-no; it's known as 'breaking the wall'. As soon as you do it you're finished. You're automatically categorised as a 'fan', as one of 'them'.

Alex believed that the secret of getting on with celebs was to treat them just as you would a 'normal' person. I'd lost count of the number of times he said, 'They're just human beings, dude, no different from you and me.' But that wasn't it, at least not exactly. After all, it's not as if the average movie star wants you not to have heard of him or her. Rather, the trick is to pretend to be *abnormal* yourself, since any ordinary person would be completely star struck. If you can keep the fact that you're impressed by them hidden they automatically assume you're someone important. It's a way of signalling that you're on the same rung of the status ladder as them. Alex's art wasn't to treat them as 'normal' people, but to persuade them to treat him as a fellow VIP.

'How the fuck did you get in?'

It was Graydon.

'Oh, er, hi there, Graydon. Yeah, er . . .'

'Was that you I saw talking to Jim Carrey?'

'Yeah it was. I told him that if there was an Oscar for . . .'

'What did I tell you about bothering the celebrities? Listen, you can stick around, but don't talk to any movie stars, okay?'

'Aye, aye, skipper.'

He stuck his finger in my face: 'I mean it.'

In order to file my *Evening Standard* story I had to dictate it to the copytakers back in London. Unfortunately, there were only two phones in Mortons and there was a queue of five or six people waiting to use each one. Still, there was nothing else for it so I took my place in the shorter of the two lines. Of course, by the time it was my turn, about ten minutes later, there were five or six people standing behind me. Would they be prepared to stand idly by while I tied up the phone for fifteen minutes? I'd just have to chance it.

After I'd got through on the freephone number I launched into my opening paragraph: 'When I arrived in Los Angeles last weekend for the Oscars, comma, I was surprised to discover that all my English friends had left town, stop. Why, question mark. Apparently, comma, it was to avoid the embarrassment of not having been invited to the *Vanity Fair* Oscar party, stop.'

I smiled apologetically at the people behind me and rolled

my eyes as if to say, 'Sorry about this, guys, but what can I do?' They glared at me impatiently.

'Could you repeat that,' said the copytaker. 'I didn't catch any of it I'm afraid.'

Oh shit.

'When I arrived in Los Angeles last weekend for the Oscars, comma . . .'

'Excuse me,' said the man standing directly behind me, 'but are you going to be long?'

'Er, I might be some time I'm afraid. It looks as though you'll have to use the other phone. Sorry.'

'Don't you have a cellphone? What kind of reporter are you?'

'Sorry,' I repeated. 'I'll try and be as quick as possible.'

I turned my back on him and continued dictating my story. After a few seconds, the people that had been standing behind me reluctantly took their places behind the people in the other queue. There were now about a dozen people waiting to use that phone and as I loudly repeated all the zingers I'd thought up about that year's Oscar nominees they shook their heads in disgust. I felt like a stand-up comedian flopping in front of a hostile audience.

When I'd finished the copytaker told me to hold while he spoke to the newsdesk. The other queue had gone down by this time but there were still several people standing in it who'd originally been waiting to use my phone. They were all watching me in anticipation, ready to dart over the moment I finished my call.

'What's your number there?' asked the copytaker. 'We're going to hang up at this end but the newsdesk wants you to wait by the phone in case there are any queries.'

Yikes!

I gave him the number but, rather than replace the receiver, I surreptitiously stuck my thumb over the cradle, thereby hanging up without appearing to do so.

'Okay, I'll hold,' I said loudly.

After I'd been standing like this for about a minute a middle-aged black woman emerged from the crowd and took her place behind me.

'Excuse me,' she said, 'I don't mean to interrupt, but are you actually using this phone?'

It was Diana Ross.

Gulp!

'Er, y-y-yes, actually. I'm on hold.'

'Because it looks to me as though you have your thumb pressed down on the watchamacallit.'

Several snorts of derision came from the other queue.

'No, no,' I said, removing my thumb. 'I was just resting my hand there.'

'In that case,' she said, 'how come I can now hear a dial-tone?'

I couldn't think of an answer.

'Busted!' cried one of my antagonists.

'Sorry, Miss Ross,' I said, handing her the phone. 'I was waiting for someone to call me back.'

As I walked away, hanging my head in shame, the people behind me broke into wild applause and out of the corner of my eye I could see Diana Ross taking a little bow.

About half an hour later I was standing by the bar, feeling thoroughly dejected, when Mel Gibson walked in. He was clutching the two Oscars he'd just won for *Braveheart* and he looked extremely pleased with himself, as well he might. There was no way *Braveheart* had deserved to win Best Picture against *Apollo 13*. I had seen it a few days earlier and, not surprisingly, hated it. Even by the standards of a film industry in which Englishmen are always cast as villains, *Braveheart* was a new low. It was a piece of anti-British propaganda, an incitement to Scottish nationalists to rise up and throw off the yoke of colonial oppression. Given that Mel Gibson had also made *Gallipoli*, he clearly had a huge chip on his shoulder about the Brits. He was an anti-Britite! I'd had four double whiskies at this point and was suddenly overcome by an urge to confront him.

I stumbled through the crowd until I was standing right behind him.

''Ere, mate,' I said, tapping him aggressively on the shoulder. 'What exactly have you got against the Brits?'

He wheeled round to face me and I steeled myself for a confrontation. *Now we'll see what you're made of, you chippy little Australian cunt.* However, instead of answering my question he transferred the Oscar he was holding in his right hand to his left, thrust out his paw and said, 'Hi. I'm Mel Gibson.'

It was completely disarming.

'Er, hi,' I said, shaking his hand enthusiastically. 'I'm Toby Young. Good to meet you.'

Once again, I'd been completely dazzled by a star's celebrity wattage. I may have had the heart of a warrior, ready to take on William Wallace on behalf of true-blue Englishmen everywhere, but I had the soul of a salivating starfucker.

Before I could regain my composure, I felt a tug from behind, as if someone was grabbing me by my collar. I half-turned, but before I could see who it was I was yanked backwards and sent sprawling into the crowd.

It was Graydon.

'Jesus Christ, Toby, I'm not going to tell you again,' he barked. 'STOP BOTHERING THE CELEBRITIES!'

20

'LET'S DISCUSS.'

Back at *Vanity Fair*'s offices two days later, I was immediately summoned to see Graydon. Oh-oh, I thought. Here it comes. He's going to bollock me for hassling Mel Gibson at the Oscar party. However, as soon as I walked in, he thrust a copy of the *Evening Standard* under my nose. It was open at the page with my story on it.

'What the fuck is that?' he demanded.

'Not sycophantic enough for you?' I asked.

By way of response, he picked it up and began to read out loud: '"When I arrived in Los Angeles last weekend for the Oscars, I was surprised to discover that all my English friends had left town. Why? Apparently, it was to avoid the embarrassment of having been invited to the *Vanity Fair* Oscar party."'

He threw the paper down on his desk and glowered at me accusingly: Well?

Jesus Christ! Some idiot on the *Evening Standard* had deleted the word 'not' from my opening paragraph, completely altering its meaning. I immediately launched into a garbled explanation, telling him how it hadn't been possible to check anything with the newsdesk because of the whole phone situation at Mortons, even relating how I'd been busted by Diana Ross. He wasn't impressed. Not only was he extremely sceptical about my excuse, he now added Ross's name to the long list of celebrities I'd 'stalked' that night. In the end I had to get the *Standard*

features editor to write a letter attesting to the fact that I'd originally included the word 'not' in my copy, even though, as she
privately confided to me, she thought it had 'read better' without
it. But he still wasn't convinced. It was just the kind of 'snarky'
thing I'd write, apparently.

'That's the last time I let you come to the Oscar party,' he
harrumphed.

I could tell that Graydon had almost completely lost patience
with me at this stage. ('Ya *think?*' as Chris Lawrence would
say.) At first, he'd tolerated my office hi-jinks as a source of
amusement. For reasons I couldn't quite fathom, he had a soft
spot for me. I was the court jester, the one person at *Vanity
Fair* who was allowed to make a fool of himself again and again
because the boss got a kick out of it. However, the joke was
now wearing thin. If I didn't pull a rabbit out of the hat soon
I could kiss my $60,000-a-year goodbye.

Fortunately, on 18 August, 1996 I finally came up with an
idea that he liked. I'd just returned from London where I'd
interviewed Ian Schrager for the *Evening Standard* – he was
planning to open two hotels in the city – and I fired off a
memo suggesting that the magazine run something on the city's
uncharacteristically upbeat mood. I quoted Schrager saying that
he'd noticed there was 'a tremendous amount of energy in
London', 'a real buzz'. I didn't have anything particularly
ambitious in mind. I thought it might make a good Vanities
piece.

Twenty-four hours later my memo came back to me with the
words 'Let's discuss' written on it. This meant Graydon wanted
to talk to me about it in person, a very good sign. (He usually
referred to my ideas as 'dog whistles' – 'You can hear them,
but I can't.') I trotted along to his office and, at his request,
went into slightly more depth about why I thought the time
was ripe for a laudatory piece about London. I talked a bit
about 'Britpop' and 'Britart' and ticked off all the usual suspects:
Damien Hirst, Noel Gallagher, Vivienne Westwood, etc.

'Okay, Toby,' he said. 'Lemme think about it.'

A few days later I was summoned to Graydon's office again, only this time it was full of people. In addition to Aimée Bell, George Hodgman, the senior articles editor, was there, as was David Harris, the art director, Gregory Mastrianni, the associate art director, and Lisa Berman, the associate photo editor. It soon became apparent that Graydon had convened this star chamber to hear my pitch. Clearly, he was considering devoting more than just a page in Vanities to London's cultural renaissance. If I could only persuade these people that the Zeitgeist was currently residing across the Atlantic, this might turn into a photographic 'portfolio' or, better yet, a 'special issue'. Exactly what my role would be wasn't clear, but whatever it was it had to be better than writing photo captions for VF Camera. Here, at last, was a chance to prove myself.

Naturally, I fluffed it. My ten-minute presentation was politely received but I could tell that they remained unconvinced. It was partly that the source was tainted. Of course *I* would sing London's praises – I was from there. It was also civic pride: they were loathe to admit that New York's claim to being the coolest city on the planet was under threat from *London*, of all places. When Giuliani famously said 'Our city can kick your city's ass' he was speaking for every New Yorker. Whatever the reason, they weren't buying it.

I was momentarily at a loss. How do you go about convincing people that such-and-such a thing is currently in fashion or, as the Condé Nasties put it, 'on fire'? I cited various bits of empirical evidence – for instance, of all the French tourists flooding in to London, 45 per cent were under twenty-five – but they weren't exactly conclusive. When it comes to the precise whereabouts of the Zeitgeist at any particular moment, the issue turns on how much weight you attach to this kind of data; the facts alone can't speak for themselves. It was more a matter of gut feeling.

I hadn't expected them to take the question of whether London really was the in place to be so seriously. Surely, when a magazine like *Vanity Fair* announces that a particular place is hot, whether it's a restaurant, a neighbourhood or a city, it's not an example of straightforward news reporting. Rather, it's an act of anointment. Even if it's not true, it *becomes* true as soon as the article appears. This is an area in which the dissemination of information has such a profound impact on the story that old-fashioned notions of objectivity and impartiality don't apply – it's the journalistic equivalent of the Heisenberg Uncertainty Principle. Yet here they were, knitting their brows, conscientiously weighing the matter up.

I was suddenly struck by a parallel between a debate about whether something's in or out and a discussion about whether something's right or wrong. I remembered from studying philosophy at Oxford that one of the hallmarks of moral pronouncements, such as 'murder is wrong', is that they're 'unverifiable'; that is, no amount of factual evidence can decide the issue of whether they're valid or not. The same appeared to be true of pronouncements about the Zeitgeist.

Then I remembered something John Maynard Keynes had written about the circle surrounding the Cambridge moral philosopher G.E. Moore. According to Keynes, Moore succeeded in dominating his disciples not because he could outmanoeuvre them in argument but simply because he had the loudest voice. Moore carried the day because he appeared to be so much more confident than anyone else. In Keynes's view, the key to persuading someone of the rightness of your moral point of view lay in asserting it as *emphatically* as possible. There was nothing more to it than that. Once your opponents got a whiff of just how *unambivalent* you were, they'd come round to your way of thinking.

Could the same principle be applied to the discussion we were having about whether the Zeitgeist had taken up residence beside the Thames? I decided to put it to the test.

'London's hot right now,' I said, trying to inject a note of definitiveness into my voice. 'It's buzzing. You can almost feel the electricity as soon as you land at Heathrow.'

'Really?' asked David Harris.

'Absolutely,' I replied.

'You think this Swinging London Mark II thing is totally for real?' asked Aimée.

'No question,' I said, looking pointedly at each person in turn. 'Make no mistake: this phenomenon is very, very real.'

It seemed to be doing the trick. They were looking at each other and nodding: He may just be on to something here. They began to crumble:

David Harris [Hesitant]: Well, maybe.

Me: Honestly, we won't regret it.

Aimée Bell [Ambivalent]: If you're absolutely sure.

Me: 100 per cent positive.

George Hodgman: It sounds right to me.

A silence descended on the group. A consensus had emerged. London was on fire.

'Fuck it,' said Graydon. 'Let's do it.'

It was agreed that the March 1997 issue of the magazine would contain 25 pages devoted to London's second coming, consisting of a 5,000-word essay and a dozen or so photographic portraits of the city's most prominent movers and shakers. Thus the *Vanity Fair* 'Cool Britannia' issue was born. (From such small acorns, great forests are felled.) And who says philosophy has no practical application in the real world?

21

COOL BRITANNIA

At last, I had a proper role at the magazine. Cool Britannia, that vacuous catchphrase of the summer of 1996, had proved to be my saviour. Admittedly, I hadn't been put in charge of the whole project – that job had gone to Aimée Bell – and I hadn't been asked to write the story either – that honour went to Aimée's husband, David Kamp. Nevertheless, I was given an official title: I was Aimée's 'number two'. It was better than being stabbed in the heart with a sharp pencil.

'Try not to fuck this up,' warned Graydon.

I got an inkling of just what being Aimée's number two involved when we flew to London at the beginning of November to organise the photo shoots that would form the centrepiece of the special issue. Aimée and David flew business class, while I was stuck in economy. I wouldn't have minded so much if Aimée hadn't taken her newborn baby and the baby's nanny along with her. They, too, flew business class. When I complained about this Aimée explained that she didn't want to be separated from her baby girl for the duration of the flight and wherever the baby went, her nanny had to go too. Oh right, I thought. Heaven forbid that you should be stuck holding your own baby for five and a half hours! In fact, though, that wasn't the real reason. Aimée simply didn't want to offend the nanny by sticking her in economy. It was a brutal reminder of my place in the food chain: Aimée cared more about her nanny's

191

feelings than mine. ('Duh!' as Chris Lawrence would say.)[1]

Everyone in the *Vanity Fair* group – and more people flew out to join us over the course of the next few weeks – stayed at The Dorchester apart from me. I was relegated to my bedsit in Shepherd's Bush. The magazine also set up a temporary office in the hotel, an expensive perk. It involved renting a suite at a cost of hundreds of pounds a day and having the hotel kit it out with desks, phones, fax machines, etc. And bear in mind that we were there for almost a month. Still, Aimée had Graydon by the short and curlies. He wanted her in London overseeing the photo shoots so this was the price he – or, rather, Condé Nast – had to pay. I would conservatively estimate that the Dorchester's bill when *Vanity Fair* checked out was £100,000. Let Si get that.

There were eleven photo shoots in all, ranging from the Spice Girls to Tony Blair, and I was supposed to be in charge of all but two of them. I say 'supposed' because most of them unravelled at the last minute when one or more of the participants dropped out and Aimée had to take over. It soon became apparent why Graydon had wanted her in London: she was an organisational genius. I'd never encountered anyone as ruthlessly efficient as her before. No matter what it took, she got the job done. At one point, she needed to talk to me urgently about something but couldn't raise me on either my landline or my mobile. The reason for that was simple: I was in my flat in Shepherd's Bush sleeping off a hangover and I'd disconnected/switched off my phones. But Aimée wasn't so easily avoided. She hatched a plan to hire a minicab to go round to my bedsit and get the driver to stand on the doorstep and ring the bell until I answered the door. When I eventually emerged, blinking into the light, the driver would thrust a mobile into my hand with Aimée on the other line. Luckily, Henry Porter, *Vanity Fair's* London editor, managed to talk her out of this, but even so. Matt Tyrnauer had once described her, affection-

---

[1] Aimée Bell denies this. She swears her nanny flew economy. Evidently, I completely imagined this slight.

ately, as a 'stern Irish taskmistress' but that scarcely does her justice. She's the Terminator.

The shoot that gave me the biggest migraine was the one involving Damien Hirst and Marco Pierre White. It should have been a doddle because they were about to open a restaurant together – Quo Vadis on Dean Street – but it was a complete nightmare. In the end, Hirst would only agree to do it if his friend Keith Allen was included in the portrait and that was a deal-breaker for White. Aimée decided it was more important to get Damien Hirst in the issue than Marco Pierre White, so I agreed, at which point Hirst added a third person to the mix: Alex James, the bassist from Blur. Oh great, I thought. Who's next? Your Mum?[1]

Luckily, the group never got any larger than this and at 11 a.m. on 7 December I rendezvoused at the Groucho Club with the photographer and we went upstairs in search of 'The Boulevardiers', as the three subjects had been dubbed by Aimée. We found them in the billiard room nursing terrible hangovers. The bar of the Groucho hadn't opened yet so I was immediately dispatched to buy a bottle of vodka. It was the first of many that they would consume over the course of the day. As soon as they got stuck into the vodka Keith Allen and Damien Hirst started clamouring for cocaine so I called up a dealer I knew and had him deliver four grams. Would that be enough? Could I expense it? I had no idea.[2] Trying to get these three men to change into a succession of different outfits and pose for the photographer after the vodka had taken its toll was far from easy. I felt like an ineffectual supply teacher presiding over a class of naughty schoolchildren. I didn't help matters by dipping into the cocaine myself.

---

[1] In fact, Hirst did insist as a condition of doing the shoot that I agree to send a copy of the Cool Britannia issue to his Mum. When the issue eventually came out four months later I dutifully dispatched it to Mrs Hirst.

[2] I was too cowardly to raise this with Aimée so I ended up paying for the coke out of my own pocket.

I was quite shocked by just how unkempt 'The Boulevardiers' were. If I'd seen them wandering down the street in Manhattan, I'd have assumed they were homeless people. Even at 11 a.m. they were bleary-eyed and unshaven. Their skin, particularly Damien Hirst's, was dry and flaky and their lips were covered in cold sores. They smelt as if they'd spent the night on the floor of the Coach and Horses, rolling around in dog ends. Unlike celebrities in New York, who tended to be better groomed than ordinary mortals, they were significantly grubbier than your average Londoner. It was as if they were saying to the world: 'We're so famous we don't need to make an effort. We can still get laid even though we smell like goats!' It was probably true. A better name for the three of them would have been 'The Toxic Avengers'.

At the conclusion of the shoot, at around 6 p.m., I had to get them to sign release forms. It was a formality, really – the magazine could still publish their photographs without their written consent – but I knew Aimée would be annoyed with me if I didn't get their signatures and I didn't want to fall any further in her estimation. However, they point blank refused to do it. It was completely nonsensical: if they didn't want to appear in the magazine, why had they spent the previous six hours posing for a *Vanity Fair* photographer? But the moment they got an inkling of how badly I wanted them to do it they folded their arms and refused to sign. Judging from the smirks on their faces, they obviously thought they were being extremely funny.

I completely lost it. I went 'shouty crackers'.[1] How could they behave like such complete cunts after I'd spent the entire day bending over backwards to accommodate their every whim, including supplying them with drugs and alcohol? They may have thought their behaviour was cool but in fact it was no different from that of any coterie of pampered, over-indulged celebrities who made everyone's life difficult just to prove how important they were. It wasn't as if they were doing *Vanity Fair*

---

[1] This is Hugh Grant's term for a hissy fit.

a favour. Damien Hirst had actually asked if Keith Allen and Alex James could be in the picture. Presumably, it was because they both needed the publicity so what was the problem? Why were they making my job so difficult?

In the end, Hirst relented and motioned for me to hand him one of the release forms. He scrawled what I took to be his signature and then handed it back. I thanked him profusely and then read what he'd written: 'Suck my big dick'.

At that point I could have happily chopped him up with a meat cleaver and tossed the pieces into a vat of formaldehyde.

In retrospect, perhaps Damien Hirst's ambivalence about being in *Vanity Fair* was understandable. One of the reasons these icons of Swinging London Mark II made my life such hell was because they didn't want to give the impression that they valued the attentions of a glossy, New York magazine. Cool Britannia was a home-grown phenomenon and they didn't need the reinforcement of being written about in *Vanity Fair*, thank you very much. Still, I couldn't help feeling that they protested a little too much. There was something unmistakably provincial about it. To a large extent, New York has replaced Paris in Balzac's dictum that unless a thing has been noticed in Paris it hasn't really happened.

This goes back to the question of what the pronoun 'it' refers to in the phrase 'where it's at'. The Zeitgeist isn't a straight-forward, tangible entity, the features of which can be determined by a simple examination of the facts. Rather, various different people – journalists, fashion designers, financial analysts, etc – take a stab at defining it and a consensus eventually emerges. Among these trendspotters, the Condé Nasties occupy an exalted position; they speak with the voice of authority. If *Vanity Fair* announces that London is on fire, then, to all intents and purposes, it's on fire. On the other hand, if London's so-called cultural renaissance goes completely unnoticed by anyone outside the city, then the whole thing is a bit of a non-event. (If Liam Gallagher falls over in a pub and there are no journalists around to witness it, did it really happen?)

I don't think I'm exaggerating the importance of the New York media in this equation. Even Swinging London Mark I, a genuine historical event, didn't take root in the popular imagination until it was documented in a 1966 *Time* magazine cover story headlined 'London: The Swinging City'. Manhattan is the capital of the world in the sense that Rome was 2,000 years ago and when it comes to deciding who's in and who's out, what's the Next Big Thing and what's 'so ten minutes ago, dahling', the New York glossy posse are the sibyls that everyone listens to. They may not start trends, but they decide which ones will catch fire and which will fizzle out. In the global kingdom, New York is the home of international court society. As John Lennon said, 'If I'd lived in Roman times, I'd have lived in Rome. Where else? Today America is the Roman Empire and New York is Rome itself.'

Of course, this state of affairs is widely resented outside Manhattan and this often takes the form of non-New Yorkers claiming they don't give a fuck about what a bunch of 'fashion Nazis' in Manhattan think. Indeed, the whole Swinging London Mark II phenomenon, insofar as it was a genuine event, was sparked off by a rebellion along precisely these lines, with people like Damon Albarn, Jarvis Cocker and Alexander McQueen self-consciously rejecting American influences and re-asserting their *Britishness*. Throughout the eighties and nineties all the best popular music, not to mention the best movies and the best TV, was coming out of the States and by 1996 the youth of Britain had become thoroughly sick of this state of affairs. Cool Britannia was a cry of independence, a howl of protest against the all-enveloping cultural hegemony of the United States, yet, paradoxically, it didn't really mean anything – it hadn't really *happened* – until it was noticed by the American media.[1] That explains the schizophrenic attitude of people like Damien Hirst, Keith Allen and Alex James: they wanted to

---

[1] In addition to *Vanity Fair*, articles about Swinging London Mark II appeared in *Newsweek, Vogue* and *W*.

assert their indifference to the attentions of glossy, New York magazines, and yet they wanted to be photographed striking this insouciant pose in *Vanity Fair*. Like rebellious school-children, their protest wouldn't have counted unless it was registered by the authorities. Unfortunately, in this scenario I was cast as the toothless substitute teacher.

The experience of working on the Cool Britannia issue did have its compensations. The biggest of these was undoubtedly Sophie Dahl, and that's not a reference to her size. I met Sophie through Isabella Blow, an eccentric British fashion guru whom Aimée had hired as a 'consultant' on the issue.[1] Apparently, Issie had first stumbled across Sophie when she'd alighted from a taxi in Chelsea laden with shopping bags and Sophie, who happened to be walking past, asked her if she needed any help.

'I saw this great big blow-up doll with enormous bosoms,' recalled Issie. 'I just could not believe the size of her bosoms.'

Neither could I. From the first moment I set eyes on her I dubbed her 'Sophie Double D'. With her voluptuous, Coca-Cola bottle figure, her winsome smile and her long, blonde tresses she reminded me of a fifties screen goddess, though I quickly discovered that she was completely without guile. She was direct and unaffected in a way that most beautiful 19-year-olds just aren't. She didn't have that jaded crust that so many models have thanks to all the attention they get from lecherous, middle-aged men. She was like a little girl wandering around a wood full of bears carrying a honeycomb, seemingly unaware of just how tempting she was. Her innocence was all the more surprising given her background. Her mother, Tessa Dahl, a famous society beauty, had Sophie when she was twenty and didn't allow the presence of a mewling infant to cramp her style. By the time Sophie was thirteen she'd attended ten different schools and spent time in India living on an Ashram. Yet she

---

[1] A picture of Issie was subsequently used without her consent by a Soho dominatrix, the Mysterious Mistress Nina, to advertise her 'services'.

was so sweet and down to earth there was something almost wholesome about her.

Aimée and I decided to include Sophie in a portrait called 'The Hedonists' featuring the staff of *Loaded* and various 'It Girls'. This shoot, which took place immediately after the one featuring 'The Boulevardiers', proved almost as much of a headache thanks to the antics of James Brown, *Loaded*'s 31-year-old editor. At one point, he and Martin Deeson, a *Loaded* contributor, got into an argument and Brown ended up punching Deeson in the face. I noticed that Deeson didn't retaliate, in spite of being almost twice the size of Brown. Perhaps there were more humiliating places to work than *Vanity Fair* after all. At least Graydon had never taken a swing at me.

The photographer on the shoot was David LaChapelle and it took place in a studio in Harlesden where LaChapelle had constructed an elaborate set based on the milk bar in *A Clockwork Orange*. At one point, one of his assistants came over to me and said James Brown had an 'unusual request'.

'What?' I inquired.

'You better ask him.'

It turned out he wanted some cocaine. Fortunately, I had some left from the Damien Hirst shoot so I offered to give him some in the loo.

'Don't be daft,' he said in his thick, Yorkshire accent. 'Just rack 'em up right here.'

We were in the middle of the set accompanied by three members of *Loaded*'s staff, four It girls and a small army of technicians. Over to one side, viewing this exchange with mounting impatience, was LaChapelle himself, a well-known 'twelve-stepper'. The idea of taking coke in front of all these people was INSANE.

'I'm not going to do it here,' I told him. 'If you want some come to the loo.'

'I'm not going anywhere,' he said, folding his arms.

In a sense this was a ridiculous threat since I didn't want him to go anywhere. I wanted him to stay right where he was. But something told me that James – 'two fists' – Brown would almost certainly start misbehaving again unless I humoured him. The fact that he was acting like such a prima donna was a bit of a shock. Damien Hirst behaving like a rock star was one thing – he was the most celebrated young artist in the country – but James Brown? He was just a magazine editor, for Christ's sake. Everyone associated with Cool Britannia, it seemed, was on a massive ego trip. Could this be a side effect of all the cocaine they were taking?

Oh fuck it, I thought, and chopped out two lines.

There were audible intakes of breath all round: Were we really going to snarfle it up right there in front of everyone? I knew it was a reckless thing to do but it was at the end of a long day and I didn't have the stomach for another confrontation. Brown handed me a £5 note and together we bent down and inhaled the drug.

Flash!

What was that? I brought my head up just in time to see a grinning David LaChapelle emerge from behind his camera. The fucker had taken a photo. Jesus Christ! What a perfect illustration of Swinging London Mark II! I had a terrible premonition of opening a collection of LaChapelle's photographs in ten years time and seeing a picture called 'The Cokeheads'. The caption would read: 'Toby Young, a contributing editor of *Vanity Fair*, gives *Loaded*-editor James Brown a line of coke during a photo shoot for the *Vanity Fair* Cool Britannia issue. This photograph appeared in an exhibition in New York in January, 1997. Toby Young was fired shortly afterwards. James Brown is now the editor of *Vanity Fair*.'

22

A COKE STROKE

I had managed to avoid the devil's dandruff in New York but it hadn't taken me long to fall into bad habits in London. No wonder Britannia had suddenly become Cool: the whole country was engulfed in a blizzard of white powder.[1] There was even a new bit of cockney rhyming slang to describe the drug: 'Gianluca', a reference (in name only) to the Chelsea footballer Gianluca Vialli (Gianluca Vialli = Charlie).[2] In pubs and bars across the city it took longer to get into the loos than it did to get a drink. Old Compton Street at 6 a.m. on a Saturday morning was busier than Madison Avenue during rush hour. It seemed the 'tremendous amount of energy' Ian Schrager had detected in the capital was chemically induced. London wasn't merely swinging; it was tapping its foot and grinding its teeth as well.

The high point of my Cool Britannia experience occurred in the wee small hours of the morning on Christmas Day in an illegal, all-night drinking club on Great Windmill Street known

---

[1] This isn't as much of an exaggeration as it sounds. In May, 2001 *The Face* published a survey of 1,000 young adults that showed that almost 50 per cent of 16 to 25-year-olds in Britain had tried cocaine. In the south east, it was as high as 86 per cent.

[2] One of the photo shoots I tried to set up was going to consist of Gianluca Vialli, Gianfranco Zola, Roberto Di Matteo and Ruud Gullit posing with Nick Hornby, Frank Skinner and David Baddiel. Unfortunately, it didn't come off.

as the Pink Panther. During the day it was an Italian pizzeria called Café Bar Sicilia, but after midnight it became the Pink Panther – or, as it was known to my friends in the City, 'CBS Asset Management'. It was run by a legendary underworld gangster called Jan who had once been known as 'Soho's clip joint King' and toured his empire in a Rolls Royce Silver Shadow. In recent years, however, he'd fallen on hard times and the Pink Panther was the last remaining jewel in his crown. But what a jewel it was! It had a crack den in the basement, an all-night bar on the ground floor and a gambling den on the floor above. It was a one-stop shop for vice. It had been a favourite haunt of mine for years before I moved to New York and now here I was again, right back at my old table.

At around 3 a.m. a girl sat down opposite me and introduced herself as Lena. She was the kind of girl you dream about bumping into after a heavy, all-night drinking session: extremely pretty, about 19 years old and, best of all, very, very lonely. She had been packed off to London by her Serbian parents a few months earlier and was living in a hostel in Balham. She had a job in a bar in Soho and had come to the club at the end of her shift. I asked her what she was intending to do on Christmas Day and she said she was going to spend it in the hostel, huddled in front of a black-and-white television set with the other waifs and strays. I told her she couldn't possibly do that. Why not come back to my place instead? I couldn't take her to lunch with my family, but she could stay in my nice, warm flat watching my big, *colour* television. She wavered, evidently a little worried about going home with a complete stranger, so I told her not every Englishman she met was a scoundrel. Some of us were gentlemen.

She ended up coming home with me where, needless to say, I had my wicked way with her. Nevertheless, the following day I made good on my promise, cooking her breakfast and setting her up in front of the telly with the remote control in one hand and a box of chocolates in the other. She was still there when I came home at about 10 p.m. I felt incredibly guilty that she'd spent Christmas Day on her own – I should have taken her to lunch with my family, damn it! – but she didn't seem to mind. On the contrary, she seemed touched that I'd let her stay in the flat.

She went home on Boxing Day and I didn't speak to her again until New Year's Day. Again, it was about 3 a.m. and I'd come home empty-handed after a night of carousing. Suddenly it occurred to me to call Lena. She was in, but she said she couldn't possibly come round because (a) she was in bed in her pyjamas, (b) it was below freezing outside and (c) she didn't have any money. I told her not to be silly. If she gave me her address I'd send a mini-cab round to collect her and pay for it when it dropped her off. She didn't even need to worry about getting dressed. After all, when she got here we'd be going straight to bed.

She agreed – eventually – and after arranging for a cab to pick her up I sat down on my sofa to wait for the doorbell to ring. I poured myself another Scotch and checked the clock on the video recorder. It was 3.23 a.m.

After what seemed like a few seconds I woke with a start. I looked at the clock: 11.28 a.m. Oh no! Then I noticed the message light blinking on my answering machine. With enormous trepidation I pressed 'Play'.

'Toby, this is Lena. Where are you? I'm in the phonebox on the corner of your street. I just tried your doorbell and there was no answer.'

Beep.

'Toby, what's going on? The taxi driver says I owe him £30 and he won't leave until I pay him. Please, you have to come and help me.'

Beep.

'The taxi driver has gone. I asked him to take me home but he said no. I begged him but he said he would only take me if I had sex with him. I'm now in the phonebox in my pyjamas and it's very cold. I am frightened, Toby. What am I going to do?'

Beep.

'Toby . . . sniff . . . I hate you . . . sniff . . . I hate all English men . . . sniff . . . you are all bastards . . . sniff . . . never call me again.'

Click. Dial-tone.

Oh. My. God.

I called her immediately but a friend of hers answered and said she was too ill to come to the phone. In the background I could hear someone coughing. How on earth had she got home? Had she walked? As far as I knew, she didn't even have any shoes on. I was mortified. How could I have done such a terrible thing? I had persuaded this girl to trust me and as a result she'd been stranded in Shepherd's Bush in her pyjamas at 4 a.m. with no money and no means of getting home. So much for being an English gentleman. I was the devil!

As it turned out, divine retribution was only moments away. After I'd removed my head from my hands I got a Diet Coke out of the fridge and gulped it down straight out of the can. Strangely, I could only taste it with the right-hand side of my tongue, as if the left-hand side had lost all sensation. Had I burnt my tongue the night before? I didn't remember having done so but that was no guarantee that I hadn't.

I decided to examine my tongue in the bathroom mirror but as soon as I saw my reflection I realised that there was something slightly odd about my whole face. I looked like . . . I couldn't . . . I did! I looked like Sylvester Stallone! The left-hand side of my face was completely immobile. I tried smiling but only the right-hand side of my mouth went up; I tried blinking and, sure enough, only my right eye moved. What the fuck was going on? This was no ordinary case of 'showbiz flu'. Half my fucking face was paralysed!

My first thought was that I'd had a 'coke stroke'. Among regular cocaine users this is high on the list of fears, right up there with destroying the wall between your nasal passages. According to my extremely sketchy understanding of these matters, a coke stroke is a mini-stroke induced by excessive use of nose candy. I tried lifting my arms up and, while I couldn't be sure, my left arm did feel slightly floppy. My left leg, too, felt odd. *Oh shit!* There was no doubt about it. I'd had a coke stroke.

The first person I called was my sister Sophie who is a nurse. She told me she thought it was unlikely that I'd had a mini-stroke – there were a number of other, more likely explanations for the symptoms I was presenting – but if I was really worried I should take myself down to the nearest Accident and Emergency department and get a doctor to examine me.

I jumped in my car and drove to the local hospital where I spent one of the most miserable afternoons of my life. As I waited for a doctor to see me, I was convinced I'd done myself irreparable harm, a direct consequence of all the alcohol and cocaine I'd taken during the eight weeks I'd spent in Swinging London Mark II. For the past ten years I had woken up each Monday morning and stared at my face in the mirror, amazed that the excesses of the previous weekend hadn't taken a greater toll. I often told myself, only half jokingly, that there must be a portrait of me in an attic somewhere in which the devastating effects of my drug and alcohol abuse were all too apparent. Well, my dissolute lifestyle had finally caught up with me. I'd turned into that portrait. I was condemned to spend the rest of my life looking like Sylvester Stallone.

Aaaaaaaaaaaaaargh!!!

'Bell's Palsy,' announced the doctor when I finally got to see him. 'It's an inflammation of the seventh cranial nerve. It normally clears up within a fortnight and never recurs. I shouldn't worry about it if I were you. In 95 per cent of cases it's no more serious than a head cold.'

This news should have made me happy but after wallowing in self-pity for the previous four hours I felt slightly disap-pointed. *No more serious than a head cold?* Half my face was paralysed, for fuck's sake. He'd only examined me for a grand total of a minute. Was he sure? What about my floppy arm? Was that due to Bell's Palsy as well?

'In your imagination,' he said, matter of factly.

What about cocaine? Was my condition related to excessive use of Bolivian marching powder?

'Why?' he replied. 'Have you got any?'

Typical, I thought. In Cool Britannia even the doctors are up to their noses in white powder.

Naturally, I wasn't satisfied with this diagnosis and called my sister to find out how I could get a second opinion. Did she know a good neurologist? Could she arrange for an MRI scan within the next twenty-four hours? What if I'd had a coke stroke and this doctor simply hadn't spotted it?

'You don't need a second opinion,' she laughed. 'It's obviously Bell's Palsy.'

Nevertheless, she promised to come and see me that night and when I got home I called Lena again and managed to persuade her to come round so my sister could take a look at her as well. By the time my sister arrived, at about 9 p.m., Lena was snuggled up in my bed with a cup of Lemsip, a state of affairs that slightly undermined my credibility as a patient. Indeed, what little sympathy my sister had for me completely evaporated when Lena told her what had happened the previous night.

'Frankly, you deserve to have had a coke stroke,' she said, after taking Lena's temperature.

One of the few inconvenient things about Bell's Palsy is that it's sensible not to fly until it's completely cleared up so I had to postpone my return to New York. This in turn led to a dramatic phone call to Aimée Bell in which I explained that I'd be out of the office for the foreseeable future because half my face was paralysed.

'You're kidding?' she said. 'Is that, like, a side-effect of cocaine?'

Oh Christ, I thought. She's obviously heard about the James Brown incident.

Later that day, Graydon called to find out if I was okay.

'Are you sure it's nothing serious?' he asked. 'I don't mean to belittle your doctors over there, but your health service isn't exactly the best in the world. Why don't you come back here and get yourself thoroughly checked out at a proper hospital?'

'I don't have any health insurance,' I said.

'Don't worry about that. I'll take care of it.'

Suddenly, I was filled with remorse. What had I done to deserve such kindness from Graydon? Of course, I couldn't take him up on this offer, not when it was just for the purposes of giving me peace of mind. To do so would have placed me too far in his debt. But it was very reassuring to know that in the event of suffering from some more serious illness he'd be there for me. I had no doubt that Graydon, a man in his late forties who still smoked twenty cigarettes a day, had a network of medical contacts in place ready to deal with any emergency. How many other bosses would put that network at the disposal of their employees, particularly one as useless as me? I felt wretched that I'd done so little – nothing, in fact – to justify his faith in me.

23

WHAT THEY DON'T TEACH YOU AT THE ELEPHANT & CASTLE JOURNALISM SCHOOL

When I returned to *Vanity Fair*'s offices in New York I was immediately summoned to the headmaster's office. I knew it: he *had* heard about the James Brown incident. I steeled myself for being 'reamed out'. What could I say in my defence? That we just pretended to be snorting cocaine as a joke? He would never buy that. Ah well. At least I'd have an excuse to bring up the question of whether I could expense it. In total, I spent £240 on the wretched stuff!

However, as soon as I saw his face I realized that this wasn't what he wanted to see me about at all. He was chuckling to himself and staring at me as if I was some funny-looking creature in a zoo – a duckbilled platypus, perhaps.

'Toby,' he said, 'you have a brown thumb.'

'What's that?' I asked.

Chuckle, chuckle.

'It's the opposite of a green thumb,' he explained. 'Everything you touch turns to shit.'

Apparently, he'd had a long chat with Aimée Bell and she'd told him that every single photo shoot I had been involved with had come unstuck at the last moment. I thought about this for a second and realised it was true. For one reason or another,

all nine of them had fallen apart and only Aimée's timely inter-
vention had saved the day. The Cool Britannia issue had been
my last chance to prove myself and I'd completely blown it.

'I don't think it's really working out,' said Graydon.

Oh, oh, I thought. Here it comes. I knew from experience that
this was code for 'you're a complete waste of space'. In public,
when the Condé Nasties are asked what happened to some former
employee they always say 'it didn't work out'. In private, they're
a little more blunt. For instance, I once asked Aimée what had
happened to Ann Harrington, Elizabeth Saltzman's predecessor.
'Her?' she replied. 'We threw her out the window.'

'Don't worry,' continued Graydon. 'I'm not going to fire you.
I'll renew your contract and keep you on the masthead, but
maybe you should think about doing something else.'

I nodded sadly. I couldn't fault his treatment of me. All things
considered, he had been remarkably patient and now that he'd
finally reached the end of his tether he was giving me what
sounded like an indefinite notice period. I got the sense that in
spite of the fact that I'd let him down in every conceivable way
he still liked me. I certainly still liked him.

I can't say I was surprised. In the year and a half that I'd spent
at *Vanity Fair* it had become increasingly clear that I was totally
unsuited to work at a glossy, New York magazine. Navigating
the shark-infested waters of Condé Nast required sonar equip-
ment that I simply didn't possess. As a contributing editor, I hoped
to overcome this disadvantage by contributing rather than editing,
but my efforts to persuade Graydon to use me as a writer had
come to nothing. Indeed, by January 1997 I'd been paid $85,000
and contributed no more than 3,000 words, making me the
highest-paid writer in the history of the magazine. On a dollar
per word basis I was paid more than Dominick Dunne who was
rumoured to be on a contract worth half a million a year. When
it came to being 'let go', it wasn't a question of if but when.

So why didn't it work out? Well, first of all there were my
sophomoric hi-jinks. Being laddish, even if it was ironic, just

wasn't a suitable way to behave at a magazine where hetero-sexual males were an endangered species. Antics I considered hilariously funny were seen as boorish and gauche by my colleagues. I remember one occasion on which I upset an Asian-American staffer by calling up the Shanghai Tang, David Tang's ultra-chic designer clothing store on Madison Avenue, and ordering Chinese food: 'Is that the Shanghai Tang? Can I get one crispy Peking duck, one egg fried rice . . .' If *Vanity Fair* was an opera company, I was the guy wandering around backstage asking the men why they were wearing tights and trying to look up the girls' skirts. For me, the fashion world was primarily an excuse for making up puerile jokes: 'Have you heard the one about Victoria's Secret? I could tell you but I'd have to kill you.'

I often felt like a character in a sitcom, except there was no audience and no laugh track. Time and again, I'd crack some joke that would fall completely flat. Take the following exchange that took place in the fashion department after Pippi had just received a phone call:

Pippi [to Elizabeth]: It's Alec Baldwin's people. They want to know if you can be his date at the Costume Institute Ball next week.

Me: Alec Baldwin's *people*? What is it, a conference call?

Pippi: Pardon?

I'd imagined that *Vanity Fair* would be peopled by the modern day equivalents of Dorothy Parker, Robert Benchley and Edmund Wilson, all of whom had worked for the magazine in the past. I naively thought that my irreverent attitude would delight my colleagues and that, after work, they'd invite me to their favourite speakeasies where we'd trade one-liners between sips of martinis. In fact, they just thought of me as a misfit, someone who had no place in a professional, office environment.

It's not that the magazine's staff are stupid. On the contrary, they're all pretty smart. It's just that they're depressingly well-adjusted. The writers who fill the magazine's pages aren't frus-trated novelists and playwrights who think of themselves as slumming it *en route* to higher things; they regard themselves as extremely successful journalists at the top of their game. Even the fact-checkers, who are generally more intelligent and better educated than their superiors, are surprisingly content. As I observed the magazine's employees day-to-day, smiling benignly as they went about their business, I often wondered how it was that a group of such apparently sophisticated people were able to devote so much energy to producing an upscale supermarket tabloid. How did they preserve their sanity while thinking up cover lines like 'Jemima and Imran: The High-Stakes Marriage of Pakistan's Camelot Couple'? Were they all on Prozac?[1]

Of course, there are exceptions to this rule. The *Vanity Fair* contributing editors include many fine writers for whom nominating someone to the magazine's 'Hall of Fame' – a monthly tribute to some do-gooder – is not the pinnacle of their careers. In particular, there are the two front-of-the-book columnists: James Wolcott and Christopher Hitchens. They're like the two smartest kids in school, with Jim lobbing wisecracks from the back row and Hitch leading a campaign to allow smoking in the sixth form common room. I remember bumping into Hitch once in the corridor outside my office. He looked slightly the worse for wear, as if he'd just rolled out of bed, so I asked him how he was. 'It's too early to tell,' he replied. Needless to say, it was the middle of the afternoon.

Hitch was the only *Vanity Fair* writer who I ended up getting pissed with at the bar of Elaine's, and it's worth bearing in mind that he's a Brit. The old-fashioned New York journalist, a harum-scarum roustabout whose status is 'somewhere between a whore and a bartender',[2] has been replaced by a clean and sober careerist with a summer house in the Hamptons. If he has any qualms about accepting his place in the Manhattan food chain it's not because he questions its legitimacy; it's

---

[1] The answer is probably yes.
[2] This is part of a quote attributed to Sherman Reilly Duffy by Ben Hecht. The quote in full is: 'Socially, a journalist fits in somewhere between a whore

because he has 'a problem with authority', nothing a quick trip to a therapist won't fix. All those qualities I'd associated with 'Noo Yawk' newspapermen – rebelliousness, independence of mind, sympathy for the underdog – have been replaced by their exact opposites. Whatever romance once attached itself to the profession has long since vanished. In New York, the people who once thought of themselves as 'us' have become 'them'.

The upshot was that I felt increasingly alienated. At times, it seemed as if Chris Lawrence and I were the only people at *Vanity Fair* who felt remotely superior to the guff we were producing every day. Was this really why we'd slogged our way through the Great Books at university? So we could devote our lives to making celebrities look good? One of our running jokes was to imagine what a glossy magazine that genuinely reported on the lifestyles of the rich and famous would be like. In between articles on 'eye jobs' and 'testicle tucks' would be photographs of zonked-out movie stars tripping over empty bottles of Zoloft as they chased their children's friends around their swimming pools. We called this imaginary magazine *Vanishing Hair*.

Of course, working for Condé Nast did have its compensations. The longer I spent at *Vanity Fair*, the more Graydon's first room analogy made sense. At times, it really did feel like being in a VIP section. I remember the joy that Chris Lawrence and I felt on discovering that one of the contributing editors we occasionally saw around the office had written the screenplay of *GoldenEye*.[1] His name was Bruce Feirstein and he was just about the most unlikely person to have been involved with a James Bond film I'd ever set eyes on. Generally speaking, the Jews at Condé Nast could be divided into two categories: those that aped the clothes and manners of the East Coast Wasp Establishment and those who remained stubbornly unassimilated. Bruce Feirstein was firmly in the latter camp. He looked

---

and a bartender but spiritually he stands beside Galileo. He knows the world is round.' *A Child of the Century* (New York: Simon & Schuster, 1954).

[1] We hadn't seen *GoldenEye* at this point.

like Woody Allen. He gave the impression that his mother had written him notes as a schoolboy to get him off games.

However, of all the Hollywood *machers* that came into the office Bruce was the only one who gave Chris and me the time of day. By the time we'd screwed up the courage to introduce ourselves he was writing *Tomorrow Never Dies* and he told us a story about one of the Bond girls in that movie. He'd been asked by Barbara Broccoli, one of the producers, to take the actress out for dinner in Los Angeles. She was lonely and didn't know anyone and Broccoli thought Bruce might like her – she was a 21-year-old model after all. Bruce said that at first he found her quite hard work but towards the end of the evening her fresh-faced innocence had completely won him over. As he was dropping her off back at her hotel he was suddenly overcome by a feeling of protectiveness and decided to warn her against all the sexual predators on the celebrity circuit.

'They may seem sweet and charming,' he said, 'but to them you're just fresh meat. They'll eat you alive.'

'That's so funny,' she squealed. 'That's exactly what Dennis Rodman said!'

The Chicago Bull and author of *Bad As I Wanna Be* had already had her for lunch.

Occasionally, *Vanity Fair* did live up to my expectations. On certain days, working there felt like living in a production of *The Women*, the brilliant satire of New York society written by Clare Boothe Luce, a former managing editor of the magazine. For instance, on one occasion I overheard the following exchange between two women scanning the morning papers in *Vanity Fair*'s publicity department:

First woman: Some plane went down over the Atlantic. 256 people killed.

Second woman: Anyone on it?

First woman: Nah.

Another memorable scene unfolded when Darryl Brantley, the assistant in the party planning department, mistakenly included an unflattering item about Graydon in 'the gossip pack', a digest of the day's gossip that was distributed to every member of staff first thing in the morning. When Graydon found out he ordered Darryl to retrieve every single gossip pack, delete the offending item, and redistribute them, with the result that everyone immediately headed down to the lobby to buy the rag that had printed the story in the first place.

At bottom, the reason things didn't work out for me at *Vanity Fair* is because I never took the magazine or the world it operated in very seriously. I couldn't help but regard Condé Nast as a fundamentally comic institution and I didn't have the wherewithal to conceal this from my colleagues. It wasn't just the subject matter of the magazines that struck me as absurd – will argyle socks be the Next Big Thing? – but the absolute certainty with which these predictions were made. It was as if the glossy posse were a kind of priesthood, consulting the Delphic Oracle and announcing their findings to the world. What enabled them to make these pronouncements? How did they *know* what would be in and out next season? In their eyes, it was their sensitivity to changing fashions, their Zeitgeist radar, that qualified them to work for Condé Nast and I just didn't have this sixth sense. Indeed, not only did I lack it, I couldn't bring myself to believe that anybody really had it. The idea that changes in fashion were dictated by some invisible hand just struck me as mumbo jumbo, on a par with the belief in primitive societies that all change has a divine origin. In the temple of the Zeitgeist, I was a heretic.

Before I started working for *Vanity Fair* my view of the glossy posse was that, far from tracking the Zeitgeist and honestly reporting their conclusions, they were just doing the bidding of various commercial interests. For instance, I thought that when Anna Wintour proclaimed that fur was back in fashion she wasn't announcing her conclusions after a long session with her crystal ball, she was simply saying what furriers wanted to hear, primarily so they would advertise in *Vogue*. If people like Wintour occasionally anticipated a trend correctly it was only because their predictions carried so much weight they ended up becoming self-fulfilling prophecies. Of course, I recognized that the Condé Nasties had to *pretend* there was more to it than this. If *Vogue*'s readers didn't believe that Wintour was attuned to the Zeitgeist, if they thought she was simply in cahoots with the fashion industry to put one over on them, her words wouldn't have any authority. It's only because Condé Nast's trendspotters are believed to have their fingers on the pulse that Condé Nast magazines are read by over seventy-five million Americans each month. But I assumed that behind closed doors, in the privacy of their corner offices, the glossy posse would acknowledge that it was all a huge con trick. I thought that the game played on Madison Avenue was a variant of the one played further south in Manhattan, the one known as 'Wall Street bilks Main Street'.

However, after a few months at 350 it became apparent that I was mistaken about this. I had credited the Condé Nasties with far too much self-awareness – they aren't nearly as cynical as that. Admittedly, they occasionally say what advertisers want to hear, they even accept bribes in the form of luxury goods, but they still think of themselves as spotting trends rather than creating them. They're a little like a corrupt priesthood: the fact that they abuse their authority doesn't mean they've lost their faith. On the contrary, they believe in the crap they're peddling. As far as they're concerned, they work in the national weather centre of trend forecasting and their job is to predict what's just over the horizon. Needless to say, this process isn't nearly as straightforward or objective as they imagine it to be. Objectively speaking, trends are created by people behaving in a particular way, but in order for that to happen they must think of themselves as following or anticipating trends that already exist. The real skill of the Condé Nasties is their ability to persuade people by a variety of ingenious means that their view of what's in and what's out is based on something real; that it is, in some sense, true. Ultimately, the reason they're able to pull this off is because they're convinced of it them-selves. They're true believers. According to Tina Brown, 'Si's navel is plugged into the *Zeitgeist*.' They're under the impres-sion that the vicissitudes of fashion have a mysterious, almost supernatural source. They honestly imagine that changes in popular taste occur in response to the tune played by some unseen piper.

The belief in this invisible hand – whether it's called 'the Zeitgeist', 'the collective unconscious' or 'the popular will' – constitutes the glossy posse's religion. It accounts for why they're so mesmerised by whatever's in fashion. I don't just mean 'fashion' in the narrow sense, though God knows they wouldn't be seen dead in last season's outfit, I mean whatever's 'very now' across the board, from the latest gadgets to the newest clubs. By wearing the hippest styles, humming the latest tunes and eating at the hottest restaurants, they believe they're staying in touch with something significant and profound. In their eyes, the 'it' in the expression 'where it's at' refers to a mysterious, intangible entity that has many of the same prop-erties as a divine being. It's invisible and yet it's everywhere; it's in the world and yet it's not quite of it. Above all, it seems to dictate that they behave in one way and not another. In short, it's a distant echo of God's will. Doing the bidding of the Zeitgeist confers status on them in the same way that being a member of the Elect confers status within certain Christian sects; to be in fashion is to be in a state of Grace. Strange as it may sound, lurking within the Condé Nast buzz factory is something that closely resembles the God of Judaeo-Christian theology.

Above all else, it was this religion I couldn't take seriously. To a greater or lesser extent, it's a faith that all New Yorkers share. As V. S. Pritchett wrote, 'There is no place where newness is so continuously pursued.' It's an extreme form of the materialism Tocqueville warned against in *Democracy in America*, an obses-sion with bodily pleasures at the expense of the immortal soul, except instead of being the opposite of Christianity it contains traces of the belief system it has replaced.[1] The men and women who work at Condé Nast are the High Priests of this cult and it was obvious to them that I was a non-believer. It was one thing to sneer at the daily absurdities of life at 350 – that was bad enough – but to be openly contemptuous of the beliefs on which the whole edifice was predicated . . . that was too much! They might not be able to burn me at the stake, but they wasted no time in throwing me out the window.

---

[1] 'Democracy favours the taste for material enjoyments. This taste, if it becomes excessive, soon disposes men to believe that all is nothing but matter; and materialism in its turn serves to carry them toward these enjoyments with an insane ardour. Such is the fatal circle into which democratic nations are propelled.' Alexis de Tocqueville, *Democracy in America*, eds Harvey C. Mansfield and Delba Winthrop (Chicago: University of Chicago Press, 2000) p. 519.

24

MIDGET JONES'S DIARY

My prospects in the dating arena followed a similar trajectory to my career. When I first arrived in New York I thought the world was my oyster – at least, it would be after I'd eaten a dozen or two. By all accounts I'd entered a single man's paradise. I'd heard that an unmarried woman in her thirties in Manhattan is more likely to get struck by lightning than find a husband. With all those sad singletons around, how hard could it be to get laid?

The answer, I discovered, was very hard indeed.

When New York women complain that there's a shortage of men in the city what they mean is there's a shortage of tall, unattached, rich men who still have their own hair. As a short, bald, William Hague look-a-like with no visible means of support, I wasn't considered much of a catch. My efforts to seduce Park Avenue Princesses by styling myself 'the Honourable Toby Young' had come to nothing and even normal women – 'civilians' in Condé Nast parlance – seemed unimpressed by my *Vanity Fair* credentials. Contrary to the impression I had before setting out for the land of opportunity, New York women do not go home with men they meet in bars, at least not ones that look like me.

Part of the problem was that, to the jaded ears of Manhattan's battle-weary female population, the tongue-in-cheek chat-up lines I'd perfected in London's clubs and pubs sounded like so much sexist crap. (Me: 'My eyes were wandering in this direction and I thought I'd come and pick them up!' Her: 'Fuck off.') I felt like Austin Powers, the snaggle-toothed secret agent who was frozen in the Swinging Sixties and brought back to life in a more abstemious era. It quickly became apparent that the only way I was going to stand any sort of a chance with American women was if I asked them out on a series of dates.

I'd spent a year and a half in Manhattan at this point and still hadn't mastered the intricacies of the American courtship ritual. To tell the truth I wasn't entirely sure what a date was. If two men and two women went out to dinner, was that just a group of friends getting together or a 'double date'? If you asked a woman out for a drink, did that count as a date, or was it a 'non-date date'?

As a general rule, if the woman called me up and cancelled a few minutes beforehand I could be pretty sure that what we were about to do together would have constituted a date. I'd heard the most ridiculous array of excuses in the short time that I'd been active on the singles scene. On one occasion a woman had told me she couldn't leave her flat because her newly acquired kitten had 'abandonment issues'.

An additional problem in New York media circles is that so many people are writing books about dating you can never be sure that the person you're with hasn't agreed to go out with you purely for research purposes. For instance, a girl I know called Tammy was invited out for a drink by someone called Lawrence Larose. Six months later he and another writer published a book that was supposed to be a reply to *The Rules* called *The Code: Time-Tested Secrets For Getting What You Want From Women Without Marrying Them*. One piece of advice offered to would-be swordsmen, Tammy discovered, was to ask a woman out on a 'non-date drinks date' to assess whether it was worth inviting her out properly.

Needless to say, Tammy never heard from him again.

On the few occasions that I'd managed to persuade New York women to go out on a date with me I'd found the whole experience extremely uncomfortable. The trouble is, being British, I'm very easily embarrassed. There's something far too direct about going out to dinner with someone solely with a view to assessing their suitability as a sexual partner. Up until this point, my *modus operandi* had been to sneak up on women and, when they weren't looking, rugby tackle them into bed. American women, I soon learnt, prefer a more upfront approach. I always marvelled at how unselfconscious they were about sizing me up. They invariably had a checklist of questions that they shamelessly ran through over the course of the evening. What did I do for a living? What part of town was my apartment in? What kind of car did I drive? It was less like a romantic encounter than an extremely tough job interview. By the time the check arrived I was surprised they hadn't asked for a urine sample.

My efforts to meet these executive recruitment officers in less formal circumstances usually came to nothing. For instance, on one occasion I decided to ask a girl I liked in the *Vanity Fair* Research Department to join me and three other couples for dinner, thereby taking some of the pressure off. However, I knew she'd only say yes if the restaurant I invited her to was on fire – she was a Condé Nasty, after all – so I decided to book a table at Balthazar, a 'hot boîte' that had just opened on Spring Street. The only way to get a reservation was to call a secret number that its owner, Keith McNally, had given to a few select people and, after a certain amount of grovelling, I managed to persuade Elizabeth Saltzman to give it to me. When a man answered the phone I assumed my most confident air and asked if I could book a table for eight the following Friday.

'How did you get this number?' he demanded.

'Keith gave it to me,' I replied.

'This is Keith speaking,' he said. 'Who is this?'

That threw me. I hadn't expected the owner to answer the phone. I blurted out my own name which clearly meant nothing to him.

'We don't do tables for eight,' he told me. 'Our maximum is six.'

'Can I book a table for six then?' I asked.

'No,' he snapped.

'Well, what's the maximum I can get?'

'I dunno,' he replied. 'One?'

I almost took it just to get a look at the place.

Even when I'd managed to come through the first date experience relatively unscathed, I was still a long way from the finish line. A quick kiss on the doorstep was about the most I could hope for. As a rule of thumb, I didn't expect to get beyond the threshold until the third date and, even then, it was unlikely to be for anything more exciting than a quick snog on the sofa. It was as if they were still following the pattern they'd established in High School, even though some of these women were well into their thirties. In Manhattan, once you've embarked on the dating rat run there are no short-cuts to getting the cheese.

This was in stark contrast to the wisecracking dames of the Roaring Twenties. In the 'Introduction' to *The Collected Dorothy Parker*, Brendan Gill writes: 'The young women who set the pace were called sophisticated, though few of them were; their shocking motto was "Anything Goes", and they meant it.' The era was summed up by the poet Edna St Vincent Millay: 'We were very young, we were very merry, /We went back and forth all night on the ferry.'

The only success I'd had at this point was with the Red Hot Chilli Pepper. After our aborted date she'd called the following day and invited me to lunch.

'Whereabouts?' I asked, expecting her to name some over-priced, uptown bistro.

'My place, of course,' she replied.

Evidently, she was feeling a little contrite after her behaviour the previous night. It was the middle of the day and I'd been planning to spend the afternoon at the gym, but the thought

220

of her $20,000 tits proved irresistible. I was soon snaking my way uptown on the subway.

Her apartment was in a fairly seedy-looking building on the Upper West Side but whatever misgivings I had about having schlepped all the way up there were soon cast aside when she answered the door. She was wearing nothing but a white towel and it was no bigger than a dishcloth. Without saying a word, she took me by the hand and led me directly to her bedroom. She was obviously feeling *really* contrite! Okay, I thought. This time it's going to happen.

When we got there she stood in front of her bed and, like a proud artist unveiling her latest creation, whisked the towel aside.

'You like?' she asked.

She was in her late thirties but she had the body of an 18-year-old glamour model. She looked like a perfectly proportioned woman of average height who'd been shrunk by 33 per cent apart from her breasts. They'd been enlarged – *literally*. Yet this was no ordinary boob job. The surgeon who'd created them was the Michelangelo of Miami Beach. They looked 100 per cent natural, like the breasts of a well-endowed Tahitian princess. Not even porn stars had tits this good. Lowering my eyes to take in the rest of her magnificent body I finally discovered what a Brazilian bikini line looked like: there, nestling six inches beneath her belly button, was a small patch of pubic hair no bigger than a caterpillar.

'Come here, Toe'ee,' she said, stretching out her hands. 'I'm feeling so horny.'

As you might expect from a twenty-year veteran of bacchanalian debauches on both sides of the Atlantic, the Red Hot Chilli Pepper had some unusual requests once we got between the sheets.

'Stick out your tongue,' she said as I was making love to her. For some reason, _____ couldn't reach orgasm unless she could see my tongue. As events took their course, and I momentarily forgot myself, she repeated this demand with more and more urgency: 'Stick out your tongue, Toe'ee. *Stick out your tongue!*'

Before long, I was on the home straight, pounding away for all I was worth.

'Oh, Toe'ee,' she cried, apparently in the throes of ecstasy. 'Now you're speakin' my language. NOW YOU'RE SPEAKIN' MY LANGUAGE!'

I called the Red Hot Chilli Pepper every day for a week after this but, alas, she refused to go out with me again. I may have been able to speak her language, but I was evidently far from fluent. Perhaps I should have offered to 'lend' her another $250.

After eighteen months on the New York singles scene, and with only one notch on my bedpost, I began to think that being struck by lightning might actually be preferable to going out on another date. I complained to Candace Bushnell about this, pointing out that the reality of single life in Manhattan fell far short of the permissive world she depicted in *Sex and the City*. Where were the happy-go-lucky good time girls that appeared in her column?

'You know what?' she said. 'You should try dating models. They're much easier than you might think.'

It had to be worth a try.

The only models I knew were the ones I'd met in the course of working on the *Vanity Fair* Cool Britannia issue. One of the shoots I'd been in charge of, 'The Blueblood Beauties', had involved photographing four British supermodels at Blenheim Palace. After the shoot they were supposed to be travelling back to London in a minibus but I offered them a lift in the Jag I'd hired courtesy of *Vanity Fair* and they all leapt in the back. For the next ninety minutes I found myself cooped up with Iris Palmer, Honor Fraser, Jodie Kidd and Jasmine Guinness. It doesn't get any better than this, I thought, as we sped towards London on the M40. For one terrible moment I had an urge to steer the car into the path of an oncoming lorry. At least my male friends would be jealous when they heard the news. In my mind's eye I pictured the headline in *The Times*: 'Toby Young Killed With Four Supermodels.'

Then I realized what it would actually say: 'Four Supermodels Killed With Unknown Journalist.'

Still, I decided to take Candace's advice to heart. Of the four, Honor Fraser had been the most friendly, partly because I knew her cousin, a New York-based merchant banker called Aeneas Mackay. The other advantage Honor had, at least in my eyes, was that she had enormous breasts. She may have been a 'Blueblood Beauty' but she had the figure of a Page Three girl.

When Aeneas told me Honor was going to be in town one weekend I begged him to set me up with her and we ended up having dinner at Indochine, a fashionable restaurant on Lafayette Street. (He booked it.) Aeneas had invited another model, Ines Sastra, and afterwards I suggested we all go to Hogs & Heffers, a motorcycle bar in New York's meatpacking district. The chief virtue of this establishment was that the staff encouraged the female patrons to remove their bras and hang them on a 'bra tree' behind the bar as soon as they walked in. With a bit of luck I'd get to see Honor's tits!

When we arrived there was a long line of people waiting to get in and Honor asked me if there was anything I could do. I boldly marched up to the front of the queue and introduced myself to the doorman, a grizzled biker in full Hell's Angel gear.

'Do I really have to wait on line?' I asked him. 'I'm on the list.'

He looked a little sceptical so I leant forward and, in a conspiratorial whisper, added: 'I'm with two supermodels.'

'The only list you're on is the stoopid list,' he bellowed. 'Back a the line.'

Needless to say, I went home alone that night.

After striking out with Honor, I decided drastic measures were called for. It didn't seem to matter who I set my sights on, whether a supermodel or a fact-checker, I always ended up shooting myself in the foot. It was time to hire a 'dating coach'.

I'd read about an agency called First Impressions Inc that offered its 'clients' practical advice on how to improve their seduction skills. For $195, First Impressions would arrange a 'simulated date' with one of their 'dating consultants', all of whom had PhDs in Psychology, after which you'd be taken back to their offices, deposited on a sofa and gently told why you hadn't been getting laid for the past eighteen months. It sounded like just what the doctor ordered.

I called First Impressions and got put through to Dr Ann Demaris, the 38-year-old co-founder of the company. After I told her what a hopeless case I was she agreed to take me on herself and a few days later an information pack arrived informing me I was to pretend that an agency called 'The Café Dating Service' had set me up with 'Susan Green', 'a professional . . . interested in film, art, travel, animals, and painting as a hobby'. Rather off-puttingly, I was also asked to sign a 'Participation Agreement' where I acknowledged that 'the date is purely a simulation and that there will be no physical contact between myself and the dating consultant'.

At 3 p.m. the following Sunday, 'Susan' and I met at the Paninoteca Café on the corner of Prince and Mulberry in Little Italy. My first thought on seeing 'Susan' was that she hadn't made much of an effort. She looked like a Woody Allen heroine who'd forgotten to take off her gardening clothes. Then I remembered that I was the one supposed to be making a good impression. I sat down diagonally opposite her and instantly realized I'd made a mistake. Why hadn't I sat down opposite her? Sure enough, back in her office, Dr Demaris picked up on this. 'It sends a message that you find me repulsive,' she explained. 'It says, "I want to keep some distance from you."'

Throughout our initial encounter I felt at a disadvantage because of the peculiar situation. It was as if I was auditioning for a particularly demanding dramatic role while 'Susan' sat there, scribbling notes on her mental clipboard. Of course, in this respect it was exactly like being on a date with a typical New York woman.

Before going back to the agency's offices to hear Dr Demaris's verdict she gave me a form to fill out inviting me to rate my own performance. In response to the question, 'Overall, how do you think you came across during the date?' I wrote: 'Not interested enough in "Susan". Easily distracted. Nervous. Opinionated. Bilious. Celebrity-obsessed. Dishonest. Occasionally amusing but too often laughed at my own jokes. Aggressive. Manic.'

I thought I'd been tough on myself.

Back in her office, after the obligatory preamble about what an 'interesting conversationalist' I was, Dr Demaris cut to the chase. 'Here are the things that would have been *even better if*,' she said, emphasizing the last three words. I sat bolt upright.

'You're a little bit challenging,' she explained, tactfully. 'I think you might intimidate people a little bit. You seem kind of intense.'

In other words, *lighten up*.

'I felt the conversation was pretty balanced in terms of who was doing the talking,' she continued, 'but most of it was about your interests. The other person might feel you're not really interested in them, that they're just an audience for you.'

You're an ego with a digestive system.

'You do have a little bit of a negativity,' she said. 'Just be aware that you communicate a little bit of a negative sense. That's generally not as universally appealing as positivity.'

You're bitter and twisted.

'You didn't talk about your nasty ex-girlfriends or your crazy mother,' she continued, trying to sound 'positive' herself. 'I don't need to know about *that* on the first date.'

At least you didn't puke on my dress.

She summed up: 'Displaying interest is your biggest developmental opportunity. "Susan" didn't come away feeling that you had a special interest in her or that you wanted to learn more about her.'

You have an acute case of Narcissistic Personality Disorder. Get help.

I'm probably exaggerating a little, but in her own, rather circumspect way, Dr Demaris was brutal. No wonder I'd been striking out. I came across as a self-absorbed, cynical egomaniac.

Naturally, I decided to retaliate. Wasn't the whole premise of First Impressions misguided? Surely, women decide within the first fifteen seconds of meeting you whether they want to take things any further and, if they decide you're not up to snuff, nothing you say or do will make the slightest bit of difference.

Not so, countered Demaris. 'Just knowing that someone's attracted to you makes them more attractive,' she said. 'If you're attracted to someone and you let them know that, that's going to increase your appeal. It just works that way.'

I remained sceptical – 'negative' as Dr Demaris would say – and at the end of our ninety-minute session I told her that in order to put her theory to the test I'd need to go out on a real, non-simulated date and put her advice into practice.

'D'you want me to set you up?' she asked brightly.

Oh, oh. Alarm bells started ringing. After everything she'd just said, what kind of basket case would she fix me up with?

'What's your type?' she inquired.

Now the correct answer to this question is 'Helena Christensen' but on the only occasion that I'd said that the person offering to fix me up had laughed and said, 'No wonder you're single!' On the other hand, when I'd told another 'Yenta' that I didn't care what the woman looked like just so long as she was intelligent she had fixed me up with the kind of woman Chris Lawrence described as 'a heinous troll'. How could I phrase my answer accurately without seeming shallow?

'The important thing,' I replied, 'is that she should be a real challenge, someone I wouldn't normally be able to get to first base with without the benefit of your excellent advice. In order to really put this to the test, she has to be *drop dead gorgeous*.'

'Let me sleep on it,' she said.

It must have been a disco nap because when I got home there was a message on my voicemail: 'I have just the person for you: Jennifer. She's a total knockout.'

I called Jennifer and we arranged to meet at Piadina, an Italian restaurant in the West Village, the following Friday. How would I recognize her? She told me she was a brunette, about five foot four and, ahem, *full-figured*. In other words, a little minx with ginormous tits. Just my type!

Typically, by the time Friday came around, I'd forgotten all the advice Dr Demaris had given me and reverted to my old self. Like most men, my view is that the most vital factor in determining the success or failure of a date is the outfit. I belted-up my Levi 501s, pulled on my Gieves & Hawkes cavalry boots, selected my best shirt – an expensive, blue Italian number from Harvey Nicks – and topped it off with a single-breasted, navy blazer from Brooks Brothers. Cool!

I arrived at Piadina at 8.25 p.m., five minutes before Jennifer was due, and commandeered the best table in the house. I ordered a good bottle of wine, poured myself a glass, put my feet up on the chair opposite, and assumed a nonchalant, bored expression. I was ready to go into battle.

When she still hadn't shown up at 9.10 p.m. I checked my voicemail. 'You have no new messages,' it said. (It occurred to me that if Nora Ephron ever made a romantic comedy about my life it would be called *You Haven't Got Mail*.) Infuriatingly, I hadn't brought Jennifer's number with me so I couldn't call her and I couldn't go home to get it in case I missed her. I'd have to sit tight.

At 9.45 p.m. I checked my voicemail again. Nothing. I ended up waiting until 10.30 p.m., by which time I'd finished the wine and was on to my second Black Label on the rocks. There was no question about it. She'd stood me up.

I called Jennifer a few days later and she claimed she'd come to Piadina at 8.30 p.m., waited fifteen minutes, then gone home. Yeah, right, I thought. What was more likely was that she'd come to the restaurant, peeked through the window, had a good look at me, and decided to take a rain check. I'd been right all along. It all comes down to the first fifteen seconds!

But how could she have rejected me in my 'result' outfit? I

called the First Impressions 'Style Consultant', a man called Gregg Levine, and asked him where I'd gone wrong. 'I tend to advise people to stay away from the jeans-and-sports-jacket look,' he said, brutally dismissing my whole sartorial philosophy. 'It's too *Seinfeld*.'

The following week I read in the *Village Voice* that a porn star called Houston was looking for 400 volunteers to help her break the world's gang-bang record. I thought about calling her manager then decided against it. Knowing my luck, she'd probably take one look at me and scream 'NEXT!'

25

'I'M SORRY, SIR, THAT CARD'S BEEN DECLINED.'

Meanwhile, back on the career front, things weren't looking too good. My *Vanity Fair* contract came up for renewal on 1 April, 1997 and, as promised, Graydon re-employed me, though only for three months instead of the usual six. As of 1 July, he explained, my name would be kept on the masthead but I'd lose my office and my monthly salary would be reduced from $5,000 to $1,000. That was less than I was paying in rent. Luckily, I still had my *Evening Standard* column, but even so. It was time to seek alternative employment.

I thought I'd start at the top and fired off a letter to Howell Raines, who was then the editorial page editor of *The New York Times*.[1] Within the American journalistic community, *The Times*'s op ed page is considered the most prestigious slot in the business. You don't get paid much – it's such an honour, you're supposed to do it for $150 – but in terms of book contracts, other writing assignments and, most importantly, *invitations to appear on television*, it's worth its weight in gold. I'd heard that Raines was looking for a 'humour' columnist so I included half a dozen squibs I wrote on spec in the hope he

---

[1] Raines is now the executive editor of *The New York Times*, the paper's top job.

might consider me for the job. I stuck the whole package in a *Vanity Fair* envelope – at least that way it would make it into his in-tray – and dispatched it via the Condé Nast mailroom.

Six weeks later the envelope arrived back on my desk. Howell Raines's address had been scribbled out and someone had scrawled 'Return to sender' underneath with an arrow pointing to my address in the top-left-hand corner. I tore it open only to find my original letter, along with the six articles, arranged in exactly the same order I'd sent them. There was no covering letter, not even a rejection slip. The only evidence that the material had been read was that every single spelling mistake and grammatical error had been corrected in red, felt-tip pen. Clearly, I wasn't *Times* material.

I decided to send Graydon a final memo. After all, it's customary to grant the condemned man a last request. Maybe he'd let me write a thousand-word Vanities piece as my swan-song. It was worth a try.

Dear Graydon,

While I was in LA, I came across a guy called Abdul who offers a rather unusual service to men out on first dates. Apparently, for a fee of $300 he'll pretend to pick a fight with you and then allow you to beat him up. Why don't I call up *Playboy*, pretend I want to write one of those hackneyed magazine pieces in which I go out on a date with the Playmate of the Year and then hire Abdul to work his magic?

Rather than just have him attack me once, I could get him to change into different outfits and attack me again and again over the course of the evening. Naturally, each encounter would end with me beating the crap out of him. (This might cost a little more than $300, but perhaps we could get a bulk rate.) Just how long would it take the Playmate of the Year to figure out something funny was going on? My guess is quite a long time.

Not surprisingly, this memo did not come back to me with the words 'Let's discuss' written on it. By this time Graydon had washed his hands of me. 'Toby's like a piece of gum,' he told a *New York Times* journalist three years later. 'He lingers on the bottom of your shoe.'

As my career nosedived, and with no prospect of a girlfriend on the horizon, I did what any self-respecting Englishman would do in the circumstances: I turned to alcohol. I've always been incapable of drinking in moderation, but up until this point I'd managed to restrict my bingeing to the weekend. Now, with no real need to go into the office every day, I began to drink during the week as well. Slowly but surely I was turning into a dipso-maniac.

One of the more alarming symptoms of my advancing alco-holism was that I'd frequently be unable to remember what I'd done the night before. By the time I got up, which was rarely before noon, there was nearly always a voicemail message from one of my drinking buddies – usually Anthony Haden-Guest – asking if I was alright. When I called him back the conversa-tion would go something like this:

Me: Why wouldn't I be alright?

Anthony: Don't you remember?

Me: Remember what?

Anthony [Cackling]: Ha, ha, ha.

Not a good sign.

On one occasion Anthony had called to tell me that I'd been found the previous night in one of the bathroom stalls at Wax, an ultra-chic nightclub in SoHo. The owner of the club had discovered me unconscious, with my trousers round my ankles, as he was closing up. The poor man had had to pull my trousers up, hoist me over his shoulder and put me in a cab. The reason Anthony knew about this was because the owner had called him to get my address at 5 a.m. Apparently, in my inebriated state I'd been unable to remember it.

I knew things were spiralling out of control when one day, out of the blue, I received a call from Molly Jong-Fast, the

19-year-old daughter of Erica Jong. 'I've heard you're, like, this *legendary* alcoholic,' she said, getting straight to the point. Apparently, a 'mutual friend' had tipped her off that I 'would be, like, this rilly, rilly nice guy' if only I stopped drinking. Did I want to go come to a 'meeting' with her?

'What kind of meeting?'

'You know, an AA meeting.'

Oh my God, I thought. It's finally happening. Someone's trying to drag me off to Alcoholics Anonymous.

'Whereabouts?' I asked.

'You live in the West Village, right? How about Perry Street?'

'Ah,' I said. 'That could be a problem.'

My flat was in Perry Street and shortly after I'd first moved in I'd discovered that the building across the street served as a meeting place for the local chapter of AA. After a night of heavy drinking I'm prone to feelings of intense self-loathing so the sight of these twelve-steppers filing into meetings all morning wasn't exactly welcome. What was particularly irritating was that afterwards two or three of them would often sit on a bench beneath my bedroom window to discuss their 'progress', making it impossible to sleep.

I tried moving the bench a few times but after a couple of days it would always find its way back to its original spot. Eventually, however, I hit on the perfect solution: I bought an air-conditioner and installed it directly above the bench so it dripped on anyone beneath it. Soon, the bench found a new home and I could sleep off my hangovers in peace.

I was so pleased with this victory I included an item about it in my *Evening Standard* column – a grave mistake. A few days later I was leaning out of my bedroom window when a Hell's Angel emerged from a doorway across the street. 'Hey, Toby,' he shouted, pointing an accusatory finger at me. 'We've got your article pinned up in here!'

Molly Jong-Fast would have to look elsewhere to indulge her Florence Nightingale complex.

*

As my descent into alcoholism continued, I took a great deal of comfort from the theory that all drunks are protected by a guardian angel. No matter how pissed I got, I always seemed to find my way home at the end of the night even though I could never remember how. This always struck me as faintly miraculous.

However, on the night of 24 July my guardian angel deserted me. The scene in question unfolded in an overpriced vodka-and-caviar bar called Pravda on Lafayette Street. I'd been drinking with Bruno Maddox, the 27-year-old British editor of *Spy*, and in my cups had offered to pick up the tab. This turned out to be a mistake. The bill, when it arrived, was for far more than I had on me and by that time Bruno was long gone. Fortunately, I'd received a new credit card in the post that morning and handed it over.

'I'm sorry, sir,' said the manager, a few minutes later, 'that card's been declined. D'you have another?'

I didn't, regrettably. However, I remembered that in the letter that had accompanied the card it had said that in order to 'activate' it I'd have to use it once in an 'ATM'. If the manager would be good enough to give it back to me, I'd pop out to the nearest cashpoint and solve the problem.

'Sorry, sir,' he replied, clutching the card to his bosom. 'I'm going to have to keep this as surety until you've settled your tab.'

'But I can't settle the tab unless you give me my card back!'

'With all due respect, sir, that's not my problem.'

The sensible thing to do at this point would have been to leave the card there and return the following day with some cash. In my wallet, which I'd left at home, I had plenty of other cards. However, I'd been knocking back the Stoli all night and was in no mood to be 'sensible'.

I lurched towards the manager, snatched my card out of his hand and made a run for it. I'd momentarily forgotten that the entrance to Pravda is at the foot of a long flight of stairs and that I'd have to climb these stairs in order to make my escape.

I got about half way up when my legs were whipped out from under me by the manager and I tumbled back down to the bottom. I leapt to my feet again and this time made it to the top, only to be intercepted by a bouncer standing on the street. *Whack!* He floored me with a right hook. A moment later he was joined by the manager and together they started beating the crap out of me.

Within seconds a squad car pulled up and two cops leapt out and bundled me into the back. Before I had a chance to tell my side of the story, which admittedly was pretty flimsy, my two assailants told the policemen exactly what had happened. Nevertheless, when the policemen got back in the car I decided to launch into my version of events.

'Officers, let me begin by saying . . .'

'Shut up, you mook,' said the more senior of the two, swivelling round in his seat and jabbing his finger in my chest. 'You're under arrest, okay?'

For one terrible moment I had a vision of spending the night in 'the Tombs', New York's infamous underground prison. *No, please. Anything but that!*

Thankfully, instead of arresting me they drove me home, waited for me to retrieve my wallet, then drove me back to Pravda so I could pay my bill. During the five years I spent in Manhattan this was my only brush with 'New York's Finest' and they behaved with exemplary restraint. Graydon, on the other hand . . .

'What the hell d'you call that?' he asked, two days later, thrusting a copy of the *New York Post* under my nose. My drunken exploits had made an appearance in that morning's Page Six.

'I got in a bar fight,' I explained.

'A bar fight?' repeated Graydon, running his eye over my battered face. 'You're too short to be getting into bar fights.'

'You should see the other guy,' I said proudly. 'Not a scratch on him.'

He didn't laugh.

'Listen, Toby, I'm gonna have to take your name off the masthead. This kind of thing isn't good for the magazine's image.'

I gulped. My days as a *Vanity Fair* contributing editor were over.

'What the hell happened?' asked Graydon. 'I gave you the opportunity of a lifetime and you fucked the dog.' (I later worked out that 'fucked the dog' was Graydon's way of saying I'd done nothing.)

'I'm not sure,' I replied. 'Why exactly did you hire me in the first place?'

'I have absolutely no fucking idea,' he said.

It was fitting that this was the final straw. In *Vanity Fair*'s heyday, back in the Roaring Twenties, barroom brawling was practically *required* of the magazine's contributors. The most celebrated names on the masthead had all been notorious drunks. Indeed, the reason Frank Crowninshield, *Vanity Fair*'s legendary editor of that era, had employed Robert Benchley and Robert E. Sherwood was because their boozing had rendered them *unemployable* by anyone else. Now, it seemed, it was a hanging offence. Compare this to the way Herman J. Mankiewicz was treated by *The New York Times*. In 1925 Mankiewicz returned to the paper after seeing *School For Scandal* and was so drunk he fell asleep at his typewriter in the middle of writing his review. The upshot was that *The Times* appeared the following day without the customary first-night notice. Nevertheless, Mankiewicz managed to talk the assistant managing editor out of firing him by presenting him with a bottle of Scotch.

Thank God I still had my *Evening Standard* column! As long as I held on to that I'd be okay. At this point I'd been doing it for over two years and I'd really hit my stride. Admittedly, I'd only ever received one 'herogram' from the editor, Max Hastings, but I had no reason to suspect he was unhappy. I'd become a mainstay of the paper. They'd even stuck a poster of me on the London Underground, for Christ's sake. No, I was safe as houses there.

'I've got some bad news,' said the *Standard* features editor, calling from London a few weeks later. 'We're discontinuing the column. It's a purely budgetary decision. We just can't afford to keep you on. Sorry.'

Click. Dial-tone.

26

ALEX THROUGH THE LOOKING GLASS

I woke up one afternoon towards the end of September, after a monumental session the night before, to discover that Alex de Silva had left me a voicemail message: 'Call me immediately, dude. I have big, *big* news.' With some reluctance I returned his call. He never phoned unless he had something to brag about – Alex is one of those people who is all broadcast and no reception.

Alex: Hey, buddy. What's the matter with your voice? You sound like you've got a serious hangover.

Me: No, no, just a cold.

Alex: Anyway, guess what? I sold a script!

What?

That couldn't be true. He'd only graduated from the USC screenwriting programme a few months earlier. How could he possibly have sold a script?

Me: What are you talking about?

Alex: You know how I told you I'd teamed up with _____ _____?

_____ _____ was a Welsh comedian who'd unexpectedly found success in an American sitcom. Alex had befriended him and they'd talked about collaborating on a screenplay. But as far as I knew they hadn't actually got going on one yet.

Me: Vaguely.

Alex: Well we've written this comedy about a gay Welsh

dog groomer who comes to LA to enter this dog-grooming competition. It's called *Woof!* Anyway, about six weeks ago my agent . . .

Me: Wait a minute. You've got an *agent*? Since when have you had an *agent*?

Alex: Ages, dude. You should get one yourself. Seriously. So my agent sends out this script, yeah, and, at first there isn't a great deal of interest. The reaction is very positive and everything, but who wants to make a quirky little film about a gay Welsh dog-groomer, you know? Then *The Full Monty* opens and guess what? It's a massive fucking hit! And quirky British comedies are the Next Big Thing. So suddenly *Woof!* becomes a hot property. We're talking *on fire*, baby. [Him as well?] The next thing I know, every fucking studio in town wants to be in business with us.

Me: You're kidding?

Alex: It's true, dude, it's fucking true! My life has just become *surreal*. You won't believe this, but at one point, me and _____ were on a conference call with Harvey Weinstein, Arnold Rifkin and the President of Paramount I mean, we're sitting there in my shitty little apartment and three of the biggest players in Hollywood are on the other end of the phone! It was un-fucking real. At one point, we actually put them on hold so we could fall about laughing. It was just unbelievable.

Me [Stunned]: You're right. I don't believe it.

Alex: I'm telling you. It was like a scene in a movie or something.

Me: So who d'you sell it to in the end?

Alex: Paramount. They weren't offering the most money but they seemed to really understand what we were trying to do in the piece, you know?

The piece? My God. He was already beginning to sound like a Hollywood arsehole.

Me: So how much money *did* you get?

Alex: It's not about the money, dude. We could have sold it for a million dollars but we felt it was more important to be in business with the right people. [Mr Integrity.] Paramount really rolled out the red carpet for us. It just felt right, you know?

Me: Come on. How much?

Alex: I'm not going to tell you.

Me: $50,000?

Alex: [Laughing]: Listen, I really can't tell you. [Pause] But it was more than $50,000.

I knew it. The little bastard was absolutely *dying* to tell me.

Me: $100,000?

Alex: More.

Me: $150,000?

Alex: More.

Bloody hell! That was more than I'd earned in my best year ever.

Me: Just tell me how much.

Alex: It was around the $250,000 mark, but this really isn't about getting rich. This is about achieving your dream. I come to Hollywood to try and make it as a screenwriter and – bingo! – I hit the jackpot straight out of the gate.

Me: That's a mixed metaphor.

Alex: What?

Me: You can't hit the jackpot straight out of the gate. In order to win a jackpot you have to . . .

Alex: Whatever, dude. Aren't you happy for me?

Me: Er, yes, yes, of course I am.

Jesus H. Christ! What did Alex have that I didn't? We'd both been in America for two and a half years and while I'd been fired – twice! – he'd sold a screenplay. It was as if our fates were mysteriously intertwined and every time I suffered some setback he was catapulted forward. What would happen if I suddenly discovered I was HIV positive? Would he win the lottery?

Alex: I mean, this is amazing, right? My movie is actually going to be made. Actors are going to be speaking my lines. It's unbefuckinglievable.

Me: Unbefuckinglievable.

27

FORGOTTEN BUT NOT GONE

Alex's good news would have depressed me under the best of circumstances but coming as it did so soon after my double whammy it left me reeling. Here I was in the financial centre of the world at the height of the nineties stock boom and I was virtually destitute! How did that happen? In the bat of an eye I'd gone from having an office, two expense accounts and a combined salary of £85,000 a year, to being a freelance hack with no fixed income. I'd just turned thirty-four and yet I had no career to speak of. I had no inheritance to fall back on, no trust fund, nothing. My only asset was my bedsit in Shepherd's Bush and that was mortgaged up to the hilt. All I had to show for my two and a half years in New York was an alcohol problem. If things got any worse I was in real danger of slipping below the poverty line.

Manhattan was a particularly bad town to be unemployed in as 1997 drew to a close. The amount of money being earned on Wall Street that year was staggering.[1] A 32-year-old girl I'd been at Harvard with told me her stock portfolio had increased by 65 per cent since the beginning of 1997, bringing her net worth up to $40 million. Nevertheless, she assured me that in the circles she moved in her $40 million was considered chump

---

[1] 1997 was the biggest year Wall Street had had to date, with the American securities industry earning $12 billion.

241

change, or 'tip money', as she put it. In 1996 Teddy Forstmann of Forstmann Little & Co had made $100 million, Tom Lee of Thomas H. Lee Company had made $130 million and Henry Kravis of Kohlberg Kravis Roberts and Co had made at least $265 million – and all were on course to do better in 1997. At the very top of the pile, George Soros was expected to clear half a billion.

Wherever I looked, New Yorkers seemed to be hurling their credit cards around in an orgiastic frenzy of consumerism. Many of that year's must-have Christmas purchases, such as Dolce & Gabbana's $3,200 cashmere cardigans, had already sold out. At Patroon, a recently opened midtown restaurant, a colleague of mine overheard three Wall Street types celebrating the closing of a deal by loudly ordering a bottle of 1953 Château Margaux for $1,725, a magnum of 1953 Haut Brion for $2,325 and a bottle of 1961 Château Pétrus for $5,800. Short of lighting up cigars with hundred-dollar bills, their consumption could not have been more conspicuous. I felt like a penniless eunuch in the cornucopia of sex and money.

In the words of George S. Kaufman, I was forgotten but not gone.

My misery was compounded by a telephone call from Chris Lawrence telling me he'd been issued with strict instructions not to sign me in to the Condé Nast building. 'Graydon's worried about you stealing office supplies,' he explained. However, lest I think he'd gone over to the other side, he quickly added: 'Don't imagine for a minute that I'm going to pay any attention to that. If you need to come into the building for any reason, any reason at all, I'll still sign you in no problem.'

Graydon was worried about me *stealing paper clips*? One minute I was a trusted employee, the next I was a petty thief? Apparently, once you were thrown out of the first room it was only a matter of time before you ended up in Riker's Island. It was at this point, I'm ashamed to say, that I began to miss the English class system. I yearned for the social safety net that was provided by my membership of the educated bourgeoisie back home. In London, thanks to my BBC accent and the fact that I'd been to Oxford and Cambridge, I could still look forward to being treated with some respect even though my career was in the toilet – or, rather, the *lavatory*. Thanks to my class background, I had an identity that wasn't affected by how well or badly I was doing. My social standing was independent of my professional status.

The various setbacks I suffered at the end of 1997 brought home to me the extent to which New Yorkers judge you according to how well or badly you're doing. When I'd first arrived and people had asked me what I did at parties, a noticeable change would come over them when I said I worked at *Vanity Fair*. They'd stop looking over my shoulder for a second and give me the once over. Occasionally, they'd even talk to me. Evidently, I was someone worth knowing. However, after I was taken off the masthead I vanished from the radar screen. Being neither rich, successful, good looking, nor well connected, I wasn't worth bothering with. No sooner had the words 'I'm just a freelance hack' come out of my mouth than the person I was talking to was hastily backing away, wondering how they could politely ask for their business card back. It was a sobering experience. I'd assumed that people liked me for who I was, not what I did, but in Manhattan you are what you do.

Why do New Yorkers attach such importance to the state of your career? To a certain extent, they define each other according to the usual demographic categories – gender, ethnic origin, religious background, etc – but these things pale into insignificance besides the jobs they do. It's as if there are no alternative sources of identity. In particular, they don't define people according to what class they belong to. New Yorkers are more interested in where you're going than where you're from. They make no bones about this. If you're in a position to help them, they're more than happy to help you, inviting you to parties, introducing you to their friends, plugging you in to their networks. But if you have nothing to offer in exchange you might as well not exist.

For Tocqueville, the absence of class distinctions was one of the chief differences between Britain and America and while he generally approved of this he worried that it could lead to excessive significance being attached to things like professional status:

> In democracies, where citizens never differ much from one another and naturally find themselves so close that at each instant all can come to be intermingled in a common mass, a multitude of artificial and arbitrary classifications are created, with the aid of which each seeks to set himself apart, out of fear of being carried away into the crowd despite himself.

Of course, in the eyes of most New Yorkers this is a small price to pay for living in a classless society. In contemporary America, meritocracy occupies the status of a 'sacred first principle'[1] and Manhattan is frequently held up as a shining example of it. Indeed, this accounts for why New Yorkers judge people according to how well or badly they're doing. Unlike in Britain, where the class system impedes social mobility, there's nothing to prevent the hardworking from rising to the top or the indolent from falling to the bottom. This belief is particularly strongly held by Manhattan's most successful residents since it implies that they've got where they are purely on their own merits. They even refer to themselves as 'meritocrats'. In their eyes, just as those who are doing well deserve to be praised, those who are doing badly only have themselves to blame.

I've always been rather ambivalent about meritocracy – and not just because I'm a beneficiary of England's class system. During my spell in New York I enjoyed shocking people by telling them that the word 'meritocracy' had originally been

---

[1] Nicholas Lemann, *The Big Test: The Secret History of the American Meritocracy* (New York: Farrar, Straus and Giroux, 1999), p.343.

coined for the purposes of damnation rather than praise. They would always dispute this until I played my trump card: my father invented it.

He coined it to describe a nightmarish society of the future in his 1958 bestseller *The Rise of the Meritocracy*. In my father's view, equality of opportunity is a snare and a delusion since it makes it less likely that equality of outcome, the 'hard' form of equality he believes in, will ever come about. If everyone starts out on a level playing field then the resulting distribution of wealth, however unequal, will be regarded as legitimate. According to him, a meritocratic society is no better than an aristocratic one since it is just as hierarchical. Indeed, it is considerably worse since the richest segment of the population don't suffer from any feelings of guilt. Unlike those who have inherited their wealth, they think their good fortune is thoroughly deserved. In my father's book, a work of fiction that purports to be a PhD thesis written by a sociology student in 2030, the absence of *noblesse oblige* in the meritocratic society of the future eventually results in a bloody revolution in which the workers overthrow their new masters.

In contemporary America, those who've reached the top are every bit as pleased with themselves as the doomed ruling class in *The Rise of the Meritocracy*. Their self-satisfaction is exhibited in all sorts of ways. For instance, the residents of what's known as 'the trifecta' – New York, Washington and Los Angeles – refer to the rest of America as 'the fly-over states' and describe themselves as belonging to Thomas Jefferson's 'natural aristocracy'. They believe they've made it because they've been blessed with an abundance of talent and think of those poor creatures who live outside the trifecta as belonging to an inferior species. At *Vanity Fair*, my colleagues frequently made fun of those who live in the fly-over states, claiming that they age faster, become balder sooner and are more likely to succumb to cancer.

One sure sign that America's plutocrats don't suffer from any feelings of guilt about their wealth is that they're completely shameless about flaunting it. You only have to visit the

Hamptons, the exclusive summer resort about seventy miles East of Manhattan, to witness bourgeois triumphalism at its most naked. As you watch a succession of millionaires glide past in their Porsche 911 convertibles, each chariot containing a more beautiful blonde than the last, you get the impression that it's only a matter of time before these 'Masters of the Universe' tattoo their net worths on their foreheads. According to Tom Wolfe, the Hamptons exists primarily to provide New Yorkers with an opportunity for this kind of display. 'The first great advantage of summering in the Hamptons,' he confided to a journalist from *The Sunday Telegraph*, 'is simply to tell everyone else in the office that you will be there and not here.'

Before moving to Manhattan I'd always been rather suspicious of the tendency of Britain's top dogs to play down their privileged status. Why should modesty and understatement be synonymous with good taste? My view – not particularly original – was that this utilitarian style had originally been developed by the British aristocracy as a way of minimising the resentment caused by their prosperity. At a time when power was restricted to members of the lucky sperm club, the aristocracy had prudently adopted a set of manners that prohibited the flaunting of their good fortune. It was one of several cunning ploys they came up with to avoid the fate that had met their cousins across the Channel. Of course, the British aristocracy's power has long since dwindled, but their social code has proved remarkably resilient, influencing the behaviour of their bourgeois successors.[1]

---

[1]'Compared with the aristocracies of Spain, Austria, and France, the British aristocracy was, on the whole, unusually public spirited and socially responsible. And compared with the Prussian *Junkers*, it was much less inclined to pursue its own class interests at the expense of the nation as a whole. To that extent, indeed, it deserved Tocqueville's encomium as the most liberal aristocracy in the world.' David Cannadine, *The Decline and Fall of the British Aristocracy* (London: Picador, 1992) p. 703.

However, now that I'd seen the alternative – a ruling class that regarded its wealth as completely legitimate – I began to think again. Whatever its historical origins, wasn't self-effacement more attractive than self-advertisement? It certainly seemed that way to me at the end of 1997.

The immodesty of New York's most prosperous residents wouldn't have been so objectionable if they really had *earned* their success. But just how meritocratic is American society? If the word is taken to denote equality of opportunity then America doesn't fare very well. The richest 20 per cent of American households have fifteen times as much income as the bottom 20 per cent and a child born into the richest segment will have a smorgasbord of opportunities that aren't available to one born into the poorest. To take the most obvious example, does anyone really imagine that George W. Bush ascended to the Presidency on merit alone? Interestingly, one of Bush's first acts as President was to announce the abolition of inheritance tax, enabling the richest 20 per cent to pass on the whole of their estates to their children, untouched by the government. The unfettered transfer of assets from one generation to the next is hardly conducive to the creation of a meritocracy. This is in contrast to Britain, where the aristocracy was decimated by the taxation policy of the 1945–51 Labour Government. It increased inheritance tax to 75 per cent for those leaving over £1 million, forcing large numbers of aristocrats to hand their houses over to The National Trust. Today, even after eighteen years of Conservative rule from 1979–97, inheritance tax still stands at 40 per cent.

Liberal-minded educationalists have attempted to eliminate the effect of America's gross economic inequality by basing college admissions on a standardised intelligence test – the notorious SAT (Scholastic Aptitude Test) – but this has been a mixed success. There's plenty of evidence to show that a child's SAT score is at least partly determined by the socio-economic status of its parents. There's even a nationwide company called Princeton Review that, for a hefty fee, will instruct children on how to perform well in their SATs. One of the women I befriended in Manhattan, Dr Katherine Cohen, was a 'college counsellor', a highly lucrative profession that involves coaching the children of affluent Americans on how to get into the university of their choice. Kat, who once worked for the admissions office at Yale, charges $28,995 for her 'platinum package'.[1] To quote Will Hutton, the ex-editor of the *Observer*: 'The network of privileged private American schools, together with the now commonplace £20,000 a year coaching in examination and interview techniques, has meant the American upper-middle class has gained a suffocating stranglehold on entry into the best universities. The much-criticised British system looks near Utopian in comparison.'

It seems clear that America is a long way from achieving equality of opportunity, but can it be described as meritocratic in some other, less ambitious sense? Perhaps all that's meant by the word is that America isn't saddled with a class system. However, on cursory examination, even that claim is dubious. The East Coast Wasp elite – the 'Episcopacy' – is still immensely rich, there's still a great deal of nepotism in American's Ivy League universities and a cabal of powerful families still dominates American politics. (In the New York media, there's even something called 'the Harvard mafia'.) Nevertheless, all this really tells us is that a self-perpetuating upper-middle class elite exists in America and few keen-eyed observers would dispute that. Indeed, there's a whole library of books devoted to the subject, the most famous being *The Theory of the Leisure Class*

---

[1] According to an article about her in *New York* magazine: 'Kat, as her awestruck protégés call her, is part of a prosperous new breed of private counsellors who are helping the children of the rich attain their birthright of getting accepted to the Ivy League college of their choice.' Ralph Gardner Jr, 'The ultimate college admissions coach', *New York*, 16 July, 2001.

by Thorstein Veblen.[1] It's not widely known, but the forerunner of *The Sloane Ranger Handbook* was a book called *The Preppie Handbook* about the equivalent clique in America.

The question is: how much social mobility is there? Looked at this way, the picture begins to improve. Even Karl Marx, referring to the America of the 1850s, acknowledged that 'though classes, indeed, already exist, they have not become fixed, but continually change and interchange their elements in a constant state of flux'. According to Jonathan Freedland, author of *Bring Home the Revolution: The Case for a British Republic*, America enjoys far higher levels of social mobility than Britain. He cites the statistic that, of all the people in the bottom 20 per cent of the US income scale in 1975, only 5 per cent were still there in 1991. Another survey conducted in the mid-eighties showed that 18 per cent of families in the bottom 20 per cent moved out *in a single year*. In general, those at the bottom of American society only stay there for a very short time.

But in the past decade many American economists have begun to challenge statistics such as these. In 1992, for instance, an economist called David Zimmerman revealed that this flattering self-portrait was fundamentally inaccurate. 'It seemed to me economists were measuring the university student who was poverty-striken for a few months before landing a job,' he pointed out. When he conducted his own research he discovered that a person's long-term average income status was primarily determined by their parents' earnings. Of children born into the bottom quintile, 40 per cent stayed there for the duration of their lifetime, while 29 per cent moved up just one level; of those born into the highest quintile, 41 per cent stayed where they were, with only 17 per cent dropping down a level. Income

---

[1]For a brief overview I recommend Paul Fussel's *Class: A Guide Through the American Status System* (New York: Touchstone, 1983).

inequality is now higher in American than anywhere else in the industrialised world. The chance of a worker who starts out in the bottom 20 per cent moving in to the top 60 per cent is lower than in any country in Europe – and less than half that in Britain.

During the time I spent at *Vanity Fair*, I witnessed countless examples of just how unmeritocratic New York society is. For instance, the only personal assistants hired between the years 1995–97 who were promoted up through the ranks were Patricia Herrera and Evgenia Peretz. Though undoubtedly able and intelligent, these two women weren't conspicuously more talented than any of the other personal assistants hired in the same period. However, they both shared an advantage the others lacked. Patricia was the daughter of the fashion designer Carolina Herrera and Evgenia was the daughter of Marty Peretz, the owner of *The New Republic*. In New York, as in London, it's not *what* you know but *who* you know that counts.

Evidently, America can stake no greater claim to being a meritocracy than Britain. This makes the triumphalism of its most successful citizens totally indefensible. America is a faux meritocracy in which abhorrent levels of inequality are justified by an appeal to a principle of social justice that, however sacred, has yet to be implemented. To use a baseball analogy, America's most successful citizens were born on third and think they've hit a triple.

The crucial difference between Britain and America isn't that we have a class system; rather, it's that Americans believe their country to be meritocratic whereas we don't. In Britain we acknowledge that the socio-economic status of your parents can have a crucial impact on your life chances, whereas the majority of Americans believe they all compete on a level playing field. In fact, it's not quite accurate to say that they 'believe' this, since it's so patently false. Rather, it's an article of faith, an example of what Plato called 'a noble lie'. It's a national myth designed to make the extreme levels of inequality dictated by untrammelled market forces more acceptable and to dispute it would be downright unpatriotic. That anyone can rise to the top, no matter how humble their beginnings, is what makes America great. 'We have come closer to a true meritocracy than anywhere else around the world,' wrote Warren Buffet in a letter to *The New York Times* on 14 February, 2001. Of course, he probably does believe that since it means his $28 billion fortune is thoroughly deserved.

This national myth isn't without some positive benefits. It probably accounts for why America has such a vibrant economy. If people believe that hard work alone can propel them to the top then, obviously, they'll work that much harder. New York is full of hungry, ambitious people scrabbling for their piece of the action, a fact that helps explain why the city has such tremendous vitality. Contrast this with London where the existence of the iniquitous English class system is everyone's favourite excuse for failure. If someone hasn't fulfilled their potential, why, it's because they weren't born with a silver spoon in their mouth!

On balance, however, Britain's more accurate self-understanding strikes me as overwhelmingly preferable. The fact that we acknowledge that your chances in life are profoundly affected by who your parents are means we're less inclined to judge people according to how well or badly they're doing. We're less worshipful of success than Americans are and, more importantly, less contemptuous of failure. The aristocratic tradition of *noblesse oblige* has been preserved in Britain precisely because we don't believe it's a meritocracy. Unlike America's top dogs, the better off in our society tend to feel a bit guilty and embarrassed about their good fortune, as if they don't quite deserve it. As a result they're fairly considerate and, on occasion, even kind towards the less fortunate. Indeed, more than one British historian has traced the origins of our welfare state to precisely these paternalistic sentiments.[1]

---

[1] See in particular Correlli Barnett's *The Audit of War: The Illusion & Reality of Britain as a Great Nation* (London: Macmillan, 1986).

Contrast this with America, where anyone who isn't doing well is automatically dismissed as a 'loser'. Kurt Andersen, the ex-editor of *Spy*, summed up the attitude in an interview in the *Washington Post*: 'Today, if you're not making money, you're some kind of sap.' The casual, unthinking cruelty with which successful New Yorkers treat cab drivers and waiters, not to mention their personal assistants, was something I witnessed every day. In contemporary Manhattan the concept of 'the deserving poor' is an oxymoron.

After a tour of duty in New York even our godforsaken Royal Family starts to look quite appealing. The fact that our sovereign is selected by an accident of birth is a constant reminder that there's something completely irrational about how well you do in life's game of Snakes and Ladders. What could be more absurd than making a member of the lucky sperm club the head of state? If we abolished the monarchy Britain wouldn't suddenly become a classless society overnight, as some republicans appear to believe, so why not preserve it as a symbol of just how *unmeritocratic* our society is? America may have an elected head of state but the present incumbent inherited the office just as surely as our own Queen did. It's important that the symbols of our national identity should reflect the unfairness of life in Britain, since the alternative – the pretence that everyone starts out with an equal chance – leads to the belief that the distribution of wealth is entirely legitimate. In its own, rather primitive way the monarchy ameliorates the extreme outcomes dictated by contemporary capitalism.

The same could be said of all the remnants of Britain's *ancien régime*. Since New Labour came to power in 1997 there has been a sustained assault on the English class system, from the reform of the House of Lords to the 'modernisation' of the High Sheriffs of England and Wales. However, like so many of Tony Blair's reforms, the changes he has made have been almost entirely cosmetic. By attacking the most visible manifestations of the class system, he has done nothing to lessen its grip on

British society. Indeed, four years after the Labour Party came to power Britain is no closer to being a meritocracy than it was. All Blair has achieved is to provide our society with a thin patina of fairness, leaving the structure put in place by Margaret Thatcher largely untouched. If anything, by making Britain appear more meritocratic, he has set back the cause he claims to believe in. As my father pointed out in *The Rise of the Meritocracy,* people will only clamour for social justice if they *perceive* their society to be unfair. In attempting to make Britain more like America, Blair is ensuring that the extreme levels of inequality tolerated across the Atlantic will soon be acceptable in Britain.

Given how nostalgic I was feeling about *ye olde country* towards the end of 1997 I seriously considered jumping on the next plane home. Why not just accept that I didn't have what it took to take Manhattan?

Well, to begin with, I couldn't face the looks of smug satisfaction on the faces of my friends. Moving from London to New York is a bit like moving from Newcastle to London. However badly you're doing, you can't move back to Newcastle. It's just too humiliating. In my mind's eye I pictured a welcoming committee of my friends meeting me at Heathrow as I stepped off the plane: 'See! We told you you'd never make it in New York.'

Then there would be Alex's *Schadenfreude* to contend with. I knew for a fact that he felt as competitive with me as I did with him, even if he was better at concealing it. If I went home now, just weeks after he'd sold his first screenplay, it would look like I was throwing in the towel. Just because he'd won the first six rounds didn't mean he was going to win the match. (It merely made it *overwhelmingly likely*.) Unless I was actually knocked out, I intended to stay in the ring for the full twelve rounds.

Finally, and most importantly, I still thought I might make it. Even though I was sceptical about America's claim to be a meritocracy, I hoped I might be one of the lucky few who breaks through. I was suffering from the same self-delusion as everyone else trying to shin their way up the greasy pole in Manhattan: I was *special*, I was destined to be a somebody.

This wasn't a rational belief. Statistically, I knew I had about as much chance of taking Manhattan as I did of re-growing my hair. But there were enough examples of people exactly like me who had made it to prevent me giving up hope. This is why the vast majority of Americans continue to believe their country is the land of opportunity. They all know someone who started out in very similar circumstances to their own and who's now sitting in the back of a limo surrounded by supermodels. Whenever I got into an argument with a New Yorker about just how unmeritocratic America is, they'd always fall back on this kind of anecdotal evidence: 'If America's not a meritocracy, how come this guy I was at high school with has just bought a private jet?' Above all else, it's these rags-to-riches stories that sustain their faith in the fairness of the American system. It's the most common narrative theme in American popular culture: the little guy who makes it big through sheer willpower alone.[1] It reinforces their conviction that if only they can tap into their inner strength, if only they can unleash their potential, they, too, will make it.

This fantasy is what props up the entire American edifice; it's why the elite haven't suffered the same fate as the ruling class in *The Rise of the Meritocracy*. The reason the cash-strapped masses don't start manning the barricades when they hear about the huge bonuses paid to the partners of Goldman Sachs every year is because they believe they might be as rich as that themselves one day if only their ship comes in. And God help me, at the end of 1997 I believed this too.

---

[1]'Universal opportunity has been a theme in American writing and fable and rhetoric at every point in our history.' Nicholas Lemann, *The Big Test: The Secret History of the American Meritocracy* (New York: Farrar, Straus and Giroux, 1999).

As I gazed at the cigar-chomping plutocrats pouring out of Balthazar in their $2,000 Giorgio Armani 'Black Label' suits one part of me thought, 'How perfectly ghastly!' But another, less rational part thought, 'I'll be there next year, mate. Just you wait.'

28

CAROLINE

Just as my career hit rock bottom, my personal life perked up. – *thank God!* An ex-girlfriend of mine called Nati Bondy, someone I'd been out with sixteen years earlier, called to say that her little sister had just got a job as a paralegal at a big New York law firm and would be arriving shortly. Could I find her somewhere to stay while she looked for a flat? I had a vague memory of Nati's younger sister hovering in the background one afternoon at their parents' house, clutching a copy of *Pride and Prejudice*. She was seven years old at the time. Without thinking much of it, I told Nati to give her my number. One of the hazards of living in New York if you're a Brit is that you get calls from your countrymen looking for a place to crash approximately twice a week.

Caroline Bondy had just turned twenty-three when she arrived on my doorstep on 5 October, 1997 and I liked her the moment I saw her. She had a naughty, slightly guilty look about her, as if she'd just eaten an entire box of chocolates. Her eyes, which were enormous, shone with mischief and her mouth was clamped shut, seemingly in an effort to stop herself giggling. It was as though she was a delinquent schoolgirl who'd been sent to the headmaster's office for smoking behind the bike sheds. She held my gaze steadily, determined not to blink first.

According to Nati, Caroline had just split up with her boyfriend and I was under strict instructions to introduce her

256

to some 'rich, good-looking men'. However, after catching sight of her I was determined to keep her for myself, though my prospects weren't good. In her eyes, the fact that I was so transparently middle-class made me desperately uncool. Even though she'd done her O-levels at Cheltenham Ladies College, she'd then gone to William Ellis, the same North London school I'd been to. By the time she'd gotten there though it was a fairly bog-standard comprehensive and as a result she now spoke with a perfect mockney accent and was known as 'Cazzy'. (Her father joked that he wanted Cheltenham to give him his money back.) She went on to do a degree in social anthropology at the LSE and most of her friends were either duckers and divers she'd met at 'Ellis' or impoverished, student types.

I managed to find her a flat next door to mine and took her to as many glamorous events as I could in her first week. I was hoping to impress her with my social connections but I needn't have bothered. She thought most of my friends were 'wankers' and dismissed the parties I took her to as 'boring'. She wasn't interested in the see-and-be-seen world of Manhattan's fashionable bars and restaurants. She was a tomboy, not an aspiring socialite. Indeed, she was a *Loaded* reader's fantasy come to life: a ladette with the figure of a Page Three girl. Her idea of a good time was watching a boxing match on Sky Sport then heading to the nearest pub to get pissed. Back in London, she'd drunk lager by the pint.

Caroline was totally unlike the girls I'd been pursuing in Manhattan. For one thing, she wasn't totally obsessed with her appearance. Clothes, hair, make-up – none of these things mattered to her nearly as much as they did to your average, 23-year-old New York girl. Feminine artifice wasn't part of her armoury. Indeed, she was constitutionally incapable of deception. Whenever she tried to conceal anything it was laughably obvious, like a little kid telling you they hadn't eaten the last piece of bread when their face was covered with strawberry jam. Everything about her reminded me of what I'd left behind when I embarked on my quest to take Manhattan. By the lights of New York's *beau monde* Caroline was a nobody, yet I found myself wanting to spend more and more time with her.

I waited until she was completely shitfaced before I made a pass at her – what a gent! – but even then I was STUNNED when she didn't turn me down. I got another surprise when she took her top off: she had *Baywatch* tits, perfect 34Ds. She knew it, too. As she led me to the bedroom she told me not to trip over my tongue. When we made love for the first time – or 'shagged', as she put it – I had the feeling that I was cheating fate, that somehow I'd ended up with a far sexier girl than I deserved. I mean, she was *absolutely fucking gorgeous*. What was she doing with a guy like me? I was convinced this was a one-off, a way of saying thank you for taking her under my wing, and I desperately tried to record the experience with my internal camcorder. This was definitely one for what Chris Lawrence called 'the bomb' – the beat-off memory bank.

The fact that I was in bed with a woman at all made it an *historic* event. Since my memorable afternoon with the Red Hot Chilli Pepper, I'd only managed a handful of one-night stands. After two and a half years on the Manhattan singles scene I'd discovered that New York women tend to judge potential partners according to how many desirable attributes they possess rather than what they're like as people. These were, in descending order of importance: social status, net worth, physical appearance, apartment, summer house and, a long way down the list, personality. No man is held to possess any intrinsic value – we're all just the sum of our assets.

Caroline, being from London, was different. If anything, she was an inverse snob, more likely to rule men out if they were too conspicuously successful, particularly if they rammed it down your throat as most New Yorkers tend to do. In general, she was less preoccupied with men's external attributes, however dazzling, and more interested in what they were like on the inside. That was lucky for me since on the outside I was a short, balding, unemployed 33-year-old with no money and a tiny flat. The fact that she found me funny was also a big help. American women had never laughed at my jokes – and I mean NEVER.

For instance, I was at a party on the Upper East Side in the summer of 1997 when a woman I was chatting up claimed to have spotted three well-known plastic surgeons on the way in. I took this as a cue to ask her what she would have done if she had to choose one cosmetic procedure.

'I don't know,' she mused. 'I guess I'd have my breasts reduced.'

As you can imagine, it took an almost superhuman effort of will to stop my eyes wandering in a southerly direction. She then asked me what cosmetic procedure I'd have done.

'Oh that's easy,' I quipped. 'I'd have my penis reduced.'

Okay, it was a bit obvious, but I was expecting at least a polite little laugh. Nothing. Instead, she said: 'Oh rilly? Why, d'you have a problem?'

Her eyes were as wide as saucers and I debated whether to play along. *Yeah baby. I've got a HUGE problem!* However, in the event of her coming home with me I knew it would only lead to disappointment – colossal, earth-shattering disappointment – so I told her I was only joking.

'Oh, I see,' she said. Then, as an afterthought, added: 'Hah!'

Thirty seconds later she was gone.

Luckily, Caroline found my particular brand of puerile humour quite funny and, to my astonishment, our night together proved to be the start of . . . *something*. I was going to say 'affair' but that wouldn't be quite accurate. We were less like lovers than two old friends who happened to have sex with each other. The usual excitement that accompanies the early stages of a romance, when two people discover each other for the first time, was strangely absent. We were like a happily married couple who'd been living together for at least ten years. I was perfectly content with this state of affairs – Christ, I would have accepted her on *any* terms – but it bothered Caroline. She was only twenty-three after all. She wasn't interested in a comfortable, low-maintenance relationship. She wanted fire-works.

The problem, from her point of view, was that we weren't in love. At this stage, I should have done what any sensible man in my position would have done and whisked her off for a dirty weekend in the Hamptons. Instead, I did something really, really stupid – GALACTICALLY stupid, in fact. I said I didn't believe in romantic love. It's an illusion, I insisted, an outpouring of feeling triggered by someone else but, actually, having very little to do with them. The person we imagine we're in love with is just a blank screen on to whom we project our own romantic fantasies. It's an absurd overreaction, out of all proportion to its apparent cause. In the language of psycho-analysis, we 'idealize the sexual object'. It's like being hypno-tised. As Freud pointed out, it's usually because something about the woman in question reminds us of our mothers. She becomes a 'mother surrogate' and all the libidinal longing we had for our mother, long since repressed, returns with an overwhelming force. This infatuation only lasts, at most, eighteen months and when it wears off we find ourselves involved with someone we hardly know, as if waking from a dream. Quite often, we don't even *like* them. No, I told her, love is a ridiculous basis on which to choose your partner. We were much better off in the mature, adult relationship we were in: two good friends who happened to have sex.

What was I thinking?

Admittedly, I did actually believe this. Freud's analysis of romantic love – or 'sexual love', as he called it – seemed to tally with my own experience. The last time I'd been in love had been in 1993 when I'd gone out with an actress called Natascha McElhone. The relationship hadn't lasted very long – she dumped me after three months – but my feelings for her had taken hold of me like a fever. When they eventually passed it was an immense relief; I felt like a Moony who'd been successfully deprogrammed. I was determined not to get into that altered state again.[1]

But I never should have expressed this jaundiced view to Caroline. All I can say in my defence is that I was taken in by her macho, down-to-earth persona. I thought she was part of a new generation of post-feminist women who'd rejected the traditional model of femininity in favour of something much more aggressive and masculine. I made the mistake of assuming that because she was a tomboy she wasn't into all that mushy, romantic stuff. That was for girly girls, not beer-swilling boxing fans like her. She was like a cross between Lara Croft and Tank Girl: she wasn't worried about whether her bum looked big in anything – she kicked ass!

In short, I did exactly what I've accused the women of New York of doing to me: I judged a book by its cover.

At the beginning of January, 1998 Caroline dumped me for a strapping, 28-year-old attorney at her law firm. I hadn't realised it, but he had been circling her for ages, wooing her with flowers, chocolates and jewellery. Unlike me, this wily lawyer hadn't been fooled by her tough exterior. He'd known exactly what buttons to push.

Needless to say, as soon as she delivered the bullet I realised I'd fallen hopelessly in love with her. I hadn't changed my mind about romantic love, but that hadn't stopped me from tumbling head over heels. I thought of love as being like a kind of mental disorder and believed that once its psychological roots had been exposed it would lose its power – the good old 'talking cure'. In fact, it's much more like a physical ailment: understanding its causes, or thinking you do, doesn't prevent you from catching

---

[1] Freud discusses the shortcomings of sexual love in *Civilisation and its Discontents*: '[W]e are never so defenceless against suffering as when we love, never so helplessly unhappy as when we have lost our loved object or its love.' *The Freud Reader*, ed. Peter Gay (New York: Norton, 1989) p. 733.

it. Love, is completely involuntary. How you feel about it in the abstract doesn't make any difference to whether it affects you personally. I'd arrogantly assumed that because I didn't believe in it, I was immune to its charms. I felt like the faith-healer of Deal in the famous limerick:

> There was a faith-healer of Deal,
> Who said, 'Although pain isn't real,
> If I sit on a pin
> And it punctures my skin,
> I dislike what I fancy I feel.'

As the winter of 1997/98 drew to a close, I was in a pretty bad way. Not only had I lost both my jobs, I'd lost the woman I loved as well. Even I could see that there was a pattern here: I was a textbook self-saboteur. What the hell was wrong with me? Why was the impulse to destroy myself – what Freud called 'the death instinct' – so powerful in me?

Of course, just when I thought I'd hit rock bottom things suddenly got a whole lot worse.

29

THE TROUBLE WITH HARRY

It was around noon on 16 February, 1998 that I discovered the full extent of the trouble I was in. Frank Johnson, the editor of the *Spectator*, had called earlier that day to tell me about a letter that had come for me from Theodore Goddard, a firm of solicitors acting for Harold Evans, Tina Brown's husband. That letter was now uncoiling from my fax machine like a poisonous snake. It was a response to an article I had written in the *Speccie* the previous November about Evans's departure from Random House, the New York publishing firm he'd been president of. It accused me of waging a 'campaign' to 'ridicule and denigrate' Evans and his wife and threatened to sue me for libel unless I paid all of his legal costs to date, gave a sum of money to his favourite charity and signed an undertaking that would effectively prevent me from writing about him or his wife ever again.

Well, I thought, it's finally happened. They've gone nuclear.

All my Fleet Street colleagues had warned me not to cross Evans and Brown – or 'Harry and Tina', as they're universally referred to. Since their arrival in New York in 1983, Harry and Tina have become two of the city's most formidable operators. In addition to being held responsible for the success of a glittering array of writers, there are a number of journalists who claim their careers have suffered after they've crossed them. (Tina's nickname at *The New Yorker* was 'Stalin in high heels'.)

263

I was now at the top of their enemies list. You couldn't call what I'd done 'career suicide' since my career was on the point of expiring at this point. It was more like career euthanasia. Of all the spectacular own-goals I've ever scored, this was my most dazzling piece of footwork.

I first met Tina at Oxford in 1985 when I was a cocky, 21-year-old undergraduate. She was the 31-year-old editor of *Vanity Fair* and had flown to Britain a few days earlier to investigate the death of Olivia Channon from a heroin overdose. In addition to being an Oxford Bright Young Thing, Channon was the daughter of a cabinet minister and Tina had decided that this 'scandal' was something she wanted to write about. A group of 'prominent undergraduates' had been convened at her request and we were sitting round a table at a French restaurant when she made her entrance.

'At last,' I said, rushing up to her and throwing out my arms as if greeting a long-lost relative. 'The female Toby Young!'

The others laughed – I had a reputation for saying inappropriate things – but Tina looked extremely put out. *Who is this idiot?*

'Only joking,' I said, trying a different tack. 'I'm the male Tina Brown!'

Silence.

The most successful British journalist of her generation stared at me coldly and gave a barely perceptible nod before sweeping past to greet the others. She didn't so much as glance in my direction for the remainder of the lunch. At the time I cursed myself for having blown such a golden opportunity but those students who did talk to her didn't seem to get much out of it. One boy described meeting her as being like encountering an alien life form that has the ability to absorb everything you know in a few seconds and loses interest in you the moment the Vulcan Mind Meld has served its purpose.

When I first arrived in Manhattan I thought Harry and Tina might make some effort to cultivate me, particularly after I started writing my *Evening Standard* column. It's not unusual for them to woo New York correspondents for British newspapers in the hope of getting some favourable publicity back in the old country. One such journalist likes to tell the story of how she was introduced to Harry at the 1997 Hay-on-Wye Literary Festival just before moving to Manhattan. 'So, you're heading to our fair shores, are you?' said the bluff Yorkshireman. 'Be sure to look me up when you get there.' He then handed her his business card and continued to work the room. Ten minutes later she was standing somewhere else when one of her colleagues dragged Harry over to meet her, telling her she couldn't hope for a better contact in New York. She gave Harry an embarrassed look as if to say, 'Sorry about this', but the spry 68-year-old was remarkably unfazed. 'So, you're heading to our fair shores, are you?' he said. 'Be sure to look me up when you get there.' He then dutifully forked over another business card before disappearing back into the crowd.

Perhaps the reason Harry and Tina made no attempt to contact me in 1995 was because I was working for *Vanity Fair*. There's no love lost between Graydon and New York's premier power couple. Back in his *Spy* days, Graydon published a copy of a grovelling letter Tina sent to Mike Ovitz begging him to consent to an interview. In the letter, which appeared in 1990, Tina described Ovitz in embarrassingly effusive terms, referring to his 'creativity', his 'gifted sense of talent', his 'taste', his 'extraordinary business acumen' and his 'aura of leadership'. Incidentally, for those who don't know, Mike Ovitz is a Hollywood agent.

A chance for revenge came two years later when Tina got wind of the fact that Si Newhouse had offered Graydon the editorship of *The New Yorker*. Naturally, Graydon accepted, but before an announcement could be made Tina informed Si that she was interested in the job herself. Tina ended up at *The New Yorker* – she was Si's favourite – and Graydon was made the editor of *Vanity Fair* instead. According to New York media folklore, Tina then rubbed salt into the wound by leaving a huge, blown-up picture of herself receiving a National Magazine Award on the wall of her office to greet her successor. She also encouraged *Vanity Fair*'s most distinguished authors and advertisers to move with her to *The New Yorker* and one of her associates dubbed the magazine 'Vanishing Flair'. These aggressive tactics succeeded in discombobulating Graydon and it was at least two years before he came into his own at *Vanity Fair*.

After I lost both my contracts in 1997, the only way I could make a living was to freelance for as many British publications as possible and I quickly discovered that there was an almost insatiable appetite for compromising stories about Harry and Tina. Not surprisingly, few other reporters were prepared to dish the dirt on 'the Bill and Hillary of the New York media'. A typical profile of them would begin with the journalist complaining that he hadn't been able to persuade anyone to utter a single word against them, on or off the record. Indeed, some reporters complained that no one was even prepared to be quoted saying something nice about them in case Harry and Tina then mistakenly attributed any of the less flattering, anonymous quotes to them. Few New York journalists wanted to cross the husband-and-wife team because they could supposedly snuff out a person's career with a single click of their fingers.

I'd always been sceptical about this. I thought it was just part of the myth they'd cultivated about themselves. In any event, I'd been fired from all my jobs so what could they do? I had nothing to lose. Consequently, I began to churn out gossipy stories about them. There was no shortage of material. Almost everyone I bumped into had an anecdote to tell. For instance, John Heilpern, the British theatre critic of the *New York Observer*, told me the following story one night at Elaine's. In 1985, when Heilpern was an editor at *Vanity Fair*, Tina asked him to commission a short story for the Christmas issue and, using all his charm, he managed to persuade the novelist Isaac Bashevis Singer to write one. In those days *Vanity Fair* was a much more literary publication than it is today, having published Gabriel Garcia Marquez's novella, *A Chronicle of a Death Foretold*, in its entirety in 1983. Heilpern duly passed the story along, expecting Tina to be pleased that he had managed to pull off such a coup,

but a few days later it came back to him with the words 'Beef
it up Singer' scrawled above the title in Tina's handwriting. 'I
had to gently explain to Tina,' laughed Heilpern, 'that "Beef it
up Singer" was a recipient of the Nobel Prize for Literature.'

As it turned out, I was wrong in thinking Harry and Tina
wouldn't retaliate if I peddled stories like this to the British
press. I was threatened with a libel suit unless I gave an undertaking that I would 'desist forthwith from further defaming,
denigrating and ridiculing' them. In effect, they were trying to
force me to sign a legal document that would prevent me from
writing about either of them ever again.

It seemed a ridiculous overreaction to a bit of mild provo-
cation on my part, but Harry and Tina don't like to be crossed.
According to Steve Florio, the president of Condé Nast: 'Tina's
got a Sicilian grandmother in that background somewhere.' I
should have realised I was playing with fire when Nigel
Dempster told me about an interview he'd conducted with Tina
towards the end of 1997. 'I mentioned your name and she went
completely crazy,' he said. 'She shuffled her papers and that
was the end of the interview. You caused me untold grief.'

The solicitor's letter accused me of making ten mistakes in
my *Speccie* article. In particular, Harry objected to what I'd said
about his decision to leave his publishing job. After parting
company with Random House, Harry had taken up a new position as the editorial director of the *New York Daily News* and
in my piece I'd treated his efforts to portray this as a smart
career move with some scepticism: 'It is as if John Birt suddenly
and unexpectedly left his job as director-general of the BBC to
take up a senior post in the Mirror Group.' Curiously, I'd written
almost nothing that hadn't already been widely reported in the
New York press, yet the article was singled out as an example
of my 'unprofessional campaign of fabrication and innuendo'.

In addition to this letter, Theodore Goddard also sent a letter
to the *Spectator* threatening the magazine with a libel suit unless
it gave an undertaking that it would never repeat the alle-
gations contained in my article, publish a correction and an

apology and pay a sum of money to Harry's favourite charity.

I suspect that what really set Harry off was an item that appeared in a gossip column in the *New York Post* claiming I was writing a satirical play about him and Tina. (This was true, though I hadn't got very far with it.) the *Spectator* article had appeared in the issue dated 29 November, 1997, some two months earlier, while the item in the *Post* had appeared on 21 January, 1998, just a day before Harry lodged his first, official complaint.[1] In this light, his attempt to gag me looked suspiciously like an attempt to squelch the play.

I was astonished that Harry was making such pernicious use of England's libel laws. It seemed so contrary to the spirit of the First Amendment. How could he have worked for so long in the American media without acquiring a respect for free speech? Either Harry believed in the First Amendment, in which case why was he seeking to muzzle me, or he didn't, in which case why had he accepted a job as the editorial director of the *Daily News*? It didn't make any sense. In his capacity as president of Random House Harry had published *Primary Colors*, a thinly disguised *roman á clef* about Bill Clinton. Why was it perfectly okay for Joe Klein to satirise the President of the United States yet unacceptable for me to 'ridicule' Harry and his wife?[2]

This wasn't the first time he had over-reacted to something

---

[1] Harry sent a letter to the *Spectator* dated 22 January, 1998 in which he listed thirteen 'direct fabrications' in my article. The letter, which Harry wanted the *Spectator* to publish verbatim, was more than twice as long as the piece it was supposed to be a response to. It contained a wealth of detail about Harry's career, including the name of the designer he'd hired to redesign *US News & World Report*: Edwin Taylor. It was Frank Johnson's refusal to publish this that led to Theodore Goddard's letter of February 16.

[2] Clinton's reaction to Harry's ribbing of him was somewhat more sanguine: he invited Harry and Tina to dinner. It was a state dinner for Tony Blair in January, 1998 and in her account of the event in *The New Yorker* Tina returned the compliment. She fawned over Clinton's 'height, his sleekness, his newly cropped, iron-filing hair, and the intensity of his blue eyes' and claimed he had 'more heat than any star in the room'.

he considered a personal attack. Harry's particularly sensitive about anything relating to his run-in with Rupert Murdoch. (Murdoch owned *The Times* during Harry's brief tenure as editor from 1981–82. Before this, Harry had had a very successful fourteen-year run as editor of *The Sunday Times*.) When the journalist William Shawcross sent Harry a manuscript copy of the chapter in his biography of Murdoch dealing with Harry's editorship of *The Times* Harry responded with a 27-page fax suggesting various changes that, in Shawcross's words, was 'almost as long as the chapter itself'. Not surprisingly, Shawcross ignored most of Harry's recommendations and Tina subsequently ran a blistering attack on Shawcross's biography by Francis Wheen in *The New Yorker*, an article that John Le Carré described as 'one of the ugliest pieces of partisan journalism that I have witnessed'.

Why do Harry and Tina react like this to any form of criticism? Why don't they just rise above it? They are British, after all. Unlike Americans, we're supposed to be able to take the occasional bit of ribbing. The answer, I think, is that they've spent too long in New York. They might have been able to laugh at themselves once, but that faculty seems to have deserted them in the eighteen years they've been in America. In common with all the other big shots in Manhattan, their sense of self-worth is now intimately bound up with their professional status and, in particular, how well they're *perceived* to be doing. Both Harry and Tina have become masters of spin, brilliant at conveying the impression that they have brilliant careers. In a sense, their actual careers are secondary to the business of managing the public perception of their careers; or, rather, that's what their careers now consist of. To paraphrase Oscar Wilde, they've put their talent into their work, but their genius into their press coverage.

In the world that Harry and Tina operate in the public sphere is more significant than the private one. It wouldn't even be accurate to say that, in this world, perception is more important than reality; perception *is* reality. For boldface names like

Harry and Tina, the public realm is the only one that matters. It's where they live. From the moment they become public figures, they begin to view everything through the eyes of those they imagine are following their every move. When debating whether to do something, they don't weigh it up in the way a normal person would, but assess how it will affect their reputations. After a few years of this some A-list figures end up with no interior life whatsoever. They begin to suffer from what the American Psychiatric Association's *Diagnostic and Statistical Manual of Mental Disorders* defines as 'Narcissistic Personality Disorder'.[1] They pay the ultimate price for their notoriety, which is the disintegration of the self, or, at least, the transformation of the self into something less recognisably human.

I'm not suggesting that Harry and Tina have become 'celebrity monsters', to use the technical term, only that in common with all New York's heavy hitters they're hyper-sensitive to criticism. The pugnacious atmosphere of Fleet Street, in which rival journalists take swings at each other all the time, is something they've left far behind. When someone cocks a snook at them in public, they're not inclined to laugh it off as they might have done when they were still based in London. On the contrary, they retaliate.

According to the *Spectator*'s solicitor, Harry had a pretty strong case. I was confident that my article was true, but that didn't mean I'd win if the matter went to court. According to Britain's libel laws, it wouldn't be up to Harry to prove that the disputed facts were false; rather, the onus would be on me to show that

---

[1] The symptoms of Narcissistic Personality Disorder are as follows: 1. A grandiose sense of self-importance. 2. Believing yourself to be special and only understood by other special people. 3. Requiring excessive admiration. 4. A tendency to use other people. 5. A sense of entitlement whereby you believe your requests should automatically be met. 6. An inability to empathise with other people, bordering on solipsism. 7. Being perceived by others as arrogant and haughty.

they were correct. Just because the majority of the facts in my *Speccie* piece had already appeared in various New York publications didn't prove they were true. In order to convince the jury, I'd have to persuade the sources that those publications had relied upon to testify on my behalf. Since most of those sources were anonymous and the majority of them lived in New York, the chances of that happening were pretty slim. Harry, on the other hand, claimed to have a number of witnesses waiting on the tarmac at JFK, ready to fly to London at a moment's notice. According to Theodore Goddard's letter, they included Si Newhouse, Dick Morris and Disney CEO Michael Eisner.

Nevertheless, the situation wasn't hopeless. My best strategy was to ensure that Harry's efforts to gag me received as much unfavourable press coverage as possible. In any libel case the plaintiff is always in danger of looking vain and self-important simply by going to such monumental lengths to restore his or her good name. My job was to persuade Harry that this would surely be the case if he pressed his claim. For almost a month my flat became the headquarters of a publicity campaign in which I tried to portray Harry as an evil press magnate bent on silencing his most vociferous critic. It was David and Goliath all over again.

The campaign wasn't wholly successful. As the former editor of *The Sunday Times* and *The Times*, not to mention the ex-president of Random House, Harry knew a thing or two about managing a story. In one interview after another he branded me a 'journalistic stalker', attempting to cast himself and Tina as the victims and me as an embittered loner. In the end, though, he couldn't quite make this stick. He and Tina are simply too rich and powerful to be taken seriously as underdogs. The previous year they'd bought a $3.7 million maisonette on East 57th Street and a few weeks earlier they'd put their country house in the Hamptons up for sale for $2.7 million. I, on the other hand, made a very convincing loser. In the press coverage our dispute received I was described as 'a media minnow', 'a

lowly freelance' and 'a nobody'. The David and Goliath angle
– or, as the *Evening Standard* put it, 'the liberal prince and the
pesky gadfly' – was just too good to ignore.

One unexpected consequence of the whole affair was that it
improved my relations with Graydon. As soon as he got wind
of the fact that Harry was threatening to sue me he called to
see if I was okay.

'You're not frightened, are ya?' he asked.

'Actually, I'm quite enjoying it,' I replied, trying to sound as
nonchalant as possible.

'I bet ya are, ya little fuck.'

He added that there was no reason for me to be scared since,
in his opinion, the dispute would end up making my name.

'There are two ways to make your reputation in this town,'
he announced. 'You can either do something great or destroy
somebody else's and, believe me, the second's a helluva lot
easier.'

Graydon asked to see a copy of the letter from Theodore
Goddard and, a few days later, called again, this time to marvel
at its pomposity. Indeed, it was so priggish he thought Harry's
solicitor must be having fun with his client: 'This line when the
guy says, "The impression conveyed is that Mr and Mrs Evans
are self-centred and uncaring people, only concerned about their
own welfare and advancement." I mean, that's got to be tongue-
in-cheek, right?'

I assured him it was 100 per cent sincere.

On 10 March the *Spectator* faxed me another letter from
Theodore Goddard, this one addressed to the magazine, saying
that Harry had agreed to drop his threat of legal action against
it provided it printed a letter from him in the following week's
issue. All his other demands had been dropped, including the
demand that the *Speccie* should pay his legal expenses. It seemed
he had come to his senses, at least as far as the magazine was
concerned. But what about his threat against me? The letter
made no reference to that. The Sword of Damocles still hung
over my head and would continue to do so until the statute of

limitations on libel ran out a year later. Still, I was fairly confident Harry wouldn't come after me. Above all else, it was his
image he cared about and by threatening me with a libel suit
he'd done his reputation far more harm that my *Speccie* article
had.[1] Once I'd made it clear I wasn't going to back down there
was nothing for him to gain by pursuing me. Apart from everything else, I was completely broke. I may have won this particular round in my wrestling bout with Manhattan, but I was
still on course to lose the match.

---

[1]As Quentin Letts put it in the *Evening Standard*: 'The suspicion is that Harry
Evans, whose eye for social connections was a common source of mickey
taking when he lived in London, has caught the Manhattan disease: humour-
lessness.' 'The liberal prince and the "pesky gadfly"', the *Evening Standard*,
4 March, 1998.

30

THE ST VALENTINE'S DAY MASSACRE

After Caroline dumped me I felt I really ought to do something about my problems with the opposite sex. Had I remained in London it never would have occurred to me to seek professional help but after living in New York for two and a half years I'd become infected by the self-improvement bug. In therapy-speak, I thought of myself as having an 'issue' and it was time to 'deal with it'; if I didn't 'own my problem' it would end up 'owning me'.

Not that I actually went into therapy. The answer, as far as I was concerned, was to get myself 're-branded'. I'd first come across the re-branding concept in an article I'd read in *The New York Times* that said single men in Manhattan had started consulting marketing experts to improve their dating prospects. The idea, apparently, was to treat yourself like a product that wasn't moving off the shelves fast enough and get a market research company to 're-brand' you. You put together a 'focus group' – a representative sample of the 'market' you were aiming at – and hired a consultant to find out where you were going wrong.

It was particularly urgent in my case since women in New York had come up with a terrifying new way of assessing potential lovers: they 'Googled' you. After meeting you for the first time, they plugged your name into Google, the Internet search engine, and trawled through the results. Naturally, as soon as

274

I heard about this I Googled myself and the first thing that
came up were the words: 'Is Toby Young the worst journalist
in the world?' I clicked on this and read the following:

> Sorry about this unstructured rant, but there's something
> about the words 'by Toby Young' that just pushes my
> buttons. He used to write an insanely annoying column in
> the *Standard* about his life in New York working for *Vanity
> Fair* (since sacked), which basically consisted of telling his
> adoring readers time and again how he had once more not
> been let into the fashionable party of the week because the
> 'clipboard Nazi' (somewhat repugnant phrase) 'didn't think
> I was famous enough'. I was actually moved to write a
> letter to the editor pointing out that he indeed wasn't
> famous enough.

Clearly, if anyone was in need of re-branding, it was me.

After working my way through the Yellow Pages I struck
gold: a company called Focus Suites that agreed to put me in
touch with a 'market research consultant' called Hazel Kahan.
Hazel had already helped one thirtysomething man re-brand
himself and, provided I convened the focus group, she'd
'moderate' the discussion and translate their musings into practical advice. There was only one catch: she charged $750.

'What if I write about the experience for a British newspaper?' I pleaded. 'Would you waive your fee in that case?'

'Sorry,' she said. 'It's non-negotiable.'

In the end, I managed to persuade the *Mail on Sunday* to
pick up the tab even though they decided against publishing
the resulting piece. I think the whole exercise was a little too
sad from their point of view. It wasn't a 'triumph over tragedy',
the *Mail on Sunday*'s formula for a good story. It was just a
tragedy.

In order to get the exercise under way I had to find six attractive women between the ages of 21 and 35 who were prepared
to sit down and talk about me for two hours – no easy task.

I decided to ask women I knew rather than six complete strangers. This was partly because I thought they'd offer more valuable advice, but mainly because I hoped they wouldn't be too hard on me. I also decided to tell them I'd be watching them from behind a two-way mirror, again in the hope that they wouldn't be too mean.

In retrospect, I should have realised that your friends never need much of an excuse to be rude about you.

Focus Suites was located at the top of a skyscraper on Lexington Avenue and on the day in question – St Valentine's Day, 1998 as it happened – Hazel began by asking each of the six women how they knew me. I was stationed behind a two-way mirror, notebook in hand. The first person to answer was Claire, a 23-year-old friend of Caroline's. She was one of only two English girls present so I thought I could rely on her to be sympathetic.

'I met him years ago in London and he was very drunk,' she said. 'He was just an idiot.'

Ouch!

Next up was Jane, a 27-year-old American actress who was going out with a friend of mine. I quite fancied her so I was particularly interested in what she had to say.

'I remember going round to my boyfriend's apartment one morning and this bald guy was asleep on the couch with an empty bottle of whisky at his feet,' she replied. 'I can't say I was pleased to see him there.'

Ooooof!

The third to answer was Lucy, a 33-year-old English businesswoman.

'I guess I met him probably two years ago and he didn't really make much of an impression, actually,' she said. 'Neither good or bad.'

Owwww!

I was out for the count, but that didn't stop Lorna, a 26-year-old Irish PR girl, from kicking me when I was down.

'The first time I saw him he was rolling around the floor of a nightclub with one of my friends,' she snickered. 'She was desperately trying to get rid of him so she told him she had to use the bathroom and left.'

Aaaargh!

Any illusions I'd had about them going easy on me were shattered within the first five minutes. By treating the whole exercise as a bit of a joke, they'd given themselves a licence to ridicule me. I knew then that the next two hours were going to be brutal. I just didn't know how brutal.

The next item on the agenda was my hair.

'Is he really bald or is it just that his hair's really short?' asked Candace Bushnell. Strictly speaking, Candace fell outside my 'target market' because she was over 35, but she's so damn sexy I would have given my eye teeth to go out with her. Indeed, one of the reasons I'd asked her to participate was to find out how she felt about me.

'He's progressively bald,' answered Meg, a 30-year-old art consultant.

'I can never figure it out,' said Candace, 'because he's got this little fuzz, you know?'

By this stage they'd already forgotten that I was sitting behind the two-way mirror. At least, I hoped they had. The thought that this was the censored version of what they really thought was too much to bear. From time to time, one of them would glance over in my direction and, for a second, I'd think they were looking at me. Then I realised they were just looking at themselves in the mirror.

They then got on to the subject of my flat which, fortunately, only one of them had seen. Unfortunately, it was Lucy, my condescending English friend.

'I was surprised by how clean and tidy it was,' she said. 'It was really neat and he was house proud and he was going round saying where he got all the pieces of furniture that he'd bought.'

'Was it good furniture?' Hazel asked.

'No,' said Lucy, 'but I mean it was, you know, carefully thought through.'

I made a mental note: *If you ever do succeed in picking up a girl in New York, make sure you go back to her place.*

Up until this point, the comments had been fairly light-hearted. But Hazel was a trained market research consultant and she was determined to get to the heart of the matter. What were my real shortcomings as a man?

Meg, the American art consultant, cut to the chase. 'He can't deal with sex,' she announced. 'He's very oppressed. He can't combine sex with love for somebody.'

For some reason, this comment produced a great deal of nodding all round: *That's it exactly.* Candace was particularly impressed. 'Meg is the kind of person that Toby should be going out with,' she declared, 'but Meg senses a deep problem and she doesn't want to go near him.'

'It's true,' said Meg.

'She sees through him,' added Candace.

I felt all the pain of rejection even though I'd never actually asked Meg out. It was as though a sophisticated group of consumers who were used to shopping at Harrods were being asked how they felt about some generic product from Woolworths. I was being picked up, sniffed and then discarded.

To ram the point home, Hazel then asked if any of them would ever consider going out with me.

'I certainly find Toby extremely intellectually stimulating,' said Lucy, trying to be charitable, 'but I guess I don't find him physically interesting.'

Candace was more direct. 'I never really thought about it,' she said. 'I always really thought of him as a friend.'

'But not thinking about it suggests you're not really interested,' Lucy pointed out, somewhat less charitably. 'I don't think there's something wrong with him physically . . .'

There was an awkward silence. The only thing that could be heard was the sound of sobbing coming from the other side of the mirror.

Nevertheless, Hazel wasn't finished. She decided to press Candace on this point: Was I someone she could *ever* be sexually interested in? I held my breath. It was the moment of truth.

'I can't really imagine being with Toby,' Candace replied. 'I just can't imagine it at all. He's just, you know, so much like someone I would be friends with and I would never, I could never . . .'

'You don't think of him as sexual, is what I'm hearing, as a sex person, sexual?' asked Hazel.

'*I* don't,' said Candace, italicising the 'I', as if to say 'but that's just me'.

'I don't think anybody does,' said Hazel, brightly. 'Would anyone like some more wine?'

Forget the wine, Hazel. How about some hemlock?

To be honest, I felt drained at the end rather than suicidal. It had been so much more intense that I'd anticipated. It was as if I'd been through a particularly gruelling form of group therapy. The point of the exercise, which was to help me improve my dating prospects, had got lost somewhere along the way and, instead, I simply found out what some of my friends really thought of me. I was a frog who might conceivably turn into a prince but none of them were about to kiss me to find out.

Another mental note: *Never eavesdrop on your friends talking about you. You might hear something you shouldn't.*

The following day Hazel called to give me her post-mortem.

'You're an interesting fruit but they'd rather have you peeled,' she said. 'They're more interested in the inside than the outside.'

In other words, they don't fancy me. Yes, thanks, I think I got that.

'If you were an alcoholic beverage you'd be less like a Cognac and more like a Tequila,' she added. 'A cognac is very intimate, romantic and so on, while a Tequila is an outgoing, party, sociable thing.'

So how should I re-brand myself?

'Show the serious side of yourself,' she urged. 'Show people what you're really about. Round yourself out. You have engaged these women's interest. Now you have to show you're interested in them. I don't think people see the vulnerability in you. Women want that, they want the little darkness in men.'

A *little darkness?* What was she on about?

'A little less glitz and a little more substance,' she concluded. 'Show a bit more emotion.'

So there it was. I had to become more emotionally correct. Women perceived me as being a Tequila Slammer but with a little work I could become a Tequila Sunrise. Unfortunately, the women I wanted to go out were the kind that drank Slammers. After the ordeal of being re-branded, I decided to stick to a more tried-and-tested method of improving my dating prospects: platform shoes and hair-thickening products.

31

MEN BEHAVING BALDLY

An unexpected consequence of my tussle with Harry and Tina was that it brought me to the attention of Bob Guccione Jr, the forty-year-old founder of *Spin* and son of the legendary owner of *Penthouse*. In the spring of 1998 the Gooch, as he was known, had just pocketed $18 million from the sale of *Spin* and was in the process of setting up a men's magazine called *Gear*. The success of *Loaded*, *FHM* and *Maxim* in the UK gave several publishers the idea of launching a similarly testosterone-charged magazine in the States and the Gooch intended to be first out of the gate. Although *Gear* was supposed to be slightly more highbrow than a typical British lad mag, with some serious reporting thrown in with the beer and the babes, it was essentially an American version of *Loaded*. After reading about my run-in with New York's premier power couple, the Gooch thought I was precisely the kind of 'politically incorrect' journalist he was after and offered me a job as a staff writer.

Naturally, I accepted. Okay, it was a bit of a come down from my previous job – if *Vanity Fair*'s a Cadillac, *Gear*'s a bumper car – but I was in no position to be sniffy. The Gooch offered to pay me $60,000 a year. I was back in business!

As soon as I was hired I started bombarding Guccione Jr with my usual crackpot suggestions. Unlike Graydon, though, he proved quite receptive.

One in particular caught his eye:

Dear Bob,

Ever since I started losing my hair, women have been telling me it doesn't matter to them whether a man is bald or not. 'It's not what's on your head that counts, it's what's *in* it,' one girlfriend told me. Needless to say, that did nothing to allay my anxiety. What else *could* she say? 'I'd prefer it if you had hair, but I just didn't think I could do any better'?

I'd like to conduct a social experiment to try and find out how much difference a full head of hair really makes when it comes to impressing the opposite sex. Why don't I get hold of a copy of *How To Pick Up Girls*, select the 10 best pick-up lines in the book, then go to 10 different bars in Lower Manhattan and try them out on 10 different women? The following night I could go back to the same bars and use the same lines on 10 different women, only this time with one crucial difference: I'd be wearing a wig. If I do better on the second night than the first, that will conclusively prove that women really do prefer men with hair. What do you think?

'I love it,' said the Gooch. 'Go get 'em, Tiger.'

Needless to say, on the first night I struck out with all ten women I approached. Part of the problem was that each line I came out with sounded like exactly that – a line. As soon as a New York woman realises you're using a line on her, she'll automatically shoot you down since that's better than leaving you with the impression that she's too dumb to realise what's going on. No self-respecting New Yorker would want to be mistaken for the kind of bridge-and-tunnel person that a pick-up line might actually work on.

The following night I set off with a heavy heart. I was convinced I was going to crash and burn in all ten venues again even though I was now wearing the wig. Sure enough, at the first five places I tried I went down in flames, but, strangely enough, instead of growing more despondent after each humiliating experience my confidence started to increase. Something about wearing the wig had subtly altered my personality. This wasn't just any old rug, either. It was a nine-ounce, ash-blonde mane designed by a Hollywood wigmaker. I was no longer a William Hague look-a-like who couldn't get laid in the city that never sleeps. I was an Australian surf punk who shagged a different Sheila on Bondi Beach every night!

The sixth place I tried was the Elbow Room, a dimly lit cave in Greenwich Village. The previous night it had played host to an NYU crowd and by the time I'd arrived the music was so loud I hadn't been able to make myself heard. But on this particular night it was given over to karaoke and the music had been switched off while the machine was being set up.

I spotted a girl over by the bar who I thought might be Australian, possibly because she was about to do a Tequila shot. She looked wild and sexy and I decided to try out a line I'd promised myself that I'd only use as 'an absolute last resort'.

'Are those space pants you're wearing?' I enquired. 'Because your arse is out of this world.'

She gave me a look of total amazement: *Did you really just say what I think you said?* Then, miraculously, she started smiling.

'That's the worst line I've ever heard,' she laughed. 'I can't believe you've ever picked up a girl using that line.'

'You're right,' I responded. 'I haven't.' Then, just as I was about to walk away, my new, be-wigged personality took over. I fixed her with an unflinching stare: 'Until now, baby.'

Within a few minutes we were joking and flirting and, before long, we were up on stage belting out a duet of *Wild Thing*. I felt like Jim Carrey in *The Mask*: the wig had transformed me into the life and soul of the party. She turned out to be a 28-year-old Polish-American called Krysia and while she may not have been Cameron Diaz she was still 'smokin''. After about an hour or so we started getting 'hot and heavy' in the back of the club and I began to worry that she might accidentally dislodge my wig. The only solution was to pretend to be incredibly vain. 'Hey, baby,' I said, every time her fingers wandered up the back of my neck, 'don't touch the hair, okay?'

In the taxi on the way back to my place I sobered up enough to remember that I was, after all, conducting an experiment. In the interests of science I decided to whisk the wig off to see whether she would still come home with me once she realised I was a complete Kojak. If she ran screaming from the cab that would prove that women find men with hair more attractive.

'Okay, baby,' I said, tossing the rug into her lap. 'Now you can touch the hair.'

For a second she looked completely horrified: *Who is this psychopath?* Then, just as she had in response to my opening line, she burst out laughing.

'You're absolutely fucking crazy, you know that?'

She ended up coming home with me, though she seemed to find me distinctly less attractive without the wig. The reason she went through with it, I suspect, is because she didn't want to seem like the kind of girl who's so shallow she cares about whether a guy has hair or not. Had she twigged a little earlier in the evening, she probably would have made her excuses and left.

Over the next few months, I played the monkey to the Gooch's organ-grinder. Nothing I suggested was too outrageous. I spent the night in the Voyeur Dorm, a house in Florida in which seven teenage girls took turns to strip in front of webcams that broadcast all their movements live on the Internet; I road-tested a machine that was billed as 'the lie detector of sexual orientation' which involved attaching wires to my penis and then seeing how the little fellow responded when I was shown pictures of naked men; I hung out for twenty-four hours with Bill Goldberg, a 32-year-old professional wrestler who at one point put me in a headlock and performed a 'jackhammer', his trademark move;

I even dressed up as a woman in an attempt to pick up a lipstick lesbian in the Clit Club, the centre of New York's hard-core dyke scene. Forget about Kosovo. That was the most dangerous journalistic assignment of the nineties.

Working for *Gear* was a lot of fun, but it wasn't exactly what I'd had in mind when I'd fantasised about moving to New York. I was no closer to the Algonquin Round Table than I had been in Shepherd's Bush.

Throughout my time at *Gear* my relationship with the Gooch could best be described as volatile. Six months after he hired me, he fired me. I took him out for a drink and managed to persuade him to give me another chance, but after another few months he fired me again. I like to think that this had less to do with my shortcomings as a reporter and more to do with his capriciousness as an employer. The Gooch was a highly strung character. When he fired me for the last time he also fired every other writer on the masthead with the exception of the sex columnist. But I wasn't exactly the most reliable of employees either. For instance, on June 30, 1998 I sent the Gooch the following fax:

Dear Bob,
    I'm sorry I didn't make the meeting this morning. It was one of those nights. I was with this girl until 9 a.m. When she eventually left to go to work I set the alarm for 10.30 a.m. and placed the clock radio next to my ear. I then woke with a jolt at 3.30 p.m. and my first thought was, 'Oh fuck.'
    I know it's not an excuse. I feel pathetic.

This 'excuse', in addition to being feeble, was a flat out lie. The bit about being up until 9 a.m. was true, but there was no girl present. The only thing that had kept me awake was a bottle of Johnny Walker Black.

When he'd first hired me the Gooch had talked about turning me into 'the P.J. O'Rourke of Cyberspace', but I never managed to pull this off. What he really wanted was a writer who could perform some sophomoric stunt and, in the course of writing it up, segue into a rant against political correctness. Unfortunately, that was beyond my gifts. After a brief stint as the Gooch's crash-test dummy my career was back in the toilet.com.

32

ALEX IN WONDERLAND

Towards the end of 1998 I got a call from Peter Stone, an LA journalist friend, to tell me that Alex was going out with _____ _____, one of the ten most famous supermodels in the world. I'd begun to think that anything was possible as far as Alex was concerned, but this took the biscuit. Could it really be true? I fervently prayed that it wasn't. I left a message on Alex's voicemail asking him to confirm that it was all a vicious rumour and about an hour later he called back.

Alex: Listen, dude, you're not planning to write about me and _____ are you?

Shit, fuck bollocks!

Me: Don't tell me it's true?

Alex: D'you promise you're not going to write about it?

Me: You absolute bastard!

Alex [Laughing]: Look, I know what it looks like. It looks like I've had this success, or whatever, I mean, if you want to call it that, and now I'm sleeping with a supermodel, whatever that means. Is she a supermodel? I don't know. Supermodel, model, whatever. But, you know, she's been a friend of mine for years. When I first knew her I couldn't even afford to take her out to dinner. She's just a friend who happens to be a super-model, you know? How did you find out anyway?

Me: Peter Stone told me.

Alex: How did he find out? It's meant to be a secret.

287

Me: Apparently, you went up to him at a barbecue and said, 'I'm shagging a supermodel.'

Alex [Laughing]: I never said that, dude. That's such a lie. I'd never say that. Did he really say I said that? I can't believe it. Okay, I *might* have said something like that, you know, in the first week of seeing her or something. It was just exuberance, you know? Of course, for about a week, I was excited that she was a supermodel, you know, if she is a supermodel, whatever that means. But now, you know, she's just _____, d'you know what I mean? I can't believe he said that to you.

That wasn't all he'd told me. According to Giles, Alex had also bragged that the first time he shagged _____ he was taking her from behind when she looked back at him over her shoulder and said, 'You know what, Alex? You're better than De Niro.'

Alex: Anyway, dude, you're not going to write about it are you?

Me: Not if you don't want me to.

Alex: Please. You can't. I mean, _____ would kill me. I'm begging you, okay? It just looks so bad. You know, I sell a screenplay and then the next thing you know I'm fucking a supermodel, like that's what it's all about, d'you know what I mean? It's got so little to do with anything. [Yeah, right.] Toby, you have to believe me, I'm the same fucking person, alright? I'm still driving the same shitty car, I'm still living in the same shitty apartment, all my friends are the same . . .

Me: The same shitty friends.

Alex: For fuck's sake, you know what I mean. It hasn't changed anything.

Me [Taking it in properly for the first time]: You just happen to be sleeping with _____ _____. You really have sold your soul to the devil haven't you? 'Okay, Lucifer, you can have my soul, but in return I want to live in Hollywood, sell a screenplay for a quarter of a million dollars and start going out with a supermodel.' So is that it? Have you got everything you wanted? Please don't tell me you have any more wishes left.

Alex [Laughing]: You're going to write about it, aren't you? I know what you're like, man. Jesus Christ, you have to promise me you won't.

Me: I promise.

Alex: I know you, Toby. You're probably going round telling everyone: 'Alex is shagging a supermodel, Alex is shagging a supermodel.' You are, aren't you?

Me: No, I'm not. I'm really not. [I was, actually.]

Alex: Well please don't, okay, because it's not like that, it's really not. I know it looks a lot like that, but that's really not how it is.

Me: Don't worry.

After Alex hung up it occurred to me that perhaps he *did* want me to write about it after all. I mean, if I was sleeping with _____ _____ I'd certainly want the whole world to know about it. In the end, though, possibly because I suspected he wanted me to, I didn't. Not until now, anyway.

33

THE GREEN-EYED MONSTER

The news that Alex was sleeping with _____ _____ hit me hard. My reaction was summed up by Elizabeth Kubler-Ross's description of the different stages a person goes through on learning that they've got a terminal disease: denial, anger, bargaining, depression and, eventually, acceptance. Like most heterosexual men, I'd grown up fantasizing about sleeping with models. It wasn't the act of having sex with them I found so appealing – though God knows that would have been sweet enough – but the bragging rights afterwards. To be able to walk past a newsstand, point at the cover of a glossy magazine, and say 'been there, done that' – that was my idea of heaven. Now Alex was living out this fantasy!

In *Experience* Martin Amis talks about his anxiety in 1970 that his friend Rob, who's career was 'horrifyingly meteoric', was about to project himself out of his orbit. I felt that Alex was on the point of flying out of my orbit, too. Amis ascribes this feeling to 'fear of desertion' and my friends certainly seemed to be deserting me in droves at the beginning of 1999. It wasn't just Alex. Back in London, my contemporaries were racing ahead in leaps and bounds. Until I'd arrived in New York I'd always thought of myself as being among the most successful members of my peer group, but now I was being left behind. I wasn't even in the pack of runners huffing and puffing to keep up with the leaders. I was limping along with the stragglers. Shit, I was about to be lapped.

Not a week went by without one of my Oxford classmates hitting the big time. Hugh Fearnley-Whittingstall – known at Oxford as Hugh Fairly-Long-Name – had been given his own cooking programme on Channel Four. Boris Johnson had succeeded Frank Johnson as editor of the *Spectator*. Patrick Marber had a play on at the Royal Court – his second. What had I achieved? Bog all. One particularly painful blow was the discovery that John Heilemann, a writer whose first ever byline had appeared in *The Modern Review*, had sold a book to HarperCollins for $1 million. I phoned him and left a message on his machine hoping to find out how he'd done it. He never returned my call.

Nothing had prepared me for the realisation that I wasn't one of life's winners. It seemed to come upon me all of a sudden. One minute I thought I'd achieve immortality through writing a great book or a classic movie or *something*; the next I was worrying about whether I'd ever hold down a steady job. All my self-confidence vanished in the blink of an eye. For the first time in my life I began to think failure might be a real possibility. Was I destined to be one of life's also-rans? I imagined my obituary in the *Brazen Nose,* the annual magazine of Brasenose College:

Toby Young, 58, Freelance Journalist

Toby Young, a freelance journalist, will be remembered chiefly for his occasional contributions to regional newspapers on the dangers of wonky supermarket trolleys. After a brief spell in America in the late nineties, where he claimed to have been a friend of the Oscar-winning screenwriter Sir Alex de Silva, he returned to Britain where he found occasional work as a feature writer for the *Wolverhampton Express & Star*. He took early retirement and used his savings to open a pub, The First Room, in Little Snoring, Bucks. In later years Toby was working on a volume of memoirs that has been passed on to his old college. It is hoped that these may one day be published. He never married.

I began to have this irrational fear that those friends who were doing well were reaping the rewards that had somehow been intended for me. Is this what Gore Vidal meant when he said, 'Every time a friend succeeds, I die a little'? It was as if Cupid's less romantic older brother – the Roman god of sex and money – was constantly firing arrows in my direction but kept hitting the people standing next to me by mistake. I even came up with a name for this cack-handed immortal: I called him 'Stupid'. It occurred to me that perhaps I ought to start charging people to hang out with me. *Roll up, roll up. Stand next to me for half an hour and thanks to Stupid's unfailing ability to miss his target you'll be shagging a supermodel within a week!*

According to Freud, fate is regarded as a substitute for 'parental agency': if things are going well for us we instinctively feel it's because we're loved by our parents and if things are going badly it must be because we've fallen out of favour. This is why we automatically focus on our successful contemporaries when we've suffered a string of setbacks. Aha, we think. That's why the gods have deserted us. It's because they love our siblings more! This, in turn, explains why we feel a sudden rush of elation on hearing about some terrible calamity that has befallen one of our friends. If something bad has happened to them, why, it must mean they've fallen from grace! All the more love for us. Alex was at the top of a long list of people whom I wanted something truly awful to happen to.

I wasn't so envious of Alex that I would have actually done anything to harm him, but the idea of indirectly hurting him by an act of *omission* was quite appealing. A recurring fantasy involved Alex hanging off the edge of a cliff and begging me to save his life. I would look down at him pityingly – if only you hadn't stood so close to me when Stupid was lining up his target – until his strength gave out and he plunged to his death. *AAAAAAAaaaaaaa . . . thunk!* The German psychoanalyst

Theodore Reik maintained that a thought-murder a day keeps the psychiatrist away, but I'm not so sure.

The people I envied the most were those who'd achieved something I felt capable of myself. Alex's crime was to write a successful screenplay, something that had long been an ambition of mine. (I should have been sleeping with _____ _____, damn it!) Whenever I spoke to any of our mutual friends back in London I'd try and persuade them that his success was wholly undeserved, that he was COMPLETELY TALENTLESS. I needed to convince myself that the only reason he'd made it in America was because he'd been lucky. Of course, I was protesting too much. At the back of my mind I'd begun to suspect that Alex knew something that I didn't. The little bastard seemed to have a knack for succeeding. But what was his secret?

According to Alex, it was because he'd discovered his vocation; he was doing what he'd been put on this earth to do. 'Find something you're passionate about, something you can't *not* do,' he said. 'You'll be surprised how quickly everything falls into place when you're doing something you really love.'

But this was just Hollywood gobbledegook. In the little time I'd spent in Los Angeles since arriving in America I'd come to marvel at the ability of people churning out hack work to convince themselves that they were skilled craftsmen. I'd been expecting to find a group of hard-bitten cynics cursing themselves for being such whores, but most of the writers I'd met seemed surprisingly content – just like their New York equivalents, in fact. Where was the self-recrimination that talented people were supposed to torture themselves with when they squandered their gifts?[1] Somehow, they'd managed to persuade

---

[1] Of course, the traditional complaint of Hollywood writers, that they're prostituting their talents, should be taken with a pinch of salt. To quote Hecht: 'Before it might seem that I am writing about a tribe of Shelleys in chains, I should make it clear that the movie writers "ruined" by the movies are for the most part a run of greedy hacks and incompetent thickheads.' *A Child of the Century* (New York: Simon & Schuster, 1954).

themselves that in spite of being paid half a million dollars to rewrite Adam Sandler comedies they hadn't sold out.

Of course, it was possible that they were concealing what they really thought. In Los Angeles, as in New York, to be perceived as a cynic is the kiss of death. Far better to be thought of as James Stewart than Jimmy Cagney. In Hollywood there's even a name for the career strategy that involves pretending to be more innocent than you are in order to impress people with your purity of soul: it's called 'the non-hustle hustle'. Was this Alex's secret? *Faux naiveté*?

I didn't think so. Alex might contradict himself from one moment to the next, but he believes what he says when he says it. Alex is Machiavellian alright, but it's completely unconscious. He isn't an honest, straightforward guy who occasionally says what people want to hear in order to ingratiate himself with them; rather, his whole being is geared to pleasing people. He can't be accused of putting on an act since that's all he is – an act. It's as if he has no identity beyond whatever his career requires him to be; his whole personality is completely subordinate to his will to power. When he laughs at the boss's jokes it's because he genuinely finds them funny.[1] This is the real secret of Alex's success. It enables him to form a series of close friendships with powerful people without them thinking they're being 'played' in any way. To use another Hollywood phrase, he's the perfect 'celebrity pet'.

When I next spoke to Alex I put it to him that his primary talent was the ability to schmooze people.

Alex [Sniffily]: I would have thought my 'primary talent' was being able to write. Having a powerful friend might be enough to open the door, you know, but it can't get your stuff made. I mean, Julia Roberts can't get her best friend's project made, d'you know what I'm saying? [Yes, Alex. You're saying you're

---

[1] A mutual friend of Alex's and mine in Los Angeles, told me that 'the Alex laugh', when focused on him, made him feel like 'Oscar Wilde on cocaine'.

incredibly talented.] Finally, the weird, brutal truth about this town is that in the end it doesn't matter who you know or how many barbecues you've been to with Steven Spielberg, it all comes down to *the work*. [FUCKING talented, in fact.][1]

Me: Yes, but you would think that because you've made it. If you were an unsuccessful writer you'd think the opposite.

Alex: I'm telling you, dude, it's the work.

Me: But you have to admit, you do have a suspiciously large number of celebrity friends. Are you saying it's just a happy coincidence? That you just happen to have become friends with people who are in a position to help you through sheer chance?

Alex: I know you have a hard time believing this, dude, but the people I've become friends with are the people who's work I really, really respect. There's nothing *strategic* about it.

Me: So the reason you became friends with _____ _____, for instance, is because you admire her 'work'? What, like, her work on the catwalk? It had nothing to do with the fact that you wanted to fuck her brains out?

Alex [Laughing]: Listen, dude, to me they're not these *really amazing celebs*, they're just ordinary people, you know? I don't think, 'Oh my God! I'm talking to Madonna!'

Me: Wait a minute. Hold it right there. *You know Madonna?*

I realised I could never compete with Alex. I was the diametric opposite. Instead of pleasing people who were in a position to help me I always ended up antagonising them. As with Alex though, it was completely unconscious. It was as if we responded to anyone in a position of authority in a completely different way. He wanted to please them, to win their approval, whereas

---

[1] The earnestness with which people like Alex discuss 'the work' is in stark contrast to screenwriters in the 30s and 40s. According to Pauline Kael, 'They were too talented and too sophisticated to put a high value on what they did, too amused at the spectacle of what they were doing and what they were part of . . .' Pauline Kael, 'Raising Kane', *The Citizen Kane Handbook* (London: Methuen, 1985) p. 19. Ben Hecht used to use the numerous Oscars he'd won as doorstops.

I wanted them to know that I was completely indifferent to what they thought of me. In Freudian terms, I was stuck at the Oedipal stage of my psychological development; I still wanted to kill my father. That, presumably, was why his career had taken off and mine had gone through the floor.

Or was I just fooling myself? Maybe Alex was right. Maybe it did all come down to the work. It didn't escape me that my theory of why I hadn't made it was quite flattering. It wasn't because I was lacking in the talent department, oh no, it was just because I wasn't any good at brownnosing! Still, my total inability to maintain good relations with those in a position to help me had to be a *factor*. I mean, I had hired a strippergram on Take Our Daughters to Work Day. You couldn't take that away from me. Unfortunately, even though I was aware of how self-destructive my behaviour was, I wasn't sure I could modify it in any way. Indeed, I wasn't sure I wanted to.

In *A Child of the Century* Ben Hecht notes that one of the hallmarks of all the miserable, penniless writers he knew in Hollywood's golden age was that, deep down, they didn't really want to succeed:

> Despite their wit and even talent, unsuccess was in their eyes. The need to be underdogs and rail against existence was as strong in them as their lust for fame and money. You could see it not only in their faces but hear it in the gloat with which they detailed their misfortunes.

Was that my problem? That I actually *preferred* being a loser? The thing that really frightened me was that I wasn't nearly terrified *enough* by the prospect of failure. I could feel myself becoming gradually accustomed to it, trying it on for size and deciding it wasn't nearly as bad as I'd originally thought. *Perhaps being a freelance, publishing a piece here and there, isn't the end of the world after all.* I'd discovered that it was perfectly possible to scrape by on very little money. Okay, 'scraping by' wasn't what I'd hoped for out of life, but maybe it was time to scale down my expectations.

I felt like Tom Cruise in *Born on the Fourth of July* finally abandoning the hope that he'd ever walk again.

It was time to do something – anything – before I sunk into the abyss.

34

TOUCHING BOTTOM

Naturally, I decided to up my alcohol intake. When I first arrived in Manhattan my boozing was regarded as excessive by my *Vanity Fair* colleagues, but by the standards of your average Fleet Street hack it was completely normal. However, by the spring of 1999 it was completely out of control *even by their standards*. (At one point Anthony Haden-Guest told me I had a problem!) I was putting away the best part of a bottle of Scotch a day.

This wouldn't have mattered so much if I wasn't such an *energetic* drunk. When I get shit-faced I don't just fall asleep; I become absurdly gregarious. I'm that really annoying bloke at the end of the party trying to persuade anyone who'll listen to come with him to this 'secret little place' he knows about that's 'really, really cool' – invariably some rat-infested basement in the middle of nowhere. If they refuse, and they usually do, it doesn't matter. I go on my own. When I get there I strike up conversations with total strangers and, for the next six hours, they're my New Best Friends: 'It's not just the booze talking, mate. I really, really like you.' When I eventually carry myself off to bed I make elaborate plans to meet up with them again the following day. Of course, if by chance I do end up bumping into them ever again I can't remember who any of them are from Adam.

It was around this time that I began to frequent an all-night bar called Marylou's on West 9th Street. With its subterranean atmosphere and insalubrious clientele, Marylou's is the New

York equivalent of Café Bar Sicilia, my old haunt in Soho. It's totally deserted until about 2.30 a.m. when suddenly it starts filling up and by 4 a.m. it's completely heaving. The great thing about Marylou's is that no one stands on ceremony. It's like a speakeasy of the old school where celebrities rub shoulders with gangsters, beautiful girls hang out with drug-addled musicians and journalists gossip with public officials – all united by their love of alcohol.

When I remember some of the things I got up to at Marylou's I shudder with embarrassment, but by far the worst of these was the time I picked up 'Jennifer', a 55-year-old man in drag. I can't even make the excuse that I mistook Jennifer for a woman. I've seen more convincing female impersonators at the local Australian pub in Shepherd's Bush. In addition to his pronounced five-o'clock shadow, you could see little tufts of hair poking through the holes in Jennifer's fishnet stockings. Nevertheless, I ended up taking this freak back to my flat in the West Village.

I want to make it completely clear – and I can't stress this enough – that I didn't fancy Jennifer. *Not. At. All.* It was an act of selfless charity. When I got talking to him at around 5 a.m. in Marylou's he explained that the only reason he was there was because his boyfriend had kicked him out of their flat and he had nowhere else to go. Normally, I wouldn't respond to a sob story like that, but since I was completely rat-arsed I invited him back to my place. He was my New Best Friend, after all. I really, really liked him! Besides, my flatmate, a British merchant banker called Euan Rellie, was away so I wouldn't actually have to share a bed with Jennifer. He could stay in Euan's room and, hopefully, by tomorrow his boyfriend would have forgiven him.

We went back to my flat where, naturally, we carried on drinking. However, after one and a half hours of listening to Jennifer tell me what a 'bitch' his boyfriend was, I'd had enough. I showed him to his room – or, rather, Euan's room – and called it a night. It was round 7 a.m.

Exactly one hour later, when Jennifer and I were both sleeping soundly, my flatmate returned unexpectedly. Now I should explain that Euan is a fairly typical upper-middle class professional. Educated at Eton and Cambridge, he's used to the best things in life. He was always complaining that the flat was 'fucking filthy' – even though it was pretty clean – and urging me to get 'a daily'. He kept his room meticulously tidy and forbade me to set foot in it. The idea that I might borrow any of his Savile Row suits . . . *ugh!* In addition to being anally retentive, he's germ-phobic.

You can imagine the scene, then, when Euan set foot in his bedroom. The first thing he noticed was the smell, a powerful combination of alcohol and body odour. *Yuk!* Next he saw a wig perched on his bedside table. What was that doing there? Could it be one of mine? He didn't recognise it. Finally, his eyes adjusted to the light. Was that . . . it couldn't be . . . it was! *Fucking Hell!* There, lying on top of his Peter Jones bedspread, wearing nothing but fishnet stockings, was a 55-year-old man called Jennifer!

'Toby,' said Euan, bursting into my room and shaking me awake. 'What is that *thing* doing on my bed?'

'Sorry, man,' I said. 'I didn't think you were coming back till tomorrow.'

Euan took a deep breath.

'I'm going to check in to a hotel but when I come back I expect your *guest* to have gone. I also expected you to have changed my sheets and fumigated my bedroom.'

I laughed.

'This really isn't funny,' he snorted. 'I'm really not amused by this.'

He wasn't either. He got his revenge by telling all our mutual friends that he'd come home unexpectedly one morning to find a naked man in the flat. 'I'm not saying Toby's gay or anything,' he would declare, sounding like Mr Reasonable, 'but you've got to admit, it was *fucking* suspicious.'

Needless to say, all my friends concluded I was a raging queen.

*

The Jennifer episode was embarrassing enough, but in the annals of my toe-curling drunken exploits it was nothing compared to the Easter weekend I spent in Verbier. As they say in Alcoholics Anonymous, that's when I 'touched bottom'.

I'm not much of a skier but when my friend Hutton Swinglehurst – another merchant banker – told me he was planning to drive from London to Verbier in his newly purchased BMW M3 I couldn't resist. The idea was to put it through its paces on the autoroute. He calculated that if we averaged 155mph we could make the journey in under six hours. Admittedly, that was unlikely considering 155mph was the car's top speed, but I couldn't fault his attitude. It was the kind of boy's own adventure that I loved.

I flew into Heathrow on the red eye on 2 April, 1999 and Huttie picked me up outside Terminal 3 at 9.30 a.m. We drove pretty much non-stop and while we didn't average 155mph we still made good time. It was just before midnight when we pulled into the forecourt of our hotel and, by my calculations, I'd been up for thirty-two hours. The sensible thing to do at this point would have been to go straight to bed so, naturally, we decided to pop into the Farm Club for a nightcap. By common consent, the Farm Club is the most depraved nightclub in the Alps but it was only five minutes from our hotel so it seemed like the obvious choice.

Six hours later I emerged, blinking into the light, having consumed an entire bottle of 18-year-old Macallan. By then Huttie was long gone so I set off in what I took to be the direction of the hotel. Two and a half hours later, I was still looking for it. This wouldn't have been such an ordeal if I hadn't left my jacket in the Farm, not to mention my room key *and* my wallet. As it was, by the time I found the hotel and eventually slipped into bed I was in an advanced state of hypothermia.

After what seemed like ten minutes I was woken by Huttie who was already in his ski gear.

'Come on, you lazy sod,' he said. 'We'll be late.'

I looked at my watch. It turned out I had only been asleep

for ten minutes! Then I noticed that something about my little finger didn't seem quite right.

'Huttie,' I shrieked. 'Where's my signet ring?'

He burst out laughing.

Oh no!

'Don't you remember?' he replied.

'No I bloody don't.'

'You gave it to that 16-year-old Swedish schoolgirl you proposed to last night.'

'You're kidding?'

'Nope.'

'Which 16-year-old Swedish schoolgirl?'

'The one you kept trying to snog in the Farm.'

'Jesus Christ. D'you at least know what hotel she's in?'

More laughter.

'Sorry, old boy. She went back to Sweden first thing this morning.'

The floodgates opened and the self-recrimination began. I was a pathetic fool, a worthless loser. How could I have been so careless? I felt worse that morning than I'd ever felt before in my life. My signet ring was one of my most treasured possessions. Whenever I was anxious about something my right hand was instinctively drawn to it and I found myself twiddling it between my forefinger and thumb. Now it was gone.

The loss of my signet ring was the last straw. Like Michael Henchard, the hero of *The Mayor of Casterbridge,* I vowed then and there that I would never touch another drop of alcohol. Of course, I'd made this promise dozens of times before, but this time I really meant it. No, I *really* meant it. As my prospects had declined, my alcohol consumption had increased and if I didn't stop now the downward spiral would only continue. I'd long told myself that if the going got really tough I could always stop drinking and that would provide me with the extra oomph I'd need to pull through. Well, the time had come to put that theory to the test.

302

Of course, I had my doubts about the benefits of giving up alcohol. Maybe sobriety wouldn't be the cure-all I imagined. Instead of increasing my powers by 20 per cent, as I hoped, maybe it would only increase them by 2 per cent. Nevertheless, I had to give it a try.

In part, this decision was a delayed reaction to the recent battering my ego had taken.[1] My failure to take Manhattan had left me with an acute sense of my own mortality. Before this, my life had stretched before me like an endless plain and I had no notion of it ever running out. I thought the number of chances I had to get things right was infinite. If a career path I'd embarked upon ended up leading nowhere, why, I would simply abandon it and try another! I rarely thought about the future and when I did I it wasn't ten or twenty years hence it was always just 'the future'. Now, for the first time in my life, I had a sense of time running out. Far from having a limitless number of opportunities, I'd probably used most of mine up already.

However, it was also a direct consequence of the loss of my signet ring. It may have only been worth about £100 but its sentimental value was incalculable. It bore my mother's family crest and, in my mind, it had come to symbolise my connection with her. In a sense, it was the only one I had. You see, my mother was dead.

---

[1] As Freud writes in *Civilisation and its Discontents*: 'As long as things go well with a man, his conscience is lenient and lets the ego do all sorts of things; but when misfortune befalls him, he searches his soul, acknowledges his sinfulness, heightens the demands of his conscience, imposes abstinences on himself and punishes himself with penances.' *The Freud Reader*, ed. Peter Gay (New York: Norton, 1989) p. 758.

35

OBI-WAN KENOBI

My Mum died on the morning of 22 June, 1993. It felt a bit like my birthday. The normal routines of day-to-day life were suspended and, no matter what I did, everyone was nice to me. It know it's perverse to talk about my mother's death in this way but at the time I kept thinking about it in ways I knew I wasn't supposed to.

For instance, when she was dying I was acutely conscious of the need to 'clear the air'. Nothing in particular, just the usual stuff: apologise for being such an awful son, assure her I'd be nicer to my sister, tell her I loved her. But I knew that saying these things was solely for my benefit. That is, I wanted to tell her things that I knew I'd regret not telling her; I wanted to avoid future guilt. But given that my sole motive for telling her was guilt-avoidance, would I really feel guilty in the future if I didn't take this opportunity to tell her?

Of course, I did tell her. Or rather, I tried. Crying is something you can't avoid by being prepared for it. You know you're going to cry and . . . you do. As soon as you start crying any pretence that you're trying to clear the air for the other person's benefit goes out the window. They end up having to comfort *you*. This must be the worst thing about dying: at a stage in your life when you most need time with yourself you have to spend every waking moment thinking about the feelings of those you'll leave behind. As Larkin wrote, when it comes to death 'courage . . . means not scaring others'.[1]

On the day she died it seemed important to my father and sister that I should be there for the moment of death. Why? Was it because, as seems most likely, they thought she might be dimly conscious of who was with her and want her family around? Perhaps it was the guilt-avoidance thing again: they wanted to protect me from feeling guilty in the future about not being there. Or maybe they just wanted to be with me at that moment. I imagined that death would strip life down to the essentials, cut through such painstaking examination of other people's motives, but it increases your sensitivity to that stuff. I expected to experience a Hemingwayesque indifference to social niceties and ended up feeling like Jane Austen.

When it happened, my clearest sensation was a tremendous surge of pity for my father. Sasha was lying on the bed they'd always shared and he was kneeling on the floor. (They'd been together for thirty-five years.) He was holding her hand but, shortly afterwards, he shuffled forward and, very delicately, as if piecing an eggshell back together, cupped her chin in his palm and gave her jaw a little push. It wasn't until later, when I discovered a poem my father had written about this moment, that I realised what he was doing. Even as I write these words, some eight years after the event, I can't read this poem without crying. It's called *Changing Places*.

> How glad I was to hear your voice
> Not by what you said
> 'My mouth will be wide open

---

[1] As one of the BBC's first women producers, my mother introduced the poems of Philip Larkin to a Radio Three audience long before he became famous. This comes from Larkin's poem *Aubade*: 'Courage is no good:/It means not scaring others. Being brave/Lets no one off the grave./Death is no different whined at than withstood.'

It must be closed
When I die, when I die.'

My head is leaning against yours
My hand is cupping your chin
Not to make love again
But, still tenderly, to clamp your jaw shut
After you died, after you died.

Up till a moment ago before your head became a skull
An inch away on the other side of that soft skin
Your memories were ready to jump the gap
To put on the purple or the yellow dress
Before you died, before you died.

Hitler was there to circle around with Donne,
The scent of wallflowers on a summer's night,
The cry of seagulls swooping on the ferry,
The sharp taste of garlic in your father's house
While you were still alive, while still alive.

This verse shows I could not close your mouth
You can dance again in your purple dress
Between the continents in my not yet skull
You can cup your hands to catch my head
You are not yet dead, not yet dead.[1]

That evening we held an informal gathering for some of her friends. It should have been a touching occasion, all these kind-hearted people sharing their warm feelings for my Mum, but I found myself becoming increasingly agitated. It was held in my parents' bedroom with her body still lying there and several of them said they could feel her spirit in the room. I thought: You

---

[1] This poem is one of over two dozen published in a collection of my mother and father's verse called *Your Head in Mine* (Manchester: Carcanet, 1994).

poor, deluded fools! She's dead. What are you talking about? It felt like they were inventing an afterlife for her because they couldn't bear the thought that she was gone for ever, extinct. But of course they were perfectly entitled to play whatever tricks they liked to avoid this appalling conclusion. It was me who was being odd by insisting on being so unsentimental.

This was the first indication that my reaction to my mother's death would be out of kilter with everyone else's. I didn't really grieve, not in any conventional sense. I cried whenever I thought of her but when I wasn't thinking about her it didn't seem to affect me. People told me I was in denial, repressing my grief. One man, someone I scarcely knew, told me he thought it was 'weird', the way I was reacting. I was behaving normally when I should have been staying at home and renting my garments.

At the time, I didn't feel particularly guilty about not grieving. I wasn't in any doubt about how much I loved my Mum; there just didn't seem much point in brooding on her death. (I may have been exceptional in having the choice.) My friends presented me with all the usual reasons for grieving: if you don't do it now you'll only have to do it later; it's best to get it out of your system; it helps the healing process. But this apparent concern for my welfare was at odds with the disapproval they obviously felt. The bottom line was they just thought I ought to be more visibly upset.

In public, the fact that I was expected to be grief-stricken made me even less inclined to be so. I wasn't going to start breaking down in front of people just because it was the socially acceptable thing to do. But privately, in my dream life, things were going haywire. Dreams about my Mum weren't like other dreams; she'd be so much more corporeal than people usually are. The dreams had a tactile dimension that I'd never experienced before: I was able to reach out and touch her. It was enormously comforting being able to make this physical contact with her, as if I was bringing her back from the dead. I used to wake up sobbing, feeling closer to her than I ever had in life.

*

It would be wrong to say that the loss of my signet ring triggered an outpouring of grief, but it affected me deeply nonetheless. Symbolically, it was like losing my mother all over again. When she'd died, a huge globule of love had been removed from my life for ever. It was as if the temperature of the world had suddenly been turned down a notch. Without my Mum in it, the universe seemed a much colder place. Looking at the empty place on my little finger where my ring had been reminded me of this absence. I realised just how alone my mother's death had left me feeling.

In this fragile state, I found my thoughts turning towards Caroline. Theoretically, I was aware that *something* about Caroline reminded me of my mother – why else would I have fallen in love with her? – but I'd never been able to put my finger on it. Physically, she was quite similar: same height, same figure, same eyes. She even shared my Mum's rather dry, sardonic sense of humour. Beyond that, though, I hadn't been able to figure it out.

Now it hit me: it was because she *disapproved* of me. Like my mother, Caroline was essentially baffled by my fascination with international court society. Why did I get so over-excited about the possibility of attending the opening of yet another designer shop on Madison Avenue? The boldface names I thought were so glamorous were just a bunch of 'fashion victims' in her view. Caroline shared my mother's impatience with the superficial world I was so mesmerised by; she was too down-to-earth to see its appeal. To her, it was just a colossal waste of time. It was as if, through Caroline's eyes, I could experience exactly what my Mum would have felt about the life I was leading in New York.

My mother was quite a serious person, sober and direct, without much in the way of playfulness. That isn't to say she was always in deadly earnest about everything, but she didn't share my comic view of the world. To her, its shortcomings were no laughing matter. She felt other people's suffering very keenly and she thought it was wrong to spend your life in a whirl of social engagements when there were so many more worthwhile things you could be doing. After getting a First in English at Cambridge, she became one of the BBC's first women producers – she met my father in 1958 while making a programme about one of his books. She went on to become the editor of the educational magazine *Where?* and write two novels: *A Lavender Trip*, which won several prizes, and *In the Shadow of the Paradise Tree*. In Highgate, where we'd lived from 1968–76, she'd set up a community arts centre called Lauderdale House and when we'd moved to Devon she'd started a local branch of the Anti-Nazi League. After her own glittering career, the journalistic life I'd chosen was a source of some sadness to her. It wouldn't have been so bad if I was a foreign correspondent, but all I seemed to be interested in was social tittle-tattle. I wasn't throwing my life away, exactly, but I was squandering my talents, doing something trivial and fundamentally shallow.

I began to realise how guilty it had made me feel, knowing how disappointed my mother would have been by my current life. In a sense, the reason I'd chosen the path I had after abandoning my PhD was to flout my mother's wishes. I'd been attracted to a career that I knew she thought was beneath me because it had made me feel grown up and independent to defy her. I'd cut the umbilical cord with the razor blade I'd used every time I'd taken cocaine. By doing something so *verboten*, I'd felt free.

However, I now saw that this was an illusion. The pleasure I got from each rebellious act was tainted by the guilt it inevitably gave rise to. Coming to America hadn't diminished my sense of guilt, as I'd hoped; it had only made it stronger. Somewhere at the back of my mind there was always an image of my mother's face, her brow knitted in disapproval. In the end, the cumulative impact of all this anxiety had been too much. I'd tried to escape it through alcohol, but the sense of weightlessness I got from being drunk was always counterbalanced by the terrible self-loathing I felt the following day. The fact that my mother was dead, and would never know what a worthless reprobate I'd become, made it that much worse. In death, her hold over me was far greater than it had been in life. In that respect, she was like Obi-Wan Kenobi: 'If you strike me down, I shall become more powerful than you can possibly imagine.'

It was as if she had me on a piece of elastic. During my twenties I had run away from her as fast as I could and, for a brief, heady moment, I thought I was free. However, now that I was in my mid-thirties the elastic was at full stretch and I felt myself being pulled inexorably backwards. Soon I'd be back where I started.

It suddenly became clear to me that the only way I could expunge the guilt I felt about failing to live up to my mother's expectations – my only chance for redemption – would be if I could persuade Caroline to get back together with me. Because she shared my mother's stern moral outlook, it would be as if my Mum was forgiving me. Caroline's love would be a form of absolution.

The reason Caroline struck such a deep chord wasn't just because she made such an ideal surrogate for my mother. It was also because I knew how much my mother would have liked her. I could so easily picture them together, jabbering away to their hearts' content. As Caroline became the focus of my thoughts, I had a sense of my mother pushing me towards her, almost as if she was choosing her for me. I'm not superstitious and I don't believe in life after death, but whenever I thought about Caroline I could feel my mother by my side, nodding her approval. 'This is the one, Toby,' she seemed to be saying. 'Don't let her get away.'

36

PMT (PRE-MILLENNIAL TENSION)

Caroline was single again at this point. For over a year she had seemed so happy with her strapping young attorney that I'd almost thrown in the towel, but in the spring of 1999 she rang me out of the blue and told me it was all over. He was at basketball practice and she'd decided to take this opportunity to leave him. Would I come over and help her move out?

I was round there in a New York minute. I managed to persuade her to stay at my place that night and we spent our first evening together watching *Friends* and bingeing on Häagen-Dazs. It was just like old times. At least, it would have been if she'd slept with me.

'Don't,' she said, when I inevitably made a pass at her. 'I really, really like you, but there's absolutely no way I'm ever going to sleep with you again. Sorry.'

Over the next few nights I did my best to persuade her to go back out with me. It was ironic that Caroline had been holding a copy of *Pride and Prejudice* when I'd first set eyes on her since I was now in exactly the same predicament as Darcy: I had to persuade the woman I loved to reconsider me, having made a very poor impression first time round. I did my best. I told her about the epiphany I'd had after losing my signet ring. I was in love with her and I wanted to devote the rest of my life to making her happy. Wouldn't she at least give me a chance?

311

The answer was no. She just didn't feel the same way about me as I did about her. I was safe, rather than exciting; a port in the storm instead of a bolt of lightning. Once, when I asked her how she felt about me, she said I was like 'a pair of comfy old slippers', something that almost sent me straight back on the booze. (Cheers, Caroline!)

The next time I made a pass at her she made her feelings even plainer.

'Listen, Toby, it's never going to happen, d'you understand? Ever. *Under any circumstances.*'

By the time summer came, and I still hadn't made any progress, she announced that she was returning to London to take up a place at law school. I pleaded with her to stay, but she wouldn't change her mind. The best argument I could come up with was that I couldn't trust myself not to start drinking again if she abandoned me. After I'd got back from Verbier, I decided not to join Perry AA. Instead, I decided to 'white knuckle it', as they say in the recovery movement; to go it alone. Well, not quite alone. Caroline had been incredibly supportive. I wasn't lying when I said I might relapse if she went back to London.

She was unmoved. However, she did offer to spend the week leading up to the Millennium with me. New Year's Eve would be the crucial test of my sobriety and while she couldn't be in Manhattan to hold my hand between now and then, she promised to babysit me over the Millennium. It was only July at this point, but in order to let her know her that I intended to hold her to this offer I booked an apartment in Val d'Isère from 26 December to 1 January and bought two airline tickets to Geneva. Of course, in the back of my mind I thought this would be the ideal time in which to try and get back together with her. If it didn't happen in a French ski resort on Millennium Eve, it wasn't going to happen.

Career-wise, things started to pick up in the second half of 1999. Geordie Greig, an old Fleet Street colleague, was made

312

the editor of *Tatler* and hired me to write a monthly 'Letter from New York'. Taki Theodoracopulos, the notorious Greek socialite, became the editor of a section in a weekly free sheet called the *New York Press* and offered me a column. In addition, now that I wasn't drinking I found I had much more energy to devote to my freelance activities. I started churning out two or three articles a week.

One of the biggest changes in my life was that I got a new flatmate in the form of Sophie Dahl. I had stayed in touch with Sophie after the *Vanity Fair* Cool Britannia issue and whenever I was in London I took her out to lunch. When she announced that she was coming to New York to pursue an acting career I invited her to move into my spare room and, to my astonishment, she accepted. Suddenly, I found myself living with a supermodel!

It wasn't the bed of roses I imagined. The worst thing about it were the telephone calls. From the moment she moved in, the phone wouldn't stop ringing. Ninety-nine per cent of the callers were men – and none of them wanted to speak to me. On those rare occasions when it was someone I knew, we'd have one of those awkward, embarrassing conversations in which they felt obliged to talk to me for a suitable period of time before they could politely ask to speak to Sophie. A typical conversation went like this:

Me: Hello?

Gentleman Caller [Surprised]: Oh. Hello, Toby. How are you?

Me: Fine. *How the hell are you?* I haven't heard from you in ages.

Gentleman Caller: Yeah, you know how it is. So, er, how are things?

Me: Oh, God, where to begin? You'll never guess what happened to me the other day . . .

Gentleman Caller [Interrupting]: Sorry, I'm a bit pressed for time. Is Sophie there by any chance?

Me: Oh. Yeah. Hold on. I'll pass you to her. [To Sophie]: It's Alex de Silva.

Next to Sophie's life, mine seemed almost unbearably drab. In the 1999 fall social season there wasn't a party worth going to that she wasn't invited to. Before she moved in, whenever the doorbell rang in the middle of the day it was nothing more glamorous than a delivery from Amazon.com. Now it was an endless stream of invitations. If I wanted to find out what she'd been up to the night before I only had to look in Page Six.

I spilled my heart out to Sophie about my unrequited love for Caroline and she was so touched by my tale of woe she burst into tears. Sophie was a died-in-the-wool romantic and to her there was only one thing for it: I'd have to propose. Why not pop the question in Val d'Isère? Sophie was sure that once Caroline realised how serious I was she'd soon change her mind. 'But you have to have a ring,' she insisted. 'It doesn't count unless you have a ring.'

Up until this point I'd been a confirmed bachelor. I'd briefly considered asking Syrie to marry me but had decided against it on the grounds that I'd be sacrificing far too much. I'd asked myself the following question: Am I ready to give up the possibility of having hot, monkey sex with a string of drop dead killer bimbos in order to settle down and get married? Obviously, the answer was no.

Needless to say, it's only men with girlfriends who have this rose-tinted view of single life. For some reason, we all imagine that if only we weren't shackled to the old ball and chain we'd be living the life of Hugh Hefner. Because Hef managed to pull it off, every sad sack with a dressing gown thinks that living in a mansion in Beverly Hills with a harem of topless lovelies is, at some level, an option. Consequently, when we're weighing up the pros and cons of getting married we never think of the alternative as a solitary, miserable existence punctuated by Kentucky Fried Chicken and watching repeats of *Ibiza Uncovered* on Channel Five. Rather, it's always an Austin Powers fantasy in which we're a finger-clicking lothario surrounded by a bevy of mini-skirted blondes.

After a tour of duty in Manhattan, all my illusions about the joys of being single had gone. There's something immature and a little sad about wanting to sleep with a different woman every night, particularly if you've only had about five one-night stands in your life. In your mid-thirties, chasing 16-year-old Swedish schoolgirls is undignified, not to mention illegal in the United States.

Besides, I'd fallen in love. I would have wanted to marry Caroline even if I'd had a string of women queuing up to sleep with me. I thought about Alex and all the conquests he'd chalked up in Los Angeles. If one of the ten most famous supermodels in the world had told me I was 'better than De Niro' while I was taking her from behind, would I have had a different view? I mean, apart from the view of her butt? I didn't think so. I was absolutely certain I'd met the woman I wanted to spend the rest of my life with.

I got the ring off a friend of mine in the New York diamond trade. I knew it was ABSOLUTELY HOPELESS but Sophie was right. I had to give it a go. If Caroline said no, as I was sure she would, at least I'd have some sort of closure. That will be it, I told myself. End of story. I'll be able to put the whole episode behind me as I enter the new century.

Then, towards the end of October, just a few days after my thirty-sixth birthday, Caroline left a message on my voicemail saying she'd changed her mind about Val d'Isère. She'd been invited to a 'wicked' party in London with all her old friends from William Ellis and she'd decided to go to that instead. She hoped I didn't mind that much, but she was sure I'd under-stand. The thought of spending Millennium Eve stuck in a ski resort with a 36-year-old teetotaller wasn't her idea of fun. It was the biggest party night of the century and she wanted to spend it getting 'trolleyed' with her closest friends.

At Sophie's urging, I flew to London to try and persuade Caroline to change her mind. She agreed to meet me at Rasa, a vegetarian Indian restaurant in Charlotte Street. I felt a flush of pleasure when I saw her again, framed in the doorway. She seemed to glow with warmth and vitality, like one of the children in the old Ready Brek ads. There was no awkwardness between us. On the contrary, it was as if nothing had changed. We'd always gotten on incredibly well and, in spite of everything, we still did. She may not have wanted to spend New Year's Eve with me but she still appeared to feel a great deal of affection.

She said the reason she hadn't got back together with me in New York wasn't because she didn't fancy me, as I seemed to think. It was because she didn't want to marry me. Apparently, she'd given the matter some serious thought. She told me about a conversation she'd had with her father in which she'd told him I was the first boy she'd ever met who she could see herself ending up with. However, in the end, after much soul searching, she decided that I wasn't 'the one'. Besides, she was twenty-five – much too young to get married.

'Wait a minute,' I protested. 'What makes you think I want to marry you?'

'I dunno,' she replied. 'I just get that impression.'

I was disheartened by this because it meant the chances of me persuading her to come to Val d'Isère were vanishing-to-zero. Presumably, she'd guessed that that was where I was planning to pop the question and that was the reason she'd blown me out. Nevertheless, I had come all this way so I had to give it a try. I decided that my only hope was to appeal to her charitable side. If I could only make her feel sorry for me – *really* sorry for me – there was just a chance she might change her mind.

The discussion got off to a bad start when she offered to refund half the deposit.

'Oh, there's no need for that,' I said. 'I'm still planning to go even if you don't come with me.'

She looked horrified.

'You can't possibly go on your own!'

'Of course I'll go on my own. What else am I going to do

316

on Millennium Eve? I know it won't be much fun, but I'll get through it somehow.'

I then proceeded to paint a picture of myself sitting in the apartment on 31 December, nursing a glass of Perrier and reading an airport thriller as the clock struck midnight.

'Don't!' she squealed. 'It's too depressing.'

It was working!

'I think the worst part will be sitting on the bus,' I sighed.

'What bus?'

'The bus that goes to Val d'Isère from Geneva Airport. I've already booked two seats and the idea of crawling up the mountain in that bus with an empty seat beside me . . .'

I let the image hang in the air.

'Oh, baby,' she said, her voice beginning to wobble. 'I think I'm going to cry.'

'Don't worry,' I said, wistfully. 'I'll be okay.'

She put her face in her hands. Was she crying? I couldn't tell. She brought her head up.

'Look, if I come, you have to swear, and I mean *swear*, that you won't try anything. I'd be coming as your friend, not your girlfriend.'

'Darling, d'you mean it?'

'Do you SWEAR?'

'I swear, I swear.'

'There's NO WAY I'm going to have sex with you.'

'I understand. No sex. Just good friends.'

'But do you?'

'Yes. I do.'

She gave me a long, hard stare.

'Okay. I'll come.'

37

VAL D'ISERE

My plan was to pop the question on the stroke of midnight on Millennium Eve. Okay, it was corny, but everything about proposing – the diamond ring, the chilled champagne, the bended knee – is corny. I'd been advised by Sophie to stick to the tried-and-tested formula. At the time, I'd expressed concern that Caroline might find this approach a little cheesy. Wouldn't it be better to try something original? Sophie had dismissed this with a wave of her hand: 'Women love all that stuff.' I hoped she was right.

By the time 31 December rolled around the prognosis wasn't good. It had been bad when we'd set off, but it was even worse now. We'd arrived in Val d'Isère on Boxing Day and in the few days we'd spent together she'd made it clearer than ever before what her answer would be. We'd been sharing a bed – there was only one bedroom in the apartment – but we might as well have been sleeping in different time zones for all the contact we'd had beneath the sheets. Not a good omen. If she didn't want to get back together for the duration of the holiday, what were the chances of her wanting to spend the rest of her life with me?

At one point I asked her whether she'd characterise her feelings for me as loving me but not being *in* love with me.

'Yeah,' she said. 'That sounds about right.'

I felt like I'd been punched in the stomach. I wanted to object that that was such a clichéd, *Ally McBeal*-ish way of putting it, but then I realised that it was me who'd put it that way. I tried another tack: Wasn't it possible that her feelings lay somewhere in between?

'Well, I'm obviously not *in* love with you,' she retorted. 'I mean, if I was *in* love with you I'd be going out with you, wouldn't I? What did you expect? That I'd come on holiday with you, change my mind, and end up going back out with you?'

Well, yes, actually, that is what I expected. Or, rather, hoped. She'd taken my most heartfelt wish and held it up as an absolutely laughable proposition. *Really, I mean, come on.*

I decided to make one last effort.

'Maybe you're *in* love with me but you just don't realise it,' I suggested.

She gave me a withering look.

'It must be nice to live in your world.'

Reflecting on this on New Year's Eve, I couldn't say it *was* particularly nice to live in my world. Nevertheless, in spite of the appalling odds, I was determined to go through with it. I'd come this far. The ring was in my pocket, the champagne was in the fridge. I even had on a clean pair of underpants on the advice of Chris Lawrence. 'Make sure you're wearing a fresh pair of boxers,' he'd counselled. 'If she says "yes" you're going to get laid and if she says "no" you might get a mercy fuck.'

Still, I was assailed by doubts. What if she lost her temper? She had made it completely clear what her response would be so why was I bothering to ask? Why was I forcing her to go through the unpleasantness of formally rejecting me? I was terrified that she would end up blaming herself for not discouraging me enough and decide to sever relations completely: 'There's nothing else for it, Toby. It's the only way to get it into your thick skull.' Even if I couldn't have her as a wife, I didn't want to lose her as a friend.

Nevertheless, I couldn't wimp out now. *Courage, man, courage.*

Rather than go out, I'd decided to cook Caroline supper. She's a strict vegetarian so my options were fairly limited. In the end, I'd plumped for wild-mushroom risotto and it had taken me the best part of a day to cobble together all the ingredients. The fact that I'd never cooked anything more ambitious than scrambled eggs before didn't bother me for some reason. I was confident I could pull it off.

She stood in the doorway, laughing, as I fastidiously measured everything out. I'd downloaded a recipe off the Internet but I had to allow for the fact that water boils at a lower temperature at high altitudes. Did that mean I should use more water or less? I couldn't work it out. Eventually, I managed to get everything under control and I ushered her into the dining room clutching a bottle of champagne. If she said 'yes', I was going to break my non-drinking rule. I could feel the ring burning a hole in my pocket.

'Darling,' I said, 'there's something I've been meaning to ask you.'

She looked at me expectantly. I shut my eyes and took a deep breath.

Suddenly, the room was filled with an ear-splitting, high-pitched screaming noise.

'You dickhead,' she said. 'You've set the smoke alarm off.'

I ran into the kitchen. Sure enough, the water had boiled dry and the risotto was billowing smoke. I switched off the alarm and scraped what was left of the food on to two plates. It didn't look very appetising so I grated some cheese on top and took the plates through to the dining room.

Caroline eyed her food suspiciously.

'What kind of cheese did you use?'

'Er, the normal kind.'

Wrong answer, apparently. She explained that cheese is made with something called rennet which comes from a cow's stomach lining. As far as she was concerned, the risotto was inedible (in addition to being inedible). Things weren't going according to plan. What I'd hoped would be the most romantic night of

320

Caroline's life was turning into an episode of *Mr Bean*. Still, there was no turning back now. I steeled myself for action.

'I know it's a long shot,' I said, surveying the wreckage of our dinner, 'but . . .'

'Don't,' she cried, showing me her palms. 'I don't want to hear it.'

Had she anticipated my question? *Oh God!* I decided to plough on regardless. I reached in my pocket and placed the ring on the table.

'Will you marry me?'

For a second a dark cloud passed over her brow. Oh no, I thought. Here it comes. I braced myself for the coming storm.

Then, to my immense relief, she flushed with pleasure. She took my hands in hers and gave me a huge smile, her eyes crinkling with affection. As far as I could tell it was a completely spontaneous reaction. Surely, she'd seen me coming a mile away? How could I have possibly caught her off guard? Surprisingly, though, she seemed genuinely surprised.

She began to think out loud, weighing up the pluses and minuses of being married to me. The minuses outweighed the pluses by ten to one but since I was expecting to be shot down straight away I was pleasantly surprised. I didn't really listen to what she was saying. All I could think was: *She hasn't said 'no', she hasn't said 'no'*. I felt like a condemned man who'd been granted a stay of execution.

'You look awfully pleased with yourself,' she said, noticing my silly grin.

'That's because you haven't said "no" yet,' I replied.

'Yessssss,' she said, slowly, 'but I've *implied* it.'

It was at that point that I knew she'd turned me down. I was overwhelmed with sadness but, by concentrating on a spot on the tablecloth, I managed not to cry. Or, rather, I managed not to make any pitiable snuffling noises as the tears cascaded down my cheeks. My immediate inclination was to ask her if she would consider going back out with me instead but I thought that would sound pathetic. I didn't want to come across as some wretched loser, desperate to make a sale.

Oh, who was I kidding? I had a huge 'L' carved into my fore-head.

Nevertheless, the effect of the proposal was surprisingly posi-tive. She didn't recoil as I'd feared; on the contrary, she seemed to gravitate towards me. I suppose it's not every day that a girl gets proposed to, particularly not by a boy who's gone to the trouble of buying a ring. She came over to where I was sitting and wiped my tears away with her napkin.

Then something miraculous happened: she kissed me. That's right, she kissed me!

There were rockets going off all over Europe at that moment, but they were nothing compared to the fireworks display in my head.

Hallelujah! She's kissing me!

We moved to the bedroom and she made love to me with a tenderness she'd never exhibited before. On all the previous occasions that I'd had sex with Caroline there was some part of me that wasn't engaged, that was standing back and observing the proceedings from a safe distance. Not this time. I was totally absorbed, lost in the warm folds of her flesh. This was what it was like with somebody you were completely in love with. Everything else was masturbation.

Afterwards, lying on the bed and staring at Caroline's head on the pillow, I had one of those 'Oceanic' experiences that Freud thought might lie at the root of all religions. Suddenly, everything seemed to shrink in size, as if I was travelling away from the scene at a hundred miles an hour. Except it wasn't a spatial sensation, not a linear movement. It was as if the gravity that kept my emotions in check had disappeared. It was like being in the swell of the sea, but not quite. Above all there was the feeling of being outside time, what Freud called 'the sensa-tion of "eternity"'. It was like touching something with a part of myself I wasn't normally aware of. I felt as if I'd made contact with the very essence of the universe.

*

The following morning, the first day of the new Millennium, we were sitting on a chair lift high in the French Alps when, out of nowhere, Caroline asked if I could sublet my flat in New York for three months.

'Why?' I said.

'So we could live together in London for a three-month trial period,' she replied.

Wait! Had she really said that? I couldn't believe it.

'Say that again.'

'Well, I thought, you know, we could give it a try. I *really* don't want to do the long-distance thing.'

I was gob-smacked. I'd assumed that last night's lovemaking, mind-blowing though it was, had been the mercy sex that Chris had predicted, a nice way of saying goodbye. However, it seemed she did want to get back together with me after all, at least for three months. The proposal had had a magical effect, if not quite the one I'd intended. She hadn't said 'yes' but she had thrown me a bone.

Now I just had to decide whether I was willing to leave New York.

38

GOODBYE TO ALL THAT

I desperately wanted to move in with Caroline, but I was reluctant to give up New York now that my career was finally on an upswing. In addition to my columns in *Tatler* and the *New York Press*, I was *living with a supermodel* for Christ's sake! Even though I wasn't sleeping with her, it was still hard to say goodbye to all that pulchritude. If my fourteen-year-old self could see me he'd say, 'Gimme five!' If I moved back to London, on the other hand, he'd shoot me with his Gat gun.

It wasn't as if Caroline had agreed to marry me. All she was offering was a three-month 'trial period', after which she would decide whether she wanted to take things any further. She was leasing me with an option to renew. What if she decided not to? The worst-case scenario was that I'd have to skulk back to New York in three months time, just long enough for all my friends to have adjusted to the fact that I'd left town. For years afterwards, whenever I bumped into any of them at parties, they'd say, 'What are you doing here? I thought you'd moved back to London?'

There would also be something fairly humiliating about the fact that I'd be abandoning America to be with her in England instead of the other way round. I was a 36-year-old man, whereas she was a 25-year-old woman. Shouldn't she be sacrificing her career to be with me? The brutal truth was that I had fewer ties to New York than she did to London. As a free-lance hack I could hang up my shingle pretty much anywhere whereas she was committed to being at law school for the next two years.

My greatest fear was that by turning my life upside down for the sake of being with her for three months I'd look unmanly in her eyes. Shouldn't I at least *pretend* to have a bit more masculine pride? The macho thing to do would be to stay in New York and get my career back on track, thereby proving myself worthy of her. If I could just manage to be a bit more successful by the time she graduated from law school, maybe she'd cross the Atlantic to be with me.

Oh, who was I kidding? After nine months of sobriety I had my answer to the question of how much more oomph not drinking gives you: a measly 5 per cent. I hadn't turned into Superman. I was still Clark Kent. In all likelihood I wouldn't be any closer to taking Manhattan in two years time than I was at the moment. Why throw away what would probably be my only chance of putting a ring on Caroline's finger for the sake of a ridiculous pipe dream? So what if I looked like a pathetic lapdog? She'd thrown me a bone and I intended to gnaw on it.

Subletting my New York flat didn't prove to be a problem. My male friends were queuing up to live with Sophie Dahl. Indeed, I was able to tell just how good a friend they were by counting the seconds between me telling them I was planning to move back to London for three months and their asking me what I intended to do about my apartment. I never got up to more than five.

I left New York on 28 January, 2000. My final act was to send all my friends one of those round-robin emails, reassuring them that I hadn't given up on my dream of making it in Manhattan; I'd just fallen in love. My hope was that instead of looking like a big fat loser I'd come across as the last of the great romantics. It didn't work. One of the people on the list was a scrappy entrepreneur called Cromwell Coulson and he replied to my message almost immediately, copying his response to everyone else. It read as follows: 'Another immigrant dream of success and riches in the New World is slowly shattered by the harsh realities of NYC. It's a tearjerker!'

I asked Caroline to marry me again on 21 April. This wasn't as bold an act as proposing on New Year's Eve had been, but it was still pretty optimistic. She'd told me at the beginning of the month, three weeks before the trial period was due to end, that I'd 'passed', though she made it clear that she wasn't agreeing to get engaged. All she was consenting to was to carry on living with me for the time being.

Up until this point, I'd simply put my life in New York on hold. I didn't want to give up my flat if I was going to end up back there in three months. However, after Caroline gave me the thumbs-up I set about moving back permanently and I organised a leaving party for 27 April. It was on the eve of my final trip to Manhattan that I decided to propose.

My reason for asking at that particular moment was so that, in the unlikely event of her saying 'yes', I could make an announcement at the party. That way, I wouldn't look so pathetic for initially agreeing to return to London on such unfavourable terms.

I chose to pop the question at Le Caprice on Good Friday, exactly a year after I'd lost my signet ring. As far as I'm concerned, Le Caprice is London's ultimate 'result' restaurant and I needed all the help I could get. Among other things, I didn't have a ring. When Caroline had said 'no' the first time I'd persuaded my diamond dealer friend to take it back and give me a refund. I didn't think I could get it back again for a second attempt.

In the event, the absence of a ring was the least of my problems.

'The only reason you want to get engaged,' she said, 'is so you can make an announcement at your leaving party.'

I assumed an expression of horror.

'Don't be absurd,' I replied. 'I want to get engaged because I love you.'

She didn't buy it. Eventually, I conceded she was half-right: my reason for wanting to get engaged *at that particular juncture* was in order to save face, but that wasn't why I wanted to marry her.

'So why d'you want to marry me?'

'For proper, non-cynical reasons.'

She stared at me incredulously.

'That's the most romantic thing I've ever heard,' she said.

Having missed my cue once, I wasn't about to fluff it **again**. For the next forty-five minutes I tried to explain exactly why I wanted to marry her. I loved her. I wanted to have children with her. I wanted to grow old with her. After I'd exhausted the clichés, I attempted to dig a little deeper: it had something to do with the feeling of calm I had whenever I was with her. It was as though I'd known her all my life. I only had to close my eyes to see the little girl, standing in the background, clutching a copy of *Pride and Prejudice*. The happiness I felt in her company was the pure, unaffected happiness of childhood. Somehow, through Caroline, I could return to a place I thought was lost to me long ago; when I was with her, no matter where I was, I felt at home.

She said she'd think about it.

The following morning I was lying in bed, staring at the ceiling, going over all the things I had to do in New York, when Caroline mumbled something in what I took to be her sleep.

'What was that, darling,' I said, gently pushing her hair away from her mouth.

She opened her eyes and looked at me.

'Okay,' she said.

It was the most romantic thing I've ever heard.

My leaving party was an unexpected triumph. I invited almost everyone I'd ever met in New York and a surprising number of them showed up. Looking round, I saw the faces of people who hadn't returned my calls in at least two years! That may have been because it was hosted by the legendary party-givers Richard and Nadine Johnson. Graydon Carter came, as did Matt Tyrnauer and Aimée Bell. Candace Bushnell was there with the Red Hot Chilli Pepper: 'Ola, Toe'ee.' Anthony Haden-Guest staggered in, supported by his latest squeeze. Euan Rellie even managed to dig up Jennifer and bring him along! I was relieved to hear he was back living with his boyfriend. Sophie Dahl very sweetly offered to introduce him to her leg waxer.

Chris Lawrence came, sporting a brand new pinstripe suit from 'the brethren'. He was still working at *Vanity Fair* but he was almost at the end of his tether. 'I've figured out why we never made it at Condé Nast,' he announced. 'The trick is to be good natured but not overly impressed with the brass. Our problem is we're not good natured and we're far too impressed.'

After everyone had arrived, I stood up on a chair and made a short speech announcing that Caroline had agreed to become my wife. *Hooray!* I also thanked everyone for putting up with my sophomoric hi-jinks for the past five years.

As soon as I stepped off the chair, Graydon immediately hauled me off to one side. I thought he was going to congratulate me on my good news but I was wrong.

'You ungrateful *cunt*,' he said. 'You didn't thank me. If it wasn't for me, you wouldn't have come to this fucking town in the first place.'

I wasn't sure if he was kidding or not – I could never tell with Graydon – but he was right. If I hadn't spent five years pursuing the Holy Grail in Manhattan I might never have found myself. I certainly wouldn't have found Caroline. Sometimes you have to travel half way round the world to discover that what you're really looking for is back home.

I should have thanked him.

39

RETURN TO SENDER

Filial pride can take you by surprise sometimes. Not the fact that you're feeling it, but the intensity of the feeling, the *ferocity*. It was the night of 30 October, 1999 and my 85-year-old father had come to stay with me in New York. I took him to a party given by a famous young writer and there he was, in his thread-bare, Marks & Spencer jacket, surrounded by the Manhattan glitterati. I was worried that he might be bored, but he seemed to be enjoying himself. There was certainly no shortage of beauti-ful girls.

The woman I was talking to, a journalist in her early thirties, caught me looking at him across the room and crinkled her eyes sympathetically.

'I know exactly what it's like,' she said.

'Know what what's like?' I asked.

'You know, having to look after your dad. They can be a real liability at that age.'

I felt a flicker of annoyance. What on earth was she talking about? He wasn't some out-of-control two-year-old, crawling all over the room. He didn't require any *looking after*.

Then she did something unforgivable. She rolled her eyes.

I was so furious I couldn't speak. How dare you, I thought. *How fucking dare you?* I was tempted to rattle off some of the things this 'liability' had achieved. As the head of the Labour Party's Research Department during the Second World

War and the author of its 1945 manifesto, he was one of the architects of Britain's post-war consensus. He founded the Consumers Association, the National Extension College and the College of Health. He's written over a dozen books, two of them bestsellers. He started *Which?* magazine. He has spawned dozens of organisations, enriching the lives of tens of millions of people, from the East End of London to the Horn of Africa. This man is a giant, I wanted to say, bestriding this room like a colossus. Beside him, these so-called 'movers and shakers' are *nothing*.

When my anger had subsided, though, I realised that none of these achievements would mean very much to her. They weren't particularly 'sexy'. He couldn't be considered a 'VIP', not someone *really* important like a fashion photographer or a gossip columnist. In her eyes he wasn't worth bothering with, this white-haired old man in his threadbare jacket. All he had done was change people's lives.

I knew then that I'd fallen out of love with America. I went to New York in search of the usual goodies – sex, fame and money – and thought I'd be willing to do whatever was necessary to achieve them. Back in London, against the backdrop of the literary atmosphere I'd been brought up in, pursuing this very American conception of the good life had seemed modern and tough-minded, a way of signalling my rejection of my parents' leftwing values. But after five years in Manhattan, where Donald Trump is everybody's favourite role-model, the belief-system I'd rejected began to seem more and more appealing. Perhaps a winner-takes-all society, in which the only arbiters of good taste are celebrities, isn't so marvellous after all.

Of course, that makes it sound as if I rejected America when, to a large extent, it was the other way round. For me, America wasn't the land of opportunity; it was the land of the un-returned phone call. Was it unrealistic of me to think I could take Manhattan? Maybe Frank Sinatra was right and only the very best have the talent and the drive to be 'top of the heap' in 'the city that never sleeps'. 'New York, New York' is like a clarion call to ambitious young gladiators everywhere, challenging them to compete in the biggest amphitheatre in the world. *Have you got what it takes to stand out in the Rome of the modern era?* I'd answered that call and the Emperors of Gotham had given me the thumbs down.

Obviously, I prefer to think it wasn't because I lacked the right stuff. Perhaps I wasn't smart enough to conquer Manhattan, but my stupidity took the form of making elementary, textbook errors. I feel like an athlete who never got the chance to compete because he couldn't tie his shoelaces. I honestly don't think that Alex is that much brighter than me and yet, after five years in Los Angeles, the little bastard had the whole of Hollywood eating out of his hand. Why? Because he has the essential skill I lack: he's brilliant at networking. I might have got a First in Philosophy, Politics and Economics at Oxford, but when it comes to the science of schmoozing I couldn't even get an O-level.

Still, perhaps this is just wishful thinking. It's certainly less damaging to my ego to think the reason I failed is because I wasn't enough of a brownnose. But is that really true? When I think about the five years I spent in New York, it was less that I lacked various people skills and more that I had a flare for antagonising the rich and famous. It was as if there were two people co-existing in my head, one a determined little careerist, ready and willing to do whatever ass-kissing was required, the other a demented, bomb-throwing anarchist intent on wreaking as much havoc as possible. There's no denying I did some SPECTACULARLY IDIOTIC things. Asking Nathan Lane if he was gay? *Mad.* Telling Graydon he hadn't made it beyond the first room on his trip to London? *Insane.* Provoking Harry and Tina into a full-scale nuclear war? *Stark raving bonkers.* Up to a point, these episodes were simply the result of blind ignorance; of not knowing, and not bothering to find out, the appropriate way to behave. But some of my more destructive acts seemed to be the result of the anarchic side of my character tripping the other side up, doing whatever it could to ensure I'd never end up achieving the things I'd set my heart on. I was my own worst enemy – and by the time I left New York there were plenty of competitors for that title.

Yet in failing to become a somebody, did I just remain a nobody? Or did I stay true to myself? I can't help feeling that the terrorist inside of me was the British part sabotaging the American part. The longer I spent in the States, the more British I felt. Like so many others, I thought that by moving to New York I could re-invent myself; I could become an American. It seemed entirely possible, too – for about six months. Then my Britishness started to reassert itself. It was as if I took a flight across the Atlantic and my nationality came by boat. I found myself becoming strangely irritated by stupid little things, like the fact that New Yorkers say 'in back' instead of 'in the back', apparently on the grounds that it's impolite to say anything that could be construed as a reference to the anus. In restaurants it's taboo to ask for the lavatory – you have to ask for 'the bathroom', 'the restroom' or 'the facilities'.

The desire not to give offence, to take everyone's feelings into account, expresses itself in less benign ways as well. Take the 'elevator etiquette' of the modern Manhattan workplace. If a man is standing by himself in a lift and a woman walks in he's supposed to step outside, allowing the woman to travel by herself. Far better for him to be momentarily inconvenienced than that she should feel 'uncomfortable'. New York society, I discovered, is far more rule-bound than any Londoner would tolerate. I began to realise the truth of Horace's famous maxim: *Coelum non animam mutant qui trans mare currunt.*[1]

---

[1] Those who cross the sea change the sky above them, but not their souls.

Why are New Yorkers prepared to put up with these petty regulations? Where's that love of liberty that's supposed to burn so brightly in every American breast? I was particularly shocked by the extent to which glossy magazine writers have given up their right to free speech in return for access to celebrities. Thanks to the antics of women like Pat Kingsley, the power of PRs to control what's written about their clients is now absolute. On one famous occasion, Kingsley rejected fourteen writers before deciding on one who was deferential enough to interview Tom Cruise for *Rolling Stone*. In 1992 a group of magazine editors decided that enough was enough and formed an anti-publicist alliance. The idea was that if enough of them stood firm PRs would no longer be able to dictate the terms on which each magazine was granted access. However, this alliance collapsed almost immediately and Kingsley was left feeling more secure than ever. 'The media is incapable of sticking to any code,' she concluded.

I was particularly disappointed by the spinelessness of New York hacks given how lively and out of control they used to be. I arrived with tales of the legendary bad behaviour of Ben Hecht, Herman J. Mankiewicz and Dorothy Parker swimming in my head, expecting to find their modern-day equivalents in the offices of *Vanity Fair*. I imagined this zany, madcap community where no one stood on ceremony and everyone had a wisecrack at the ready. But that devil-may-care attitude, that sense of fun, was nowhere to be found. Instead, I was confronted with a regiment of pinched and hidebound careerists who never got drunk and were safely tucked up in bed by 10 p.m. The average New York journalist today is a far cry from the large-souled heroes of the Roaring Twenties. He's a terrified conformist, an emasculated drudge. In London, I'd seen chartered accountants behave with more abandon.

After spending my first year doggedly going to every literary party I could, always searching for that elusive crowd of brilliant, fearless writers, I realised that the circle I'd been hanging out with back in London was far closer to the Algonquin

Round Table than any group of journalists I was likely to encounter in Manhattan. For all her shortcomings, Julie Burchill has a lot in common with the sassy, hard-drinking dames of the Jazz Age. She's independent-minded, iconoclastic and whip-smart, which is more than can be said for most of the hacks in New York today. In the five years I spent in America I didn't meet anyone who was more like Dorothy Parker than her.

It would be nice to think that the shortcomings of the current generation of New York hacks is a temporary aberration rather than an instance of that 'general apathy' that Tocqueville identified as an ever-present danger in democratic societies. According to Richard Klein, a professor of French at Cornell, America is simply going through a bad patch:

> We are in the midst of one of those periodic moments of repression, when the culture, descended from Puritans, imposes its hysterical visions and enforces its guilty constraints on society, legislating moral judgements under the guise of public health, all the while enlarging the power of surveillance and the reach of censorship to achieve a general restriction of freedom.

However, while there's undoubtedly a cyclical element to these cultural shifts, it seems far more likely that the gradual erosion of freedom is an irreversible process, the inevitable consequence of the triumph of equality over liberty that Tocqueville warned of in *Democracy in America*. The thicket of petty restrictions that New Yorkers willingly submit to every day is an example of what Tocqueville referred to as 'mild despotism'. Why do they put up with them? Because they enjoy the support of the majority, making them absolutely irresistible in a society as thoroughly democratic as theirs. It's a form of voluntary servitude, the means by which the majority imposes its will on the individual.

The reason we don't have so many of these rules in Britain,

at least not yet, is because the forces of democratisation haven't yet succeeded in quashing our pugnacious, independent spirit, a fact that Tocqueville would attribute to our aristocratic heritage. Of course, contemporary Britain is much less aristocratic than it was, but the manners and customs of the nobility have percolated down through the ranks, giving an aristocratic flavour to the whole. Their most precious gift has been to impart their love of liberty to every British subject, enabling our country to resist some of the more pernicious effects of that love of equality that Tocqueville identified as the defining characteristic of the age.[1]

In praising aristocratic societies, Tocqueville wasn't coming down in favour of the hereditary principle against the doctrine of majority rule. What he had in mind was the classical definition of aristocracy: the rule of the best. The reason he found eighteenth-century Britain so appealing is because it was a society in which status was largely based on what type of man you were rather than how much wealth you'd accumulated. Of course, it was patently unjust that the pool from which the best men were drawn was restricted to those of noble birth, but Tocqueville thought it might be possible to preserve this hierarchy of human types while doing away with the hereditary principle. It was his fervent hope that democracy might be combined with aristocracy to produce a society that was based on the principle of equality but in which all men still aspired to be of the highest type. As he understood it, this was the kind of society the Founding Fathers hoped they were creating in America.

In Chapter Three I talked about the excitement I felt in Stanley Cavell's class on discovering what I thought to be Thomas

---

[1] I'm not talking about *economic* equality, obviously. It's one of the ironies of American democracy that the least defensible form of inequality, the kind that condemns fourteen million children to grow up in poverty, is virtually the only form of inequality that's tolerated.

Jefferson's natural aristocrats in the classic screwball comedies of the thirties and forties. In the book Cavell wrote to accompany his class, *Pursuits of Happiness*, he talks about the link between Tocqueville's ideal citizens and the characters in these films. The reason Tocqueville prized liberty so highly is because he thought it was essential if the citizens of a democracy are to transcend the frenzied pursuit of material gain and become fully formed human beings. In a discussion of *The Philadelphia Story*, Cavell writes:

> Dreading the tendency in democracy to a despotism of the majority, a tyranny over the mind . . . [Tocqueville] looked upon the aristocrat's capacity for independence in thought and conduct, a capacity if need be for eccentricity, as a precious virtue, an aristocratic virtue by which the success of the democratic virtues is to be assessed, to determine whether in its search for individual equality democracy will abandon the task of creating the genuine individual.

According to this test, the current generation of New York journalists – the contemporary equivalents of the characters portrayed by Clark Gable, James Stewart and Cary Grant – don't fare very well. Time and again during the five years I spent in Manhattan, I had a sense of encountering people who weren't quite human. This became apparent in any number of ways. One of the most striking was the overwhelming similarity of everyone I met, as if they had all come off the same production line; they lacked that divine spark that makes all human beings unique. It sounds dreadful to say it, but it was as though they didn't have souls.

Then there was the difficulty I had in making proper friends. (No wonder, you might think, after reading the previous paragraph.) I had dozens of acquaintances in New York, people I enjoyed hanging out with, but at the end of my time there I'd only made two real friends. I found it easy to form superficial bonds with journalists in Manhattan, but nigh on impossible to establish close, lifelong friendships, partly because so few of them were willing to get drunk with me. This was brought home to me when I lost my job at *Vanity Fair* and the people I thought of as my mates suddenly fell by the wayside. Indeed, whenever I spotted an old colleague at a party and made my way towards them a look of panic would come over their faces: *Omigod! How am I gonna get away?* In the New York media world, as soon as word gets out that you've been fired no one wants anything to do with you. Just as in Vietnam the foot soldiers steered clear of anyone they held to be unlucky, so at Condé Nast no one wants to be associated with a loser. Among media types, it seems, friendship is less important than career advancement.

Perhaps the most telling indication that the people I encountered weren't quite fully formed was their lack of interest in romantic love. Obviously, there are exceptions to this, but I was astonished by how little significance they attached to Eros, particularly when it came to selecting a husband or wife. Marriage was a wholly practical affair, an alliance being entered into for reasons of material rather than spiritual gain. The ideal partnership wasn't a co-mingling of two souls in eternity but a mutually beneficial arrangement that could be dissolved as soon as it ceased to be useful. This downgrading of romantic love was the highest cost they paid for sacrificing their freedom for professional gain. As the renowned Chaucer scholar Nevill Coghill pointed out, '[L]ove is essentially an aristocratic experience; that is, an experience only possible to natures capable of refinement, be they high-born or low.'

Of course, even as I packed my bags, some part of me still yearned for the trappings of a successful New York career. I would be lying if I said I'd become completely disillusioned with the world of stretch limos and power restaurants. On one level, I still dream about becoming a boldface name in New York and sleeping with supermodels. But on another, deeper level I know that these goals wouldn't bring me lasting happiness. That was the most poignant thing about Harry and Tina, the thing several of their friends remarked upon. In spite of their brilliant careers, neither of them seemed remotely happy. On the contrary, they appeared anxious and insecure, terrified that everything they had built was about to come crashing down. According to Ben Hecht: 'There is a nervousness that goes with fame in New York. The celebrity is haunted by the fear of waking in the morning and, like an inverse Byron, finding himself unknown.'

Leaving Manhattan, I was in no doubt that Caroline appealed to the British side of my character. If her total indifference to fame and money was what made it possible for her to love me, it was also one of the reasons I loved her. I knew that in future, whenever I fretted about not being invited to some fancy party or worried that my photo byline wasn't flattering enough, one withering glance from her would be enough to cure me of my pretensions. She was like an antidote to New York. My better self couldn't hope for a stronger ally.

After I finished this book I sent a copy to my father and a few days later we had supper together at his home in Islington. I was there to receive his verdict.

He was nice about it – 'very funny' – but not particularly enthusiastic. 'Why not write a more serious book?' he asked. He reminded me of T.S. Eliot's distinction between two kinds of achievement, those for which we're acclaimed in our lifetime and those that last through the ages. Wasn't it time I stopped pursuing the cheap baubles of worldly success and went for something more substantial? He was right, of course. According to the writer Nicholas Lemann, *The Rise of the Meritocracy* has made my father 'a minor immortal'. Forget about the Hollywood gods I was so impressed by at the first *Vanity Fair* Oscar party. That's the kind of immortality it's really worth pursuing.

Still, I can't honestly say I regret the time I spent worshipping false idols. Some people are lucky enough to stumble across the right path straight away; most of us only discover what the right one is by going down the wrong one first.

EPILOGUE

At the end of May, 2000 I heard from Peter Stone, the LA journalist, that Alex had been chucked by _____ _____. Not surprisingly, that was something he hadn't called to tell me about. However, I left a message on his voicemail asking him if it was true and a couple of days later he called back.

Alex: She didn't *chuck* me, dude. It totally wasn't like that. I think we both knew it wasn't working, you know? She's totally fucked up. She's someone who's been adored, who's been flattered and fawned upon from the age of eighteen, and for what? *Through an accident of biology.* I mean, since she was eighteen she's been told how fantastic she is, how great she is, when, basically, all she's had to do is *walk down a bit of wood*, you know? And that fucks you up. I'm just glad it ended now rather than, you know, after we'd had a kid or something. Then it would have really been ugly, d'you know what I'm saying?

Me: Come on, Alex. You were sleeping with _____ _____ and now she's gone. That has to hurt.

Alex: Look, I won't pretend I'm not upset about it – I am, I'm upset, *okay?* – but I've never been as impressed with that world as you have. I mean, it really isn't all that wonderful, you know? I've been there when Tommy Hilfiger has said: 'Let's take the private jet and go to Mauritius for a week.' I've been there when Bono has said: 'Come out to Dublin to celebrate Salman's birthday.' Look, dude, I was at a screening

340

and the only other people there were Sean Penn and Brad Pitt. But you know what? The reality is so disappointing. Sean Penn is just this nasty, belligerent little drunk trying to fuck as many different women as he can. Brad Pitt's a sweet kid but after talking to him for half an hour you realise that that's all he is – a sweet kid.

Me [Awestruck]: This is what I envy about you, Alex. When you criticise that world you have total credibility. You've been there and done that. But when I criticise it, it just comes off like sour grapes. Tommy Hilfiger and Bono wouldn't even let me in the tradesman's entrance. When they saw me coming up the drive they'd unleash the Dobermans.

Alex: I know you romanticise that world but, believe me, it's just really, really hollow. Yes, there's a thrill for a while but, ultimately, you'd lose interest. I was going out with, quote unquote, one of the most beautiful women in the world, and you know what? It just doesn't mean that much after a while.

Me: I don't romanticise it – at least not any more. But I wish I'd been part of it so I could condemn it more convincingly. I'm jealous of your *authority*. Even as a disillusioned cynic you're more successful than me. It's so unfair.

Alex: You have to stop looking at the world so competitively. It's not just about winning, dude.

Me: Listen, Alex, you have to write about this. Forget about gay Welsh dog-groomers. Write a screenplay about an ordinary guy from North London who goes to Hollywood and ends up sleeping with _____ _____. At first he's totally seduced by her and the world she moves in but, eventually, he's spat out and he becomes Mr Angry, fuming and raving about how shallow she and her friends are. The Alex character could even end up stalking her and—

Alex [Exasperated]: Look, dude, she didn't *spit me out*. You've got to get that out of your head. If you really want to know, I broke up with her.

Me: You broke up with her? Jesus Christ, Alex, I would literally sacrifice my left testicle to be able to say that. 'Sure, I know _____ _____. We dated for a few months. But you know what? After a while the beauty thing got kind of tired. So I broke up with her.'

Alex [Laughing]: Well that's basically what happened.

When I last spoke to Alex he was writing a script for Adam Sandler.

ACKNOWLEDGEMENTS

I was thinking of beginning the Acknowledgements with one of those postmodernist disclaimers that call into question the whole notion of objective truth, but nearly everything that takes place in this book happened exactly the way I've described it. I say 'nearly everything' because I've occasionally given things a slight comic twist, but you'd be surprised by how little exaggeration and embellishment there is. When I flick through the book's pages and read about all the humiliating things that happened to me I wish I *had* invented most of this stuff. Unfortunately, it's a pretty accurate account of what occurred.

Wherever possible I've used people's real names, but for legal reasons I've occasionally had to change them or leave them blank. I've tried as hard as I can to get all the factual details in the book right and I'd like to acknowledge the help of Riza Cruz and Consuelo Moorsom in that regard. However, there will inevitably be plenty of mistakes. If you spot any, can you email me and let me know on howtolose@hotmail.com? That way, in the unlikely event of there being any additional printings of this book, I can correct them.

I have a long list of people I wish to thank but, regrettably, if I named them they'd lose their jobs. People who work on New York glossy magazines do so in an atmosphere of nail-biting paranoia. Indeed, an employee of *Talk*, Tina Brown's magazine, once described it to me as being like 'working for the Nixon Whitehouse'. Freedom of speech may be guaranteed by the American Constitution, but woe betide the glossy magazine journalist who attempts to exercise that right by talking about his boss. (A better name for *Talk* would be *Omerta*.) Nevertheless, I had plenty of Deep Throats and even though I can't name them here I'd like to take this opportunity to thank them. They know who they are.

Those I can name include my agent Emma Parry, my editor Alan Samson at Little, Brown, and my libel lawyer Martin Soames. Several people read the book in the course of its evolution and improved it dramatically with their suggestions, including Michael Young, Sean Macaulay, Cosmo Landesman, Chris Lawrence, Melik Kaylan, Christopher Caldwell and Cromwell Coulson. I'd also like to thank Becky Quintavalle and Rachel Leyshon at Little, Brown. Needless to say, all the mistakes, including using the expression 'needless to say' far too often, are mine.

Finally, I'd like to thank Graydon Carter. Without him, this book would never have been written.

An Outline of Piaget's Developmental Psychology
for Students and Teachers